AN
EASY GUIDE
TO THE
END
OF THE
AGE

AN
EASY GUIDE
TO THE
END
OF THE
AGE

A Visual Unveiling of Revelation

ANDREW JAMES LATEER

An Easy Guide to the End of the Age

Copyright 2025 Andrew James LaTeer

For more information, email: andrew@endtimezscribe.com

ISBN: 979-8-89694-249-8 - eBook

ISBN: 979-8-89694-250-4 - Paperback

FREE GIFT

Go to: https://www.endtimezscribe.com/

I dedicate this book to three sisters and seven brothers who are unlike any other:

First, to my sister Venitta LaTeer, one of my most steadfast fans, you never gave up on me, even after I had. That was annoying, but a blessing, Sis!

Second, to my brother William Miller, who has provided me a sanctuary wherein to write this and draw closer to my Lord and Savior, Jesus Christ.

Third, to my friend Ethan Waller, who took me in when I was in dire need and opened his heart and home to me.

Fourth, to Pastor Doug and Becky Abbey—their hearts and lives reflect the compassion of Christ! (A friend loves at all times, and a brother is born for adversity.)

Fifth, to Mr. Richard Meyers, the man whose life revealed to me the Father heart of God.

Sixth, to Pastor Dan and Cindy Schallmo, two of the boldest, most persevering, and Spirit-filled servants I have had the pleasure to serve under. It is my honor to serve with you, and I love you!

Seventh, to Pastor Joe Jansen, hearing you preach while I was under your leadership showed me some of your heart toward God, and what it means to be a man of God. I love that!

Finally, to my friend James Michael Wilson, with whom I have a bond like no other person on this earth.

Special Acknowledgments: Illustrators and Photoshop Illustrator

IMAGES FOR AN EASY GUIDE TO THE END OF THE AGE

Contents

CHAPTER 1

Birth Pangs

You little son of a sea biscuit! You don't think I can make you cry? That was the scream that reverberated through the room that day. I grew up with a stepfather who was extremely, atrociously, abusive. He was the cruelest person I have ever met in my life. Now I would like to set the stage for you because what had happened was this man beat his children regularly. I was probably around 8, 9, or 10. He would beat us regularly. There were places where he would beat us and say, "That was for nothing, just wait until you do something!" That day, after beating me, he looked at me and said, "When are you going to grow up and become a man and stop crying like a baby?" I determined in my heart that the next time that he beat me I would not cry. I would not give him the satisfaction. So, the next time he beat me I didn't cry, and I stood there before him and he looked at me and said, "You little son of a sea biscuit, (obviously he didn't use sea biscuit) you don't think I can make you cry?" Then he beat me within an inch of my life. From that point forward, all he would have to do is look at me crossed eyed and I would burst into tears. He broke me that day. That man crushed my spirit. He broke my spirit! Now my stepfather was the most cruel, abusive person I have ever known in my life. One abuse he put me through was emotional. My stepfather would tell me things like, "Andrew, you're worthless. You're never going to amount to nothing. Nothing more than a worthless piece of crap. You can't do anything right!" Let me tell you after hearing that enough times you internalize statements like that and believe those statements to be true, and that is who you are. So, when I tell you I had low self-esteem, I'm not kidding! This happens in way too many homes in America and in other parts of the world. This is a part of our national fabric and is something we do not hear about many times until it is way too late. Things like this do not make the news. They thrive in the shadows, growing like a malignant cancer. What makes it into the news is so saturated with negativity that many people have tuned out.

There is a lot of turmoil in the world these days. Many people are so overwhelmed with the barrage of negative elements in the news that they cannot bring themselves to watch it. Racism changes face and is less up front than in previous generations but is still very prevalent. Corruption in the political system is in our news regularly. Many perceive financial institutes as less trustworthy and more corrupt than ever before. Natural disasters take a toll on every society. There is the cost of rebuilding, with billions of dollars used to recover rather than build. These catastrophes hurt every nation's economy.

As we look around at current events, anyone with a conscience must be appalled at the state of our world. Murder is on the rise all over. It is so commonplace these days that we don't even stop and blink anymore. We are becoming desensitized to the ever-increasing violence in our societies. Albert Fish is a serial killer who preyed on young children. Included in his sadism was cannibalism and psychological torture.

In the instance of ten-year-old Grace Budd, Albert Fish wrote to her mother how he stripped her naked, cut her into manageable pieces so that he could cook and eat her. Declaring her butt tasted sweet coming out of the oven.[1] This was case number three of the top ten horrific true crime cases you should never web search. The Columbine massacre has become almost a household term in our country and, unfortunately, was only the highest profile among many. There are rising tensions between supporters of biblical marriage and those who advocate for same-sex marriage. The battle lines are being drawn, whether we want them to be or not.

Back in the 1950s, the big disciplinary problems in school were smoking and chewing gum in class; we've come a long way since then. The '50s were not an age of total innocence. That period had issues such as racial segregation, a lack of women's rights, and political unrest. However, the issues facing this generation and those of our grandparents are in significant contrast and are relatively tame by comparison. Many say the kids these days are starting younger and younger—meaning primarily that they are involved in things considered adult. Sex, drugs, smoking, and drinking are being engaged in by those who are barely into their teens and, for some, even before their teenage years. The generation growing up now is far more open to bisexuality. In talking with them, the consensus is that "it's all good." Anyone who has seen late-night television could not have missed all the movies and series that are rated M for mature. "Going postal" is a term everyone understands these days. Road rage is becoming more and more commonplace. There was an event many years ago of a mother who drove her children into a body of water and killed them all. Not that long ago there was a news report of a twenty-three-year-old who killed his lady friend and her child. This also is becoming so commonplace that it hardly fazes us anymore. There is the tragedy of September 11, 2001. Terrorist attacks throughout the world plague this earth.

Pornography is a billion-dollar-plus business these days. Any form of perversion a person can imagine is available on the internet. Not to mention the adult stores that are everywhere these days. The most appalling is child pornography. Children are being kidnapped and sold as sex slaves all over the world. We now have Amber Alerts for missing children. The National Center for Missing and Exploited Children was born because of devastating events in the late 1970s and early 1980s. Two abductions concerning Adam Walsh and Etan Patz, along with murders and kidnappings around Atlanta, Georgia, were the catalyst for the creation of this center.[2] A child being stolen for one sick reason or another is becoming an everyday event. This, too, has become so commonplace that it hardly even registers anymore.

But understand this, that in the last days will come (set in) perilous times of great stress and trouble [hard to deal with and hard to bear]. For people will be lovers of self and [utterly] self-centered, lovers of money and aroused by an inordinate [greedy] desire for wealth, proud and arrogant and contemptuous boasters. They will be abusive (blasphemous, scoffing), disobedient to parents, ungrateful, unholy and profane. [They will be] without natural [human] affection (callous and inhuman), relentless (admitting of no truce or appeasement); [they will be] slanderers (false accusers, troublemakers), intemperate and loose in morals and conduct, uncontrolled and fierce, haters of good. [They will be] treacherous [betrayers], rash, [and] inflated with self-conceit. [They will be] lovers of sensual pleasures and vain amusements more than and rather than lovers of God. For [although] they hold a form of piety (true religion), they deny and reject and are strangers to the power of it [their conduct belies the genuineness of their profession]. Avoid [all] such people [turn away from them]. (2 Tim. 3:1–5)

These verses describe the culture we live in today. We are close to totally fulfilling that verse, it would appear. We trust our public officials less and less because corruption has become the standard, rather than the exception. This applies to our church leaders as well. This is not to say that all our public officials and church leaders are corrupt. There are some honorable men and women in all spheres of influence. However, there are more than enough leaders who are corrupt that it leaves a sour taste in our mouths. Money, it would appear, is often the reason for the corruption, as they trade their influence in their positions of trust for monetary and other illicit gains.

Our society has a fascination with the supernatural. There are many shows about the paranormal. We have TV shows such as Ghost Hunters, Paranormal State, Crossing Over, Beyond, Extreme Paranormal, and many more. We have many new movies every year about possession based on actual events. Does that not say anything about the state of our society and how hungry and susceptible we are to the "dark side" of the supernatural?

One of this writer's guilty pleasures is a TV series called Criminal Minds. Our society has a fascination with serial killers, and the show explores the darker side of human nature. The part of the show that speaks to this writer is, if I am being honest, this dark side, amazed at how a person can think to do those things to another human being, but probably even more so, the brave men and women who stand up to the monsters and rescue their victims. However, the show reflects our society and the depths of human depravity on a scale in human history that is like the days of Noah.

Drugs and gangs are now a part of our national fabric. The use of alcohol and drunk driving are also commonplace. These are only a few of the many problems that plague our nation and the world at large. It appears our society is spiraling out of control. People everywhere are asking, "What's going on?" This book is an attempt to answer that question from a biblical perspective. Many people say that they believe the end is close, but they are unsure what all is involved at the end of the age. We have many movies and books that reflect this feeling in our society. The End of Days, with Arnold Schwarzenegger; The Day After Tomorrow, with Dennis Quaid; 2012, with John Cusack; and The Sum of All Fears, with Ben Affleck and Morgan Freeman, are just a few of the movies that reflect our interest as a society. Many say they believe the end is close, while others mock, saying, "Where is Jesus's return?"

To begin with, you must know and understand this, that scoffers (mockers) will come in the last days with scoffing, [people who] walk after their own fleshly desires and say, where is the promise of His coming? For since the forefathers fell asleep, all things have continued exactly as they did from the beginning of creation. For they willfully overlook and forget this [fact], that the heavens [came into] existence long ago by the word of God, and the earth also which was formed out of water and by means of water, through which the world that then [existed] was deluged with water and perished. But by the same word the present heavens and earth have been stored up (reserved) for fire, being kept until the day of judgment and destruction of the ungodly people. Nevertheless, do not let this one fact escape you, beloved, that with the Lord one day is as a thousand years and a thousand years as one day. The Lord does not delay and is not tardy or slow about what He promises, according to some people's conception of slowness, but He is long-suffering (extraordinarily patient) toward you, not desiring that any should perish, but that all should turn to repentance. But the day of the lord will come like a thief, and then the heavens will vanish (pass away) with a thunderous crash, and the [material] elements [of the universe] will be dissolved with fire, and the earth and the works that are upon it will be burned up. Since all these things are thus in the process of being dissolved, what kind of person ought [each of] you to be [in the meanwhile] in consecrated and holy behavior and devout and godly qualities, while you wait and earnestly long for (expect and hasten) the coming of the day of God by reason of which the flaming heavens will be dissolved, and the [material] elements [of the universe] will flare and melt with fire. But we look for new heavens and a new earth according to His promise, in which righteousness (uprightness, freedom from sin, and right standing with God) is to abide. So, beloved, since you are expecting these things, be eager to be found by Him [at His coming] without spot or blemish and at peace [in serene confidence, free from fears and agitating passions and moral conflicts]. And consider that the long-suffering of our Lord [His slowness in avenging wrongs and judging the world] is salvation (that which is conducive to the soul's safety). (2 Pet. 3:3–15)

The Bible has much to say about the end of the age, but many are confused and find it mystical and complicated. Many are curious but have no clue where to look to research this subject. This is an attempt to simplify so the average person with little to no knowledge of the Scriptures can understand what the Bible has to say about the end of the age. This writer has never seen a book where someone went in and did the hard work of gleaning prophecy about the end of the age out of all the different books scattered throughout the Bible, then consolidating the various prophecies into one book to study. This study will respectfully consider all the popular views on the subject. Included are the Scripture verses that have brought about these various views so the reader can follow along and decide for themselves.

The issue, it would appear in interpreting prophetic Scripture, is that men desire to be experts in the places that God has left unclear. Interpreting symbolism in Scripture is a prime example. One Bible scholar states that this symbol of a horse and a rider found in Revelation 6 is this or that, while another gives an entirely different interpretation to that same portion of Scripture. The Bible states that no prophecy of Scripture is up to any one person's interpretation, as it did not originate with humankind but originated with God. Only One knows all the symbols and what they mean, and that is God himself. This is like a magician's sleight of hand. While God has people looking over here, he has already disclosed what is necessary. But people's attention is focused on the unclear and on what is open to interpretation rather than what is clear. Jesus spoke to the people in parables in his day, and it would appear he is doing it still in our day. It would be hard to believe that God, in his wisdom, gives any one man or woman all the insight into any one subject. We can only press on and determine as best as we can. This is a very complex subject, and the desire here is to make it simple.

The Bible has a lot to say about the end of the age and the Second Coming of Christ. However, if you are trying to find out about that subject and are not familiar with where in the Bible to look for those passages, the attempt can be daunting. What may be surprising to those who have done little to no research on the subject in the Bible is that this concept is in different places throughout the Scriptures. Different people wrote it, separated by hundreds and sometimes thousands of years. We will look at many portions of Scripture that describe this period and what we can expect. There are scholars who state that there is more written about the end of the age than any other period of human history, including the life of Christ. If the Bible has that much emphasis on this topic, then it is vitally important. There are many similarities between each person's insights, as inspired by the Holy Spirit, but they each give us a little different perspective on the subject.

> Every Scripture is God-breathed (given by His inspiration) and profitable for instruction, for reproof and conviction of sin, for correction of error and discipline in obedience, [and] for training in righteousness (in holy living, in conformity to God's will in thought, purpose, and action). (2 Tim. 3:16)

There is ultimately one author of the Bible, which is God himself, as he inspired men of God to write. Each vessel that God spoke through brought to the work his own unique flavor and personality to the work. What is so fascinating is that when you compare what this person says about the subject as compared to what somebody hundreds—and sometimes even thousands—of years later stated on the subject, they dovetail and confirm each other nicely. This book is not an exhaustive study on the subject. I would also like to state early on in this book that I have memorized a lot of Scripture. There are many times while I am writing that a verse comes to mind, so I write it down from memory. This is not verbatim, but in general terms. I then Google where in the Bible that verse is located and add it after so that the reader can verify for themselves that what I am referencing is found in the Bible.

Is it okay to admit right up front we don't know it all? Most people who broach this subject come across as presenting their interpretation as the only one. Many who are curious on the subject know there is one glaringly obvious truth: You can't all be right! This might not be so bad if we were all saying the same thing, but as one who has read a lot of different material on the subject, I believe that such is not the case. Let us look at what we can know for sure and then speculate about what is open to interpretation. It is okay. God is all right with people using their brains and is very familiar with the fact that we seldom agree on very much. While God is interested in how we use our brain, he, it would appear, is more interested in men's and women's hearts.

> For with the heart a person believes (adheres to, trusts in, and relies on Christ) and so is justified (declared righteous, acceptable to God), and with the mouth he confesses (declares openly and speaks out freely his faith) and confirms [his] salvation. (Rom. 10:10)

It is not the brain but the heart that believes in salvation. God is initially more interested in capturing a person's heart than a person's mind. We see this repeatedly in the Gospels. It was rare that Jesus engaged anyone in a battle of wits. Most of the time, he appealed to their hearts. As an example, in John 8, the rulers of Jesus's day came to him and brought a woman caught in the act of adultery. They declared, "Moses said stone this woman, but what do you say?" They were attempting to engage him in a battle of wits. It says that "they were testing him so that they might have something with which to bring an accusation," as they had noticed he liked helping sinners. He knew the Law yet drew in the sand. Some scholars say that he was praying while doing this, asking his Father how he wanted him to answer them. Others suggest that Jesus was drawing the names of sins in the sand and as each person saw the sin they were guilty of was conscience-stricken and left (John 8:3–11, author's paraphrase).

First, if they were so interested in being fair and playing by the rules, where was the man? It would be an impressive feat indeed if the woman committed adultery all by herself, wouldn't it? So where was the man? Why didn't they bring him before Jesus along with the woman if they were trying to go by the book? In response, Jesus told them, "He that is without sin among you cast the first stone," and they all left from the oldest down to the youngest. And when Jesus was alone with her, he said, "Woman, where are your accusers? Has no man condemned you?" She said, "There is no one!" and he said, "Neither do I condemn you sin no more" (John 8:7–11, author's paraphrase). Out of all those present; he was the only one who could have legitimately cast that first stone. Instead, he forgave her. What do you suppose went on in her heart after that? What do you suppose went on in the hearts of the crowd that was ready to stone her? Do you think it was their hearts that were troubled or their minds? Do you think they went home to study the Torah and figure out how to get Jesus again? Assuredly, some did, but it was not those hearts that Jesus was after! Thank God, he loves us, yes?

Jesus compared the end of the age to a woman giving birth to a child. Anyone who's even vaguely familiar with childbirth knows that the pain and contractions start out comparatively mild compared to the last event and then build with intensity and frequency until the child is born. Matthew 24 is one of the biggest chapters on the end of the age in the Bible. This book is written for the average person who's looking around and sensing that something earthshaking is near, and they can't quite put a finger on it. It should be interesting to merge biblical prophecy on what the Bible has to say about the end of the age. It would also be beneficial to simplify as much as we can so the average person can benefit from the study.

CHAPTER 2

One Penetrating Question

One penetrating question concerning the end of the age: Did Jesus mean the literal last day when speaking of resurrecting the dead? Why? Why would that matter? Because if he literally meant the last day when he was speaking of resurrecting the dead, we have a sequence of events that are about as solid as it gets for the timeline of the Rapture and the Second Coming of Christ. Let us explore what Jesus had to say about the resurrection of the dead, and an interchange between Jesus and some dear friends about this subject:

> For I have come down from heaven not to do My own will and purpose but to do the will and purpose of Him Who sent Me. And this is the will of Him Who sent Me, that I should not lose any of all that He has given Me, but that I should give new life and raise [them all] up at *the last day*. For this is My Father's will and His purpose, that everyone who sees the Son and believes in and cleaves to and trusts in and relies on Him should have

eternal life, and I will raise him up [from the dead] at *the last day.* (John 6:38–40) (emphasis mine)

No one is able to come to Me unless the Father Who sent Me attracts and draws him and gives him the desire to come to Me, and [then] I will raise him up [from the dead] at *the last day.* (John 6:44) (emphasis mine)

He who feeds on My flesh and drinks My blood has (possesses now) eternal life, and I will raise him up [from the dead] on *the last day.* (John 6:54) (emphasis mine)

In Jesus's discourse in the sixth chapter of John, he is doing something that he unfortunately has to do frequently: challenging the misconceptions of the Jewish people. Jesus had just fed the multitudes, and they were seeking him to get more bread. In this discourse, Jesus continues to shock them by first stating that he is the bread that came down from heaven and eventually that they would have to eat his flesh and drink his blood. Many stopped following Jesus at this point. However, it is in this interaction that we hear Jesus talking about doing God's will, and a huge part of that is that those whom the Father has given to him will come to him; he will not lose even one of them but will raise them up in the Resurrection on the last day. This appears to be a teaching that many of his close friends are familiar with, although we see it clearest in John chapter 6. Here are some of Jesus's closest friends, who are obviously familiar with this teaching.

NOW A certain man named Lazarus was ill. He was of Bethany, the village where Mary and her sister Martha lived. This Mary was the one who anointed the Lord with perfume and wiped His feet with her hair. It was her brother Lazarus who was [now] sick. So, the sisters sent to Him, saying, Lord, he whom You love [so well] is sick. When Jesus received the message, He said, this sickness is not to end in death; but [on the contrary] it is to honor God and to promote His glory, that the Son of God may be glorified through (by) it. Now Jesus loved Martha and her sister and Lazarus. [They were His dear friends, and He held them in loving esteem.] Therefore [even] when He heard that Lazarus was sick, He still stayed two days longer in the same place where He was. Then after that interval He said to His disciples, let us go back again to Judea. The disciples said to Him, Rabbi, the Jews only recently were intending and trying to stone You, and are You [thinking of] going back there again? Jesus answered, Are there not twelve hours in the day? Anyone who walks about in the daytime does not stumble, because he sees [by] the light of this world. But if anyone walks about in the night, he does stumble, because there is no light in him [the light is lacking to him]. He said these things, and then added, our friend Lazarus is at rest and sleeping; but I am going there that I may awaken him out of his sleep. The disciples answered, Lord, if he is sleeping, he will recover. However, Jesus had spoken of his death, but they thought that He referred to falling into a refreshing and natural sleep. So, then Jesus told them plainly, Lazarus is dead, and for your sake I am glad that I was not there; it will help you to believe (to trust and rely on Me). However, let us go to him. Then Thomas, who was called the Twin, said to his fellow disciples, let us go too, that we may die [be killed] along with Him. So, when Jesus arrived, He found that he [Lazarus] had already been in the tomb four days. Bethany was near Jerusalem, only about two miles away, and a considerable number of the Jews had gone out to see Martha and Mary to console them concerning their brother. When Martha heard that Jesus was coming, she went to meet Him, while Mary remained sitting in the house. Martha then said to Jesus, Master, if You had been here, my brother would not have died. And even now I know that whatever You ask from God, He will grant it to You. Jesus said to her, your brother shall rise again. Martha replied, I know that he will rise again in *the resurrection at the last day.* Jesus said to her, I am [Myself] the Resurrection and the Life. Whoever believes in (adheres to, trusts in, and relies on) Me, although he may die, yet he shall live; And whoever continues to live and believes in (has faith in, cleaves to, and relies on) Me shall never [actually] die at all. Do you believe this? She said to Him, Yes, Lord, I have believed [I do believe] that You are the Christ (the Messiah, the Anointed One), the Son of God, [even He] Who was to come into the world. [It is for Your coming that the world has waited.] (John 11:1–27) (emphasis mine)

In this account, Jesus and Martha (presumably Mary and Lazarus too) have had a private conversation, and because of this conversation, Martha understands that her brother Lazarus will rise to life again on "the last day." This was apparently a standard teaching of Jesus: that the resurrected dead rise to life on the last day.

We are now going to be shifting gears to the apostle who has a unique relationship to end-time events, as the things he says on the subject relate closely to Jesus's teaching about the dead who died believing in him being resurrected on the last day.

CHAPTER 3

The Apostle Paul's Unique Apostleship Concerning the End of the Age

The Apostle Paul has a unique apostleship compared to the twelve apostles who traveled and ministered with Jesus for three years before his death. Paul is the only notable apostle who was chosen (handpicked by Jesus himself) like the twelve, but after Jesus ascended to heaven.

Jesus chose Paul to be an apostle, and Paul felt totally inadequate, largely because Paul felt he was born in an untimely fashion, unlike the other apostles:

> For I passed on to you first of all what I also had received, that Christ (the Messiah, the Anointed One) died for our sins in accordance with [what] the Scriptures [foretold], That He was buried, that He arose on the third day as the Scriptures foretold, And [also] that He appeared to Cephas (Peter), then to the Twelve. Then later He showed Himself to more than five

hundred brethren at one time, the majority of whom are still alive, but some have fallen asleep [in death]. Afterward He was seen by James, then by all the apostles (the special messengers), And last of all He appeared to me also, as to one prematurely and born dead [no better than an unperfected fetus among living men]. For I am the least [worthy] of the apostles, who am not fit or deserving to be called an apostle, because I once wronged and pursued and molested the church of God [oppressing it with cruelty and violence]. But by the grace (the unmerited favor and blessing) of God I am what I am, and His grace toward me was not [found to be] for nothing (fruitless and without effect). In fact, I worked harder than all of them [the apostles], though it was not really I, but the grace (the unmerited favor and blessing) of God which was with me. (1 Cor. 15:3–10)

Paul's Christian education was unorthodox. Paul was not there for the Sermon on the Mount; he was not there for Jesus's instruction in Matthew 24 concerning the end of the age and Jesus's return. Jesus taught Paul by direct revelations. God led Paul not to consult with those who were apostles before him, but went to Arabia, then to Damascus, and then after three years, he finally got acquainted with those who were apostles before him, as we read in Galatians. God used Paul to write almost a quarter of the New Testament; we can trust that Paul's testimony is safe:

For I want you to know, believers, that the gospel which was preached by me is not man's gospel [it is not a human invention, patterned after any human concept]. For indeed I did not receive it from man, nor was I taught it, but *I received it* through a [direct] revelation of Jesus Christ. You have heard of my career *and* former manner of life in Judaism, how I used to hunt down *and* persecute the church of God extensively and [with fanatical zeal] tried [my best] to destroy it. And [you have heard how] I surpassed many of my contemporaries among my countrymen in [my advanced study of the laws of] Judaism, as I was extremely loyal to the traditions of my ancestors. But when God, who had chosen me *and* set me apart before I was born, and called me through His grace, was pleased to reveal His Son in me so that I might preach Him among the Gentiles [as the good news—the way of salvation], I did not immediately consult with anyone [for guidance regarding God's call and His revelation to me]. Nor did I [even] go up to Jerusalem to those who were apostles before me; but I went to Arabia *and* stayed awhile, and afterward returned once more to Damascus. Then three years later I did go up to Jerusalem to get acquainted with Cephas (Peter), and I stayed with him fifteen days. But I did not see any other apostle except James, the [half] brother of the Lord. (Gal. 1:11–19)

One would normally expect a new convert like Paul to be mentored by those who were apostles before him. However, the Spirit led Paul on a different path. It is reminiscent of the Spirit leading Jesus into the wilderness to be tempted by Satan for forty days—not the normal path to launch a public ministry.

Why is any of this important? Because of all the apostles who God led to write concerning the Second Coming of Jesus, it is only Paul whose writings are specific enough to pinpoint the timing of certain events—for example:

Now in regard to the coming of our Lord Jesus Christ and our gathering together to *meet* Him, we ask you, brothers and sisters, not to be quickly unsettled or alarmed either by a [so-called prophetic revelation of a] spirit or a message or a letter [alleged to be] from us, to the effect that the day of the lord has [already] come. Let no one in any way deceive *or* entrap you, for *that day will not come* unless the apostasy comes first [that is, the great rebellion, the abandonment of the faith by professed Christians], and the man of lawlessness is revealed, the son of destruction [the Antichrist, the one who is destined to be destroyed], who opposes and exalts himself [so proudly and so insolently] above every so-called god or object of worship, so that he [actually enters and] takes his seat in the temple of God, publicly proclaiming that he himself is God. Do you not remember that when I was still with you, I was telling you these things? (2 Thess. 2:1–5) (emphasis mine)

We can debate what the Scriptures mean by the "day of the Lord," but what we cannot debate, if we take Paul's letter to the Thessalonians literally, is that day will not come until these things happen first. No other writer in the New Testament has that kind of specificity. The Gospel writers simply related what Jesus himself said about the end of the age and the signs of his return. Peter writes about scoffers in the last days, asking why he is taking so long, and stating this is God's mercy to lead us to repentance. James exhorts us to wait patiently for that day. The book of 1 John tells us the Antichrist is coming and, in some measure, is already here. The book of 2 John tells us that anybody who denies Jesus came to earth physically is the deceiver and Antichrist. The book of Revelation is a revelation of the person of Jesus, but there is not much about the book and its inherent imagery that is simple.

It would stand to reason that God would have chosen one of the twelve who traveled with Jesus to have specific inside information concerning the end of the age and Jesus's return. But God is seldom interested in how humankind thinks he should do things. Paul was at the top of his class in Judaism. A natural thought is that God would send Paul to the Jews because Paul knew their theology and culture intimately. God sent Peter, a fisherman, to the Jews, and God sent Paul to the Gentiles.

Some of what is fascinating concerning Paul is that he had experiences with God that there is no record of the other twelve having:

It is necessary to boast, though nothing is gained by it; but I will go on to visions and revelations of the Lord. I know a man in Christ who fourteen years ago—whether in the body I do not know, or out of the body I do not know, [only] God knows—such a man was caught up to the third heaven. And I know that such a man—whether in the body or out of the body I do not know, [only] God knows—was caught up into Paradise and heard inexpressible words which man is not permitted to speak [words too sacred to tell]. On behalf of such a man [and his experiences] I will boast; but in my own behalf I will not boast, except in regard to my weaknesses. If I wish to boast, I will not be foolish, because I will be speaking the truth. But I abstain [from it], so that no one will credit me with more than [is justified by what] he sees in me or hears from me. Because of the surpassing greatness *and* extraordinary nature of the revelations [which I received from God], for this reason, to keep me from thinking of myself as important, a thorn in the flesh was given to me, a messenger of Satan, to torment *and* harass me—to keep me from exalting myself! (2 Cor. 12:1–7)

Paul was "caught" up to the third heaven and heard and shown things that are inexpressible. To keep Paul humble because of the extraordinary revelations that God gave Paul, God gave Paul a "thorn in the flesh." There is a lot of speculation as to what Paul's "thorn in the flesh" was, but that question is unnecessary for our study. Since Paul was not with the other twelve during Jesus's earthly ministry, where did Paul receive instruction on the end of the age and the signs of Jesus's return? Some of Paul's insights conceivably came from experiences like this one. We cannot know for sure if this is the case; what we can know for sure, however, is that however Paul came to understand end-time events and the signs of Jesus's return that he shared that understanding with the churches in his care. He speaks with authority and specificity that the other apostles do not have.

> For we say this to you by the Lord's [own] word, that we who are still alive and remain until the coming of the Lord, will in no way precede [into His presence] those [believers] who have fallen asleep [in death]. (1 Thess. 4:15)

No one else among the apostles speaks with authority on this issue more than Paul: "We are not telling you what we think, or guess, this came straight from Jesus. Those of us who are alive when Christ returns will not meet Christ when he returns before those believers who have died knowing Christ as their Savior" (author paraphrase).

This, again, gives a sequence of events that none of the other writers of the New Testament have written about concerning the sequences of events that happen before Jesus returns physically back to earth. We would do well to give additional weight to what Paul has to say on this subject.

Let us look at these Scriptures in a different translation because some may consider the translation added for us more than the biblical author or the Holy Spirit intended.

1. For this we say unto you by the word of the Lord, that we which are alive and remain unto the coming of the Lord shall not prevent them which are asleep. For the Lord himself shall descend from heaven with a shout, with the voice of the archangel, and with the trump of God: and the dead in Christ shall rise first: Then we which are alive and remain shall be caught up together with them in the clouds, to meet the Lord in the air: and so shall we ever be with the Lord. (1 Thess. 4:15–17 KJV)

2. Now we beseech you, brethren, by the coming of our Lord Jesus Christ, and by our gathering together unto him, That ye be not soon shaken in mind, or be troubled, neither by spirit, nor by word, nor by letter as from us, as that the day of Christ is at hand. Let no man deceive you by any means: for that day shall not come, except there come a falling away first, and that man of sin be revealed, the son of perdition; Who opposeth and exalteth himself above all that is called God, or that is worshipped; so that he as God sitteth in the temple of God, shewing himself that he is God. Remember ye not, that, when I was yet with you, I told you these things? (2 Thess. 2:1–5 KJV)

3. All that the Father giveth me shall come to me; and him that cometh to me I will in no wise cast out. For I came down from heaven, not to do mine own will, but the will of him that sent me. And this is the Father's will which hath sent me, that of all which he hath given me I should lose nothing, but should raise it up again at the last day (John 6:37–39 KJV)

    a) The first bullet point states that by Jesus's own word, there will be some believers who are alive and remain at his Second Coming. We will not meet him before the resurrected dead; 1 Thessalonians 4:17 is the key Scripture where we get the concept of the Rapture. There are only a few places in the Scriptures that use the word harpazo, which is the original Greek word that means "to be seized or caught up" and is now known as the Rapture. The concentration in this study is on the words "caught up" (because it is in this framework we derive the word rapture), there are a few other instances of the word harpazo in the New Testament, but they are not in direct relationship to this study.

The word translated caught in this verse in Strong's Exhaustive Concordance of the Bible is "harpazo," which means "to seize: catch (away, up), pluck, pull, and take by force." Translated into Latin, it became the word raptus, and then raptus became the English word rapture. Five times, the word harpazo is in the New Testament:

1. Acts 8:39, when the Spirit caught up Phillip.

2. 2 Corinthians 12:2, when Paul was caught up to the third heaven.

3. 2 Corinthians 12:4, when Paul was caught up to paradise.

4. 1 Thessalonians 4:17, when the living believers are caught up with the resurrected dead.

5. Revelation 12:5, when the child is caught up to God.

   b) Bullet point two states regarding the coming of our Lord and our gathering together to him, that day will not come until after the man of lawlessness takes his seat in the temple, proclaiming himself to be God.

   c) Bullet point three states that Jesus does not resurrect the dead until the last day.

The logic here is inescapable: Jesus is coming for his people, and the resurrected believers rise from the dead before those who are alive and remain get caught up or raptured. Regarding the coming of our Lord Jesus Christ and our gathering together to him, that day will not come before the Antichrist reveals himself in the temple as God. Jesus does not raise the believers until the last day.

Even if you could believe that Jesus meant something other than the literal last day—which is highly unlikely as Jesus is the way, *the truth*, and the life (John 14:6)—the Scriptures plainly tells us that concerning the coming of our Lord and our gathering to be with him that day will not come until after the revealing of the Antichrist. The theory of two different "raptures" (once for the Church in secret and then plainly at the end of the age) is just that: a theory.

What this theory that I am proposing now hinges on depends on what Jesus meant by the last day? Could Jesus have meant the last day before the Tribulation? It's possible, but why not just say that? Without any other qualifiers the natural understanding would be the last day of the end of the age.

Jesus approached and, breaking the silence, said to them, All authority (all power of rule) in heaven and on earth has been given to Me. Go then and make disciples of all the nations, baptizing them into the name of the Father and of the Son and of the Holy Spirit, Teaching them to observe everything that I have commanded you, and behold, I am with you all the days (perpetually, uniformly, and on every occasion), *to the [very] close and consummation of the age.* Amen (so let it be). (Matt. 28:18-20) (emphasis mine)

Let us recognize that this verse is part of what Christians call the Great Commission. This is his parting instruction to his disciples. This is his last commandment before returning to the Father. This has been taught countless times. However, every sermon I have heard does not include this last part of Jesus stating he is with us all the way through to the end of the age. Is that not curious? Jesus told us to go, make disciples, baptize, teach, etcetera. Everything in the Great Commission Christians accept as Jesus's parting words to them as his disciples except that Jesus is with us all the way through until the end of the age…why is that? We accept everything except the timing part.

The experts of the law in Jesus's day thought they knew what the coming of the Messiah would look like. Jesus let them keep their preconceived ideas and simply went about his Father's business. Jesus expected his people to adjust their thinking "on the fly" as God brought prophecy to pass. Most of the experts got it wrong and found themselves outside the provision of God. We would do well not to repeat their mistake. Let us come to terms with the fact that scriptures that appear conflicted God knows fully, but we do not.

The rest of the various theories about Christ's Second Coming are worth exploring. However, the plainly written verses about Jesus's return and the Rapture need to be our focus. We have the King of kings and the Lord of lords telling us he will resurrect those who believe in him on the last day. We also have the King of kings' and the Lord of lords' protégé, Paul the apostle, telling us we do not get raptured until after the resurrected believers rise from the dead first, and neither of these things occur until after the revealing of the Antichrist. All the rest, as important as it is, does nothing to change this equation.

CHAPTER 4

Man's Preconceived Ideas

We must go into this knowing that we have some things wrong. That God would give any one person 100 percent accuracy in any area of spiritual knowledge defies logic. Our egos would be too big to be of any use to God. "We see in part; we know in part; we see through a glass dimly . . . but we see!" (1 Cor. 13:9–12, author's paraphrase). The Bible states Jesus received the Spirit without measure. None of the rest of us can make that claim.

A word about prophecy: Prophecy is a complicated matter. No one has it completely right, including this writer. The following story may illustrate this concept well.

There was once a teacher at a school for the blind who took four of her students to a petting zoo in which there was an elephant. She guided one student to the tail, another to the ear, and another to a leg, and the last one to the trunk. When the teacher asked each of her students to describe an elephant, each student's perspective differed from the other students' depending upon which part that student had contact with. (This story is an adaptation of the blind men and the elephant.)

Prophecy is similar—only God knows all the aspects of this elephant. We need to know that most people who attempt to broach this subject are sincere in their beliefs. Hopefully, the motives of their hearts are pure. However, one has one part of that elephant and someone else another. It does not make them wrong. Perspective is different due to which part of the elephant they had contact with. The Bible says in 2 Peter that no prophecy of Scripture is up to any one person's individual interpretation, as it did not originate with humankind but with God.

> [Yet] first [you must] understand this, that no prophecy of Scripture is [a matter] of any personal or private or special interpretation (loosening, solving). For no prophecy ever originated because some man willed it [to do so—it never came by human impulse], but men spoke from God who were borne along (moved and impelled) by the Holy Spirit. (2 Pet. 1:20–21)

Returning to the Scripture that states that no prophecy of Scripture is up to any one person's individual interpretation, as it did not originate with humankind but with God, I would like us to consider Jesus as an example. Jesus was speaking with the leaders of the synagogue, and he stated that their interpretations concerning him were wrong.

> You search and investigate and pore over the Scriptures diligently, because you suppose and trust that you have eternal life through them. And these [very Scriptures] testify about Me! And still you are not willing [but refuse] to come to Me, so that you might have life. (John 5:39–40)

Jesus never corrected the misconceptions and faulty theology of the leaders of his day. One of their misconceptions was that his birthplace was not Bethlehem. They believed he was from Galilee and therefore excluded him from the possibility of being their promised Messiah. Jesus never came back to them and said, "No, I was born in Bethlehem, but because of the rulers in power threatening my life, my family moved to Egypt. After a while, we resettled in Galilee." He could have set the record straight; he never did so. Jesus is not all that interested in challenging our preconceived ideas. He knows, and Scripture bears testimony, that the sincere heart will find him, regardless of our preconceived ideas.

The leaders of Jesus's day attempted to interpret Scripture about the First Coming of the Messiah and got it wrong. Jesus has promised us repeatedly that he is coming a second time. If you are a person who finds the miracles, signs, and wonders too grandiose to be believable—especially as described in Matthew 24, Revelation, and other places throughout the Scriptures—then consider his First Coming. This holds especially true if you believe in the First Coming of Christ yet struggle with the magnitude of what Jesus states is going to accompany his Second Coming if you take what he says literally. It is understandable if you are not a believer. However, if you are a believer, have you really considered the magnitude of the miracles, signs, and wonders concerning his First Coming?

He was born of a virgin! Do you believe that or just feel like people got carried away and embellished the story a little? Angels ministered to him and attended to him at his birth, baptism, and many other instances. He turned water into wine, walked on water, and fed five thousand men—not including the accompanying women and children—with a handful of fish and some loaves of bread. He healed the sick, cleansed lepers, and even raised the dead! Honestly, how many people have you known who have done even one of those things? Finally, he rose from the dead himself and now sits at the right hand of the Father, making intercession for us. Many miracles, signs, and wonders attested to his

First Coming, so is it so unbelievable that he would do likewise at his Second Coming? We have grown up hearing about all these miracles and take them for granted. We even hear it in our Christmas specials and A Charlie Brown Christmas, to the point it doesn't really hit us where we live. Have you ever considered how you would have reacted if you had been alive during the time of Christ? Would you have stood with Christ or with the religious leaders of the day? Don't be too quick to answer that because it is one thing to evaluate with hindsight and another when it is happening in the right here and now. We—or our children, or their children—may be in a position to have to make those kinds of decisions. The Bible says, "the love of the great body of believers is going to grow cold" (Matt. 24:12, author's paraphrase) The majority will not stand with Christ when push comes to shove, so let's not be quick to say we would have stood by him, as we may soon get our own chance.

Here is an example of Jesus not defending himself. He chose not to challenge the preconceived ideas of the biblical scholars of his day:

Listening to those words, some of the multitude said, this is certainly and beyond doubt the Prophet! Others said, this is the Christ (the Messiah, Anointed One)! But some said, What? Does the Christ come out of Galilee? Does not the Scripture tell us that the Christ will come from the offspring of David and from Bethlehem, the village where David lived? So there arose a division and dissension among the people concerning Him. Some of them wanted to arrest Him, but no one [ventured and] laid hands on Him. Meanwhile the attendants (guards) had gone back to the chief priests and Pharisees, who asked them, why have you not brought Him here with you? The attendants replied, never has a man talked as this Man talks! [No mere man has ever spoken as He speaks!] The Pharisees said to them, are you also deluded and led astray? [Are you also swept off your feet?] Has any of the authorities or of the Pharisees believed in Him? As for this multitude (rabble) that does not know the Law, they are contemptible and doomed and accursed! Then Nicodemus, who came to Jesus before at night and was one of them, asked, does our Law convict a man without giving him a hearing and finding out what he has done? They answered him, Are you too from Galilee? Search [the Scriptures yourself], and you will see that no prophet comes (will rise to prominence) from Galilee. (John 7:40–52)

These were the rulers, theologians, and Bible scholars of Jesus's day. But they had it wrong. If we—who are attempting to interpret the Scriptures concerning his Second Coming as thoughtful, sincere seekers—can get it wrong like they did, should we even attempt to interpret prophecy? God put prophecy in our Bible to guide us, but we need to be careful. No prophecy is of any individual interpretation, so the key is to not be so dogmatic about what you believe about any prophecy, but to get the main points the Holy Spirit is trying to convey in the prophecy. God alone knows each detail, but there is much that is clear about a prophecy without getting stuck on the details.

Let us look at some more examples of places Jesus corrected the religious leaders' interpretation of the scriptural prophecy concerning his First Coming and chose not to correct their viewpoint. Then, we are going to look at those he gave revelation knowledge concerning the prophetic Scripture of his First Coming.

In this example, a lawyer asked Jesus a question. They tested him and said, "Which are the really significant commandments given by God?" Jesus answers him with, "Love God with everything you have got and those around you like you do yourselves. These two commandments capture the intent of the law." Then Jesus turns the table on them and says, "Concerning the Christ, whose son is he?" They replied with, "He is the son of David, of course." Jesus comes back with "David calls him Lord" and quotes Psalm 110:1 (which David wrote), which says: "The Lord said to my Lord, sit at my right hand until all your enemies are under your feet." His question to them is, "If David calls him Lord, then how can he be David's son?" After this exchange, nobody challenged him with penetrating questions. (Matt. 22:35–46, author's paraphrase)

Now he cleared up a doctrinal error in this exchange and challenged their previous point of view concerning whose son the Christ was. However, there is no reference to him continuing the dialogue and showing them how he was the Christ, the Son of the Living God. He simply left it at that and gave them something to think about. Wouldn't you say this was a perfect opportunity for him to explain about the Scriptures concerning his fulfillment of messianic prophecies? There is no record that he did so. Isn't that strange?

In this next example, Jesus is talking to his disciples and asks them what the people are saying about him. They answer, "Some say you're John the Baptist and others Elijah or one of the other prophets." Then Jesus says, "Who do you say that I am?" Peter declares, "You are the Christ!" Then, with strong conviction, he tells them to "keep that among themselves and tell no one" (Mark 8:27–30, author's paraphrase).

Why does Jesus do that? Doesn't he want people to get it straight? Does it not seem strange to you that when he could broadcast to others through his willing disciples, he forbore? Not that it is unimportant that people came to know him as their Messiah in his First Coming, but the emphasis is on how they came to know. In these and other examples, it is glaringly clear that having all the complicated Scriptures figured out correctly is not a prerequisite to revelation knowledge. Who were these men, by the way? Were they the great minds of Jesus's day? No, these were fishermen, tax collectors, and a physician. So being educated doesn't leave you out, as Luke was a physician, but those who simply followed Jesus were the ones Jesus revealed himself to.

In the following example, he declares straight out to the rulers of his day that he is the Messiah, but they had already made up their minds concerning him and use his confession to sentence him to death.

The high priest during Jesus's trial asks him to reveal whether he is, in fact, the Christ, the Son of God. Jesus replies with, "You have stated the fact and in addition, I tell you that you will see me seated at the right hand of my Father and coming on the clouds of the sky." At this point the high priest tears his robe and says, "What need do we have of any further evidence? We have all heard him commit blasphemy. What do you say we should do?" They answered, "He needs to be put to death" (Matt. 26:63–66, author's paraphrase)

Now let us look at the people he revealed himself to. There was a blind man whom Jesus healed, and the people got excited and came to the religious rulers and stated, "Jesus healed this man." This man had been blind from birth, so they were looking at an incontrovertible miracle, and the people were saying, "Is this the Christ?" The religious people did not want to hear that, so they first verified that he had indeed been born blind. They brought in the blind man's parents and questioned them about whether this was their son who had been blind from birth. They said, "Yes, this is our son, and he has been blind since birth." Then they asked the parents, "How does he now see?" They replied, "He is of age. Question him yourselves," because they were afraid of being expelled from the synagogue if they confessed Jesus did the healing. The rulers would excommunicate anyone who declared that Jesus was the Christ.

They brought the former blind man in a second time and asked him again how he got healed. The man told them, and they said, "We will give God glory, but as for Jesus, we know he is a sinner." At this point the man replied, "Whether he is a sinner, I am not sure, but what I know is I was blind and now I see." They asked him again how he got healed, and he got a little testy with them and asked, "Why do you want to hear it again? Are you looking to become his disciples also?" They got mad at this point and said, "You are his disciple, but we are the disciples of Moses. We know God used Moses, but we do not know that about this man." The man was getting lippy and said, "Now here is something. We all know God does not listen to sinners. No one has opened the eyes of a man blind from birth, but you are unsure of him. If he were not from God, he could do nothing." They responded, "You have been born in sin, and yet you think you are going to teach us?" At that point, they threw the former blind man out of the synagogue. When Jesus heard they had thrown him out, he came to the man and asked him if he "believed in the Son of God," and the man asked, "Who is he that I may believe?" Jesus said, "I am the Son of God," and the man fell down and worshipped him. Jesus said, "I came into this world for judgment and to make blind eyes see and seeing eyes blind." Some rulers were nearby while this was going on and said, "Are you saying that we are blind?" Jesus told them that because they claimed they could see their sin remains (John 9, author's paraphrase)

This blind man did not need to know the messianic Scriptures and have all his theological ducks in a row. He understood the Messiah had come, and the biblical scholars did not. That really is the point! We do not have to understand it all to be ready for his Second Coming. It is enough to recognize when it is here. He was a blind beggar, and he got what the great minds of his day missed, and Jesus set it up that way.

Here is another example of someone who had absolutely no background to get the revelation of the Messiah's First Coming, and she got it.

Jesus needed to go through Samaria; this was a divine appointment. The Samaritans were outcasts during the time of Jesus. Samaritans were considered half-breeds, as they were half Israeli and half Arabian. They did not accept the rest of the Old Testament, just the Torah or the first five books. Samaritans were out of touch with God's people in Jerusalem. It was improper for a male Jewish person to address a Samaritan woman. This was especially true of this woman, as she had been with five husbands, and she was not even married to the man she was living with now. Jesus was not your typical Jewish male. Almost all the Jewish people would go many miles out of their way to go around Samaria rather than be among those they considered inferior to themselves, so the need that drove Jesus through Samaria was not geographical but a divine appointment.

Jesus was sitting by a well in Samaria and was thirsty, and eventually a Samaritan woman came to draw some water. He asked this woman for a drink, and she said to him, "How is it you ask me for a drink, as you are a Jew, and I am a Samaritan and a woman?" Jesus was alone with this woman, as the disciples had gone into town to purchase something to eat. Jesus's response to this woman's inquiry was to tell her, "If you knew who was asking, you would have instead asked me, and I would give you living water." She responded with, "Sir, you have nothing with which to draw water, so how are you going to provide for me this living water? Are you greater than the person who first built this well, our ancestor, Jacob?" Jesus skipped this question and went directly to the main point. He said, "Everyone who drinks this water will thirst again, but the water that I give shall be in a person and they will never thirst again."

This impressed the woman, and she said, "I want that water so that I am no longer thirsty and have to come all this way to get some." Jesus told her to "get her husband." She replied, "Sir, I have no husband." Jesus told her, "In this, you have spoken the truth, for you have had five husbands and the man you are living with now is not your husband." The woman said, "Sir, I perceive you are a prophet." Switching the focus off herself and her lifestyle, she tried to sidetrack Jesus with a theological question. She said, "Our ancestors worshipped God here on this mountain in Samaria, but you Jews say that Jerusalem is the proper place to worship." Jesus responded, "The time is coming when people will not worship merely here on this mountain or in Jerusalem but wherever they are at in Spirit and in Truth. My Father is seeking those types of worshippers. God is a Spirit, and those that seek to worship him must do so in Spirit and in Truth."

Now we get to the crux of the matter, as she said, "I know that when the Messiah comes, he will tell us everything we need to know and make it all clear to us." Jesus said to her, "You are speaking with him right now." The woman ran into town and told everyone, "Come and see a man who has told everything about my life to me. Is it possible that this is the Messiah?" The community could not have had a high opinion of her with her reputation. As excited as she was about the possibility of Jesus being the Messiah, it did not slow her down at all, and the people of her community came to Jesus. Some of them believed because of the woman's testimony, and others believed after listening to him for themselves. Then these people said, "Now we know that this is the Messiah, the Savior of the world." The Messiah spent two days with them before returning to Galilee (John 4, author's paraphrase)

Once again, these people are among the least likely to discern and accurately decipher the scriptural prophecies concerning the First

Coming of the Messiah. They had none of the messianic prophecies in the Psalms, in Isaiah, or in any of the other books to work with. However, these guys got it right, and the Bible scholars got it wrong. The point is, if we look at Jesus's criteria for what he was looking for regarding the prophetic Scriptures concerning his First Coming, he was not looking for anything remotely akin to perfection. They did not have to have it all figured out to please him.

Maybe we need to give ourselves a break and not feel we must have it all figured out either. There is more than enough bottom-line stuff to keep ourselves occupied with until his Second Coming. In particular, the things he says repeatedly: be faithful to the end, he who endures to the end, be watchful, pray, do good things for others when it is in your power to do so, etcetera. If we look at the life of Jesus regarding how he handled prophetic Scriptures in relationship to his expectations of those around him, we see he was not all that interested in their theological viewpoints. It is not wrong to want to delve into the Scriptures and rightly divide the Word of Truth. But getting it all figured out is not high on God's priority list. His priorities regarding prophetic Scriptures appear to differ from our own, so maybe we would do better to take our cue from him. In these examples, we can safely conclude that the currency of the kingdom of God is faith, not understanding, or intelligence.

When God gives us prophetic Scripture, we see what we want to see—and God does not stop us. Even the Apostles, with Jesus telling them straight out he must suffer many things at the hands of the authorities and on the third day rise again, could not see past their preconceived ideas until after the fact:

> Let these words sink into your ears: the Son of Man is about to
> be delivered into the hands of men [whose conduct is opposed

to God]. However, they did not comprehend this saying; and it was kept hidden from them, so that they should not grasp it and understand, and they were afraid to ask Him about the statement. But a controversy arose among them as to which of them might be the greatest [surpassing the others in excellence, worth, and authority]. (Luke 9:44–46)

He just got through telling them and instead of understanding the significance of what Jesus just told them . . . they are arguing. God does not stop us from missing what is being said, not even when we are walking with the Word made flesh. How much less should we be dogmatic in our beliefs when he is not physically among us? They got what he just plainly stated to them wrong, even after they walked with him and saw all the signs and miracles. Why was it that what he just said did not captivate them? What was already going on in their hearts and minds took priority over what Jesus just plainly told them! They were slow to believe even after the Resurrection, and only truly got it then—not before. What does that suggest to us when we look at human reasoning attempting to decipher prophetic Scripture? The religious experts and those who walked with him both missed it! The heart hears what it wants to hear.

God many times gives us insight through prophecy about things that are going to come to pass. However, it was rare when humans accurately understood what God *meant* by what God *said.* Even Daniel who was well known for understanding visions and dreams consistently asked the messengers sent to him for clarification. However, Daniel did correctly interpret the dream of Nebuchadnezzar. (Dan. 2:27-45)

As an example, Joseph had a dream about eleven stars and the sun and moon bowing down and giving him reverence. They all understood that Joseph was claiming God was lifting him up above all the members of his household. That part they got right. However, in the end God did exactly what he said when Joseph was sold in slavery to Egyptians, was promoted, went to jail, was promoted again, and eventually became the second-highest ruler in Egypt. The brothers came to Egypt because of the famine and bowed before him not even recognizing who he was. The path to how God fulfilled this prophecy no one could have foreseen. (Gen. 37–50)

We are each of us accountable to God for how we understand the Scriptures. Paul praised the residents of Beroea because unlike the residents of Thessalonica, they listened to what Paul said about the Messiah Jesus and then went back through and studied the Scriptures for themselves to check the Apostle Paul's understanding of God's word (Acts 17:11). Your favorite Bible teacher is not allowed to speak on your behalf concerning your understanding of Scripture. You and I are responsible before God for studying out these matters for ourselves.

When God told Moses to confront the rulers in Egypt, did God bother to tell Moses ahead of time what his obedience would cost him . . . or did he just let him walk into it blind? When Moses obeyed God, the rulers of Egypt made it harder on the people of Israel, and God did not spare Moses but required both the leader and the people to readjust (Exod. 5.)

Did Job understand what was going on when God allowed the enemy of his soul to test him? No. Job is a good example. What was going on in the heavenly realm, Job did not see! God expects us to trust him when things make little sense and entrust ourselves to him, as he is our faithful Creator.

The angel of the Lord told Mary that she would give birth to the Messiah, and she responded with an enthusiastic "yes." Did her heart know all that yes encompassed? (Luke 1:38). Did her heart know at that moment that thirty-three years later, she would see her son hanging on a cross? Do we believe that even then, she really understood what God was doing and why?

If we look at the example of Jesus's First Coming and his interactions with his people, there is only one safe interpretation of prophetic Scripture: Trust and adjust as events unfold. Stay close and prayerful because he does not filter his agenda through our preconceived ideas. God enacts what he has purposed and expects us to fall in line with his ways and purposes.

These extraordinary events are only going to occur once: the visible Second Coming, the great falling away, and the reign of the Antichrist. Many people during Hitler's rise to power felt sure that he was the Antichrist, and the end of the world was near. Could we go through a tough season and then have things settle down again? Of course. We could have this entire turmoil die down and receive peaceful times for hundreds or even thousands of years. You and I do not control the flow of human history. If events and unrest throughout the world continue at the pace they are currently at, then it does not appear the end is that far off. We have had many false positives before. However, let us look at a passage that has a definite time . . . even though we do not know specifically when this is:

> So, the four angels who had been in readiness for that hour in the appointed day, month, and year were liberated to destroy a third of mankind. (Rev. 9:15)

If taken at face value, there is a specific time for these events to take place, and nobody but the Father knows if that is a few years or a few millennia away.

But when the proper time had fully come, God sent His Son, born of a woman, born subject to [the regulations of] the Law. (Gal. 4:4)

God is very specific with time. While we have a lot of choice in this life that he gives us, anybody who has seriously followed God for any amount of time will attest to the fact that God leaves the timing of events in our lives in his hands and not ours.

There is a reason that in this study, we have looked at this concept of humankind's preconceived ideas in contrast to God's fulfillment of prophetic Scripture to the point of redundancy. In the American culture we live in today, our focus on God's Word has a huge emphasis on prosperity and God's personal best for our lives. There is nothing wrong with that, providing we have balance with the other truths of God's Word. If we are leaning too much in one direction, we will find it hard to adjust if God enacts events that are outside of our mindsets. The purpose is simply to be open and willing to adjust as God brings events to pass because scripturally, given the examples we have just looked at, most people miss it when the time is now.

CHAPTER 5

Jesus's Teaching on the End of the Age

After a lot of prophecies, there is an explicit instruction from the Lord regarding our response to what he is saying. For example, in Matthew 24, which we shall look at shortly, Jesus gives many prophecies about the end of the age. At the end of the chapter, Jesus gives us an explicit instruction:

Watch therefore [give strict attention, be cautious and active], for you do not know in what kind of a day [whether a near or remote one] your Lord is coming. But understand this: had the householder known in what [part of the night, whether in a night or a morning] watch the thief was coming, he would have watched and would not have allowed his house to be undermined and broken into. You also must be ready therefore, for the Son of Man is coming at an hour when you do not expect Him. Who then is the faithful, thoughtful, and wise servant, whom his master has put in charge of his household to give to the others the food and supplies at the proper time? Blessed (happy, fortunate, and to be envied) is that servant whom, when his master comes, he will find so doing. I solemnly declare to you, he will set him over all his possessions. But if that servant is wicked and says to himself, My master is delayed and is going to be gone a long time, And begins to beat his fellow servants and to eat and drink with the drunken, the master of that servant will come on a day when he does not expect him and at an hour of which he is not aware, And will punish him [cut him up by scourging] and put him with the pretenders (hypocrites); there will be weeping and grinding of teeth. (Matt. 24:42–51)

This is important—our response to what he is saying. The people living in this time that Jesus is referring to will know through experience the events of that time and will be able, with hindsight, to say, "Oh, that was what Jesus was talking about." But it is our response that is important, not our understanding ahead of time what each individual point is. God knows we will speculate about prophecy. We need to be careful that we do not get so hung up on trying to interpret each individual piece of it and become so dogmatic in our views that we repeat the mistake that the leaders and theologians and Bible scholars of Jesus's day did. They became so dogmatic about their views that when their Messiah showed up in person, he did not match their preconceived idea of what the Messiah would look like, and they rejected him, to their ruin. We would be wise not to repeat that mistake. Keep prophecy that is clear, especially what God says needs to be our response to certain events. God knows we will speculate, but do not be so narrow-minded in the interpretation that, when the actual events take place, you miss it because it does not fit your mindset.

We need to start with the Scriptures that talk about the end of the age that are the clearest first, to inform those that are less clear. Interpretations in Revelation vary. If you start with Revelation, that becomes your trajectory, the prism through which you evaluate everything else. The straightforward statements made by Jesus, Paul, Peter, and others should be the prism through which we evaluate Revelation.

A word on symbols and symbolism: They are fascinating and sensational. However, the symbols represent real things, both physically and spiritually:

> Then He left the throngs and went into the house. And His disciples came to Him saying, Explain to us the parable of the darnel in the field. He answered, He Who sows the good seed is the Son of Man. The field is the world, and the good seed means the children of the kingdom; the darnel is the children of the evil one, And the enemy who sowed it is the devil. The harvest is the close and consummation of the age, and the reapers are angels. Just as the darnel (weeds resembling wheat) is gathered and burned with fire, so it will be at the close of the age. The Son of Man will send forth His angels, and they will gather out of His kingdom all causes of offense [persons by whom others are drawn into error or sin] and all who do iniquity and act wickedly. (Matt. 13:36–41)

Jesus used symbols when talking to the crowds and explained the meaning of them privately to his disciples. These symbols represent actual times, people, and events. He chose symbols that captured the essence and nature of what he was talking about, illustrating his point to the crowds. There are many more parables that Jesus spoke of, with many more interpretations of the symbols explained, and this pattern holds true. The book of Revelation is full of symbols, and they also represent actual things, both physical and spiritual. We will look at the book of

Revelation and relate the symbols found there in the same pattern that Jesus interpreted the parables to his disciples. While there are different methods of interpretation that are used to decipher Revelation, this is the method we will use in this study. As Jesus is the primary teacher, this approach seems as tenable as any of the other methods.

A man is a physical being, and an angel is a spiritual being, and the Bible speaks of both as being real, even though we see the one and not the other. When we get to the book of Revelation, keep this in mind. While there are lots of symbols Jesus uses to show us his plan, they represent actual people, places, and things. And we do not have to know the identity of each symbol to obey the truth that is revealed in the prophecy.

The Lord, it would appear, is not in the least threatened by our attempts to interpret his Word. He knows that there are going to be many differences of opinions. That does not seem to bother him in the least. Maybe he is evaluating how we each respond to his Word. The Bible states that "he who has will be given more, and he who does not have (understanding), even what he does have shall be taken away." (Matt. 13:12, author's paraphrase)

Pretend that you are the owner of a company, and you put out a vision statement for your company. Then you tell your employees that instead of dictating what that means for them, you desire for them to choose how to incorporate your vision in their day-to-day work activities. What the employee does with implementing the vision statement of the owner says a lot more about that individual employee than it does about the owner of the company. The vision statement from the owner of the company is stable and consistent throughout the life of the company. The individual employees' interpretations of the owner's vision statement are going to be varied, each according to the person's individual abilities, personality, intellect, background, etcetera. This, of course, would never happen in real life, as we humans must be in control and dictate the terms of our vision. But God is very secure in who he is. There is a portion of Scripture in Psalm 2 where the rulers of the nations have gathered together to determine their own course and break off the bonds of the Most High God. The Bible states that "he who sits in the heavens laughs!" (Psalm 2:4) (authors paraphrase) We can make our plans, but control is an illusion, and there is only One who can say with certainty, "I am going to do this or that." Our hearts will one day stop beating, and our time will be up. We are not God and have no guarantee that what we plan will come to fruition.

I struggled for decades about whether to write this book, as there is a lot out there on the subject, and a good portion of it contradicts what the next person writes. The sincere, curious person must be mystified at all the confusion and difference of opinion. If it's all coming out of the same book and we all have the same Spirit of Truth leading and guiding us, how in the world can there be such differences in interpretation? It is imperative that we remember God has made no two snowflakes alike, much less two identical humans.

There are general truths that all sincere Christians share. For example, because of the sacrifice of God's Son on the cross, God forgives our sin, and not through any effort on our part. Other bedrock truths we share include that all have sinned and fallen short of the glory of God, there is a loving God who gave, God has angels, there is a fallen angel named Satan that is God's and our enemy, there are demons, etcetera. There are other areas of the Bible that are not so clear-cut and, therefore, are open to varying interpretation.

Going back to the example of the owner of a company issuing a vision statement, let's say that one of his tenets was that there was no sleeping on the job. It's a pretty straightforward concept. I am reasonably sure most people are going to come to the same conclusion and performance on that instruction. Now what if one of his instructions was to be innovative? What that word means to you may be drastically different from what that means to me. Each person is probably going to have a little different spin on what that's going to look like. There are many truths in the Bible that are straightforward—God is love, he hates sin, etcetera—and there are others that are not so clear: for example, in Matthew 24:28: "Where there is a dead body, there will the vultures be gathered" (author's paraphrase) We need to leave room for personal interpretation, human error, and sin, among a host of other possibilities.

Desiring not to add to the confusion, I kept waiting for certain elements to be introduced by others. I concluded it might be part of my unique snowflake to introduce those elements, and my insight was just as tenable as any of the others I had read on the subject. We do the best we can, knowing that the Bible says we will "all one day stand before the judgment seat of Christ and give an account of our lives to him" (2 Cor. 5:10, author's paraphrase) I have no desire to be wrong and find out I have led others astray and give an account to God for misleading his people. That is a scary thought and one that I take seriously. His Word states that teachers have a greater responsibility, so I struggled for decades and finally decided that in good conscience, I needed to make the attempt, as I could be wrong, but I also could be right—although, I don't think anyone is 100 percent on either side of that equation.

This topic has fascinated me for the vast majority of my life, and I have studied on and off, reading almost anything I could get my hands on concerning the subject of the end of the age and Jesus coming back again. I read all kinds of things, even when I strongly disagreed with them, as I wanted to know why people believed what they believed.

How did they come to that conclusion? He came the first time, and most people got it wrong, and he said he was going to come back again. And for whatever reason, that thought always fascinated me: What is it going to look like? When is it going to happen? Can he wait until I get married first? I had all kinds of questions!

Another thing to note is that humans often equate the power of God being with a person as an endorsement from God that God validates their theology. There is some truth in that God will not use someone significantly if they do not have a solid theological foundation. Salvation, humanity's depravity, God's holiness, God became human to die for our sins, etcetera, are parts of that foundation. But there are other areas that are not as solid, and God leaves room for various interpretations in those areas.

Let us look at some people who God has mightily used and the different denominations they represent. Why? What difference does that make? The contrast should make the acknowledgment that God uses a person based on their personal love relationship with him, and not their theology. Many of these individuals held very different theological understandings. God using us in some significant way is not an automatic endorsement that what that person believes theologically is an oracle of God.

1. Charles Finney was Presbyterian.
2. Watchman Nee was associated with the Plymouth Brethren, who have their roots in the Anglican denomination.
3. Billy Graham was Southern Baptist.
4. John Calvin was a Reformed theologian.
5. Charles Spurgeon a Reformed Baptist.

6. C. S. Lewis was Anglican.

7. Martin Luther is associated with the Lutheran denomination.

8. Benny Hinn is associated with the Assemblies of God and the Pentecostal movement.

9. Mother Teresa was Catholic.

Even if you do not particularly care for some individuals on this sample list, admit that God used them considerably in their time.

Out of all the people who speak in the Bible on the topic of the end of the age, no one is more authoritative and illuminative than Jesus himself. Before we begin the discussion of Jesus's thoughts on the end of the age, we need to set the stage. Jesus, when he talks to the crowds, mostly talks to them in parables. In Matthew 13:9–15, Jesus speaks to the crowd about the parable of the Sower and concludes with this statement:

> He who has ears to hear it let them be listening and let him consider and perceive and comprehend by hearing. (Matt 13:9)

The passages that follow, Matthew 13:10–15, are the basis for a principal in interpreting Scripture. All Scripture quoted is from the Amplified Bible, unless otherwise stated. Choosing this translation was because of the translators' attempts to be very honest in expounding on the Greek text:

> Then the disciples came to him and said, why do you speak to them in parables? And He replied to them, to you it has been given to know the secrets and mysteries of the kingdom of heaven, but to them it has not been given. For whoever has

(spiritual knowledge), to him will more be given and he will be furnished richly so that he will have abundance; but from him who has not, even what he has will be taken away. This is the reason that I speak to them in parables: because having the power of seeing, they do not see: and having the power of hearing, they do not hear, nor do they grasp and understand. (Matt. 13:10–13)

In these passages, we learn that when Jesus talked to the crowds, he talked mostly in parables. When he was talking to his disciples, he spoke plainly. In Jesus's discourse about the end of the age in Matthew 24 and 25, Jesus is not talking to the crowds but talking to his disciples; therefore, he is talking plainly and not in parables.

CHAPTER 6

Matthew 24

Jesus departed from the temple area and was going on his way, when his disciples came up to him to call his attention to the buildings of the temple and point them out to him. But he answered them, do you see all these? Truly I tell you, there will not be here one stone upon another that will not be thrown down. While he was seated on the Mount of Olives, the disciples came to him privately and said, tell us, when will this take place and what will be the sign of your coming and of the end (the completion, the consummation) of the age? (Matt. 24:1–3)

I n Mark 13:3, the Scriptures tell us it was Peter, James, John, and Andrew who asked these things privately, so this was an inner-circle conference.

Quite a few Bible scholars divide this into three separate issues:

1. When will the destruction of the temple be?
2. When will the sign of Jesus's coming be?
3. When will the end of the age be?

While this is clearly plausible, it is not necessarily accurate. The destruction of the temple was 70 CE, and many contend that the end of the age has not happened yet. There are those who suggest the end of the age has already occurred in 70 CE. But when you read about the events in the Tribulation and what the Antichrist is going to accomplish, this does not seem to add up if you apply a literal paradigm as opposed to an allegorical approach. Preterists hold the view that the end of the age has already occurred, and we will look briefly at that perspective.

They base much of this view because of Matthew 24:34: "This generation shall not pass away until all these things are fulfilled." That perspective would suggest that the generation would be Jesus's generation and those alive while Jesus taught this. In the Amplified Bible, the translation is "you, this generation (the whole multitude of people living in a definite, given period) will not pass away till all these things taken together take place." The generation that has all the signs— not just some—in evidence will not pass away before the end of the age.

Preterism is a view concerning end-time prophetic events, that some or all end-time prophecy occurred in the generation following Jesus's death, culminating with the destruction of Jerusalem in 70 CE. There are two schools of thought in the preterists' theology: full preterism and partial preterism. Full preterism is the school of thought that everything concerning the end of the age culminated in 70 CE and fulfilled all prophecies.

Partial preterism is the school of thought that some of the prophetic Scriptures regarding the Second Coming of our Lord and Savior and the judgment of God against sinful humankind have had some fulfillment during the time of the Roman invasion and destruction of Jerusalem in 70 CE. However, the fullness will occur at the end of the age. They would say that Christ came in judgment on Jerusalem, and that was *a* day of the Lord but not *the* day of the Lord.

There were around three hundred messianic prophecies that were literally fulfilled in Christ's First Coming. Why would the prophecies concerning his Second Coming become allegorical? That the Messiah would be from the tribe of Judah, that he would be born in Bethlehem, and that he would die by crucifixion are just three of the prophecies.

It is difficult to follow the train of thought that everything in the Scriptures about Christ's Second Coming in 70 CE completed all his judgment against sinful humankind. You must consider almost everything in Revelation as purely allegorical and next to nothing as literal. Matthew 24 would be allegorical as well. Angelic witnesses stated in Acts 1:11 that we would see Jesus return similarly to how he left, and Revelation 1:7 states the entire world will see him return in the clouds. There has been no record of that having taken place. It is reasonable to agree that Jesus came in judgment on the nation of Israel in 70 CE, but not that he physically came. In the book of Acts, Jesus rose from the earth from his disciples up into the clouds, and two men appeared in white robes. They said:

This same Jesus, who was caught away and lifted up from among you into heaven, will return in [just] the same way in which you saw Him go into heaven. (Acts 1:11)

Is that supposed to be allegorical also? The Scriptures tell us in a different verse where he will return:

BEHOLD, A day of the lord is coming when the spoil [taken from you] shall be divided [among the victors] in the midst of you. For I will gather all nations against Jerusalem to battle, and the city shall be taken and the houses rifled and the women ravished; and half of the city shall go into exile, but the rest of the people shall not be cut off from the city. Then shall the Lord go forth and fight against those nations, as when He fought in the day of battle. And His feet shall stand in that day upon the Mount of Olives, which lies before Jerusalem on the east, and the Mount of Olives shall be split in two from the east to the west by a very great valley; and half of the mountain shall remove toward the north and half of it toward the south. (Zecc. 14:1–4)

Jesus left from this mountain when he ascended to heaven in the disciple's sight. (Acts 1:12) It seems kind of fitting that he would return to the same spot when he comes again.

The partial preterists' viewpoint is a lot more understandable. There was some fulfillment of prophecy in the destruction of Jerusalem and the temple in 70 CE. And they leave room for the physical return of the Lord later, at the end of humankind's history.

However, to assume that the next two events are separate events is just that: an assumption. They are three separate items, but some items naturally go together in the speaker's and the hearer's mind. The easiest illustration to come to mind is asking somebody if they want rice and beans with their dinner. Although rice and beans are separate items, some people in this country think of them as one dish. In the movie Forrest Gump, Forrest says, "Me and Jenny go together like peas and carrots."[3] There are many occasions throughout the Scriptures where men of God admonished strangers, friends, and family to come in and have dinner with them. While these are two separate acts—to come in and to eat—it is one event: fellowship. Various places in the Scriptures see these two events—the coming of the Lord and the end of the age—as two sides of the same coin. Now let's continue with Jesus's statements about the end of the age in Matthew 24:

> Jesus answered them, be careful that no one misleads you [deceiving you and leading you into error]. For many will come in (on the strength of) my name [appropriating the name which belongs to me], saying, I am the Christ (the Messiah), and they will lead many astray. (Matt. 24:4–5)

Many will come in his name and lead many astray. This is maddening, as he states repeatedly how he will appear in the clouds. However, for those who do not study the Bible, it is understandable how someone with great charisma and seemingly good intentions could captivate the heart and intentions of the unaware. The Bible states:

> It is a fearful (formidable and terrible) thing to incur the divine penalties and be cast into the hands of the living God! (Heb. 10:31)

Can you imagine standing before God Almighty and explaining to him why you impersonated his Son and led many people astray? That seems an untenable position, yet many will choose to do just that.

> And you will hear of wars and rumors of wars; see that you're not frightened or troubled, for this must take place, but the end is not yet. For nation will rise against nation, and kingdom

against kingdom, and there will be famines and earthquakes in place after place; All this is but the beginning [the early pains] of the birth pangs [of the intolerable anguish]. (Matt. 24:6–8)

We have had wars and rumors of wars, earthquakes, and famines since time began. However, Jesus says that there will be an escalation in frequency and intensity just before the end of the age, and he compares this increase to a woman giving birth. This is a very general, broad-based sign that one would not want to put a lot of weight on all by itself. As we continue to look at the discourse, we are going to see many more signs mentioned by Jesus that will continue to bring into sharper focus the signs to look for at the end of the age:

Then they will hand you over to suffer affliction and tribulation and put you to death and you will be hated by all nations for my namesake. (Matt. 24:9)

It doesn't cost very much to take a stand for Jesus currently, depending on where you live. In America, we have fishes and crosses on our cars, bumper stickers that read, "Honk if you love Jesus," etcetera. What if loving Jesus caused persecution? The book of Revelation talks about Christians being beheaded during the Tribulation period. How quickly would you put that fish, cross, or bumper sticker on your car then? This is not to belittle or scare anyone but only intended as perspective. The cost of being a Christian today in America compared to this period Jesus describes is very different.

And then many will be offended and repelled and will begin to distrust and desert [him whom they ought to trust and obey] and will stumble and fall away and betray one another and pursue one another with hatred. (Matt. 24:10)

We will turn on each other and turn away from God. It is sometimes strange what a little pressure can do. Some state that pressure reveals the genuine character underneath the facade. During this time, it is going to cost to be a Christian, and many who are currently your brothers and sisters in the Lord will turn you over to the powers that be, and sometimes that will mean your death, as explained more fully in Revelation. The pressures of this time will be like the Holocaust. People had to make the hard choice of hiding Jews from the powers of that time risking their own lives to protect the Jewish people or turning Jewish people into the authorities.

And many false prophets will rise up and deceive and lead many into error. (Matt. 24:11)

In the Old Testament, there is a scene in which false prophets are prophesying to the rulers of their day and telling the rulers just exactly what they want to hear. These obviously held a position of esteem among the rulers, but God hated them. He said:

Then the Lord said to me, the [false] prophets prophesy lies in My name. I sent them not, neither have I commanded them, nor have I spoken to them. They prophesy to you a false or pretended vision, a worthless divination [conjuring or practicing magic, trying to call forth the responses supposed to be given by idols], and the deceit of their own minds. (Jer. 14:14)

There will be a time when Christian ideology and philosophy are going to be at direct odds with the established leadership of the world. The book of Revelation speaks of the Antichrist waging war against the saints, and God permits him to triumph over them until Christ returns and destroys the Antichrist. When you cross-reference Matthew 24 with the book of Revelation, you see that there are many places where they dovetail well. As events continue to unfold and the climate continues to get dark outside, this is a perfect breeding ground for false prophets to rise.

> And love of the great body of people will grow cold because of the multiplied lawlessness and iniquity. (Matt. 24:12)

The book of Thessalonians speaks of a great falling away of those who profess to be Christians in this period. Jesus is painting a picture of the climate that will be prevalent just before he returns. The world is going to be out of control, and lawlessness is going to be the law of the land. Being a police officer is going to be extremely hard then. As bad things happen, people naturally ask, "Where is God? If he is so good, why doesn't he do something?" This is the climate in which many will turn away and say, "I can't follow you anymore. It makes no sense for things to be this out of control and God does nothing!" Actually, he did what was most needful for us two thousand years ago on a cross, and now it's our turn to trust.

"Where was God when my son died?" one parishioner asked. The man's pastor, not wanting to belittle the father's pain, bowed his head and asked God how he should answer the man. God told the pastor to tell the father that he was in the same place when that man's son died that he was when his own son died. God did not leave himself off the hook regarding sacrifice and pain. As his followers, we will have our share also, and we need to trust that when the dust settles, he will balance every scale. In the meantime, our focus needs to be learning to love and trust the One who purchased us at substantial cost to himself.

But he who endures to the end will be saved. (Matt. 24:13)

Another sign to look for will be persecution of the Church and betrayal by church people against each other. Jesus speaks of multiplied lawlessness and iniquity. Again, there have always been lawlessness and iniquity. There will be a marked increase in frequency and intensity just before the end of the age.

And the good news of the kingdom (the Gospel) will be preached throughout the whole world as a testimony to all the nations, and then will come the end. (Matt. 24:14)

Another sign will be all the nations of the earth hearing the Gospel; we are close with this one right now. Severe persecution was the hallmark of the early church. This persecution included beheadings, crucifixion, being boiled in oil, etcetera, but the more persecution came against the Church, the more on fire and persuasive it became.

So, when you see the appalling sacrilege [the abomination that astonishes and makes desolate], spoken of by the prophet Daniel, standing in the holy place—let the reader take notice and ponder and consider and heed [this]. (Matt. 24:15)

Okay, some clarifications of terms are necessary here. Being "sacrilegious" is being disrespectful toward something that is viewed as holy and respectful to the average person. An abomination is something that is loathsome; it fills a person with abhorrence. Desolate is an area that is uninhabitable, devoid of life, or barren.

So when the Bible speaks of the abomination of desolation, it does not convey a concrete image in our mindsets. But basically, the imagery here is like that of a church or synagogue when vandals break in. The vandals urinate and defecate all over the altar, write obscenities on the wall in blood, rip the Bible or Torah in half and pour refuse on it, etcetera. What they have done is an abomination to that church or synagogue, and they have made the practices of that church or synagogue desolate or inoperable until cleansing occurs. We are going to look more fully at the abomination of desolation spoken of by Daniel the prophet.

> Then let those who are in Judea flee to the mountains; Let him who is on the housetop not come down and go into the house to take anything: And let him who is in the field not turn back to get his overcoat. And alas for the women who are pregnant and for those who have nursing babies in those days! Pray that your flight may not be in winter or on a Sabbath. (Matt. 24:16–20)

It is imperative that, as Christians, we pray that when the abomination of desolation takes place, it's not in the winter or on the Sabbath. Scriptures tell us exactly what that is, but the seven-year Tribulation period would obviously include some winters and many Sabbaths. The seven-year Tribulation period is actually a misnomer, as the Great Tribulation period Jesus designates occurs after the abomination of desolation. Scripture tells us that there is a seven-year covenant that the Antichrist confirms and, at the halfway point, breaks the covenant by committing the abomination of desolation. So the seven-year Tribulation period, as it has become known, is actually three and a half years, not seven. The prayer that is needed is the timing of when the abomination of desolation occurs. It is at this point that all hell breaks loose. Pray it's not under these circumstances.

> For then there will be great tribulation (affliction, distress, and oppression) such as has not been from the beginning of the

world until now—no, and never will be [again]. And if those days had not been shortened, no human being could endure and survive, but for the sake of the elect (God's chosen ones) those days will be shortened. (Matt. 24:21–22)

This is a paradoxical verse! There is comfort because God sees and, for the elect's sake, shortens the days because, left on our own and allowed to run its own course, we would annihilate ourselves. Therefore, it is scary how badly we allow things to get, but nice that God intervenes. Some would say he intervenes too late, and it is going to feel that way, but he alone holds the position of the Most High God, so we will need to trust his judgment. The scenario that Jesus paints for us in these verses would be hard to conceive in any of the previous generations, that if those days had "not been shortened," no flesh would have survived. However, since the Manhattan Project, and the potential for nuclear warfare in this present age, total annihilation is very conceivable now.

The abomination of desolation—Jesus says when we see it, there is no time for going back and getting that one last item. The picture here is like having your house on fire, and it is now too late to go in the house to grab something vitally important, such as your life's savings kept hidden in a safe. So what is the abomination of desolation? Jesus said that when you see the abomination that makes desolate, recorded by Daniel the prophet, you should run. Let's hear what Daniel has to say.

And he shall enter into a strong and firm covenant with the many for one week [seven years]. And in the midst of the week he shall cause the sacrifice and offering to cease [for the remaining three and one-half years]; and upon the wings or pinnacle of abominations [shall come] one who makes desolate, until the full determined end is poured out on the desolator. (Dan. 9:27)

Many theologians and Bible scholars agree that the he here is referring to the Antichrist, as it is part of the seventy weeks of years that God has appointed for his people in judgment. We will get into the seventy weeks of years a little later in the book.

This verse describes the Antichrist entering a strong covenant or treaty with many people for seven years. When you cross-reference this with the book of Revelation, there is another declaration of someone entering a treaty for seven years. Approximately three and a half years into the treaty, the Antichrist breaks his promise, and the treaty is void. Upon the wings or pinnacles of abominations shall come one who makes desolate. Both terms—wings and pinnacles—speak of heights, so probably this is the height of abomination. We will look a little later into the activity of the Antichrist as he performs this monstrosity and causes the people of God and their activities to become desolate.

Some at this point will say, "Well, brother, now that is an encouraging word!" I'm not trying to pretend that a lot of this is not unsettling—it is. But let's keep in mind our example of Jesus, of whom the Bible states "for the joy that was before him endured the cross!" (Heb. 12:2, author's paraphrase) Do you know what his joy was? It was you and me who were redeemed by his precious blood and brought into the family of God for all eternity. But the only way to satisfy the divine justice of God was that our sin had to be paid for, and, seeing as there was no one else pure enough to pay that cost, God paid it himself. But to get to the joy, he had to go through the cross. We will never come close to matching him and the extravagance of his gift toward us. However, without knowing all the answers, we can emulate him and go through dark times, knowing that there is joy on the other side of our cross as well.

> For His anger is but for a moment, but His favor is for a lifetime or in His favor is life. Weeping may endure for a night, but joy comes in the morning. (Ps. 30:5)

To get into why one week is equal to seven years is in the book of Numbers, and it is a biblical principle of God that when he is in judgment against his people, he counts a year for each day of whatever wrong they committed.

> And your children shall wander in the wilderness forty years, and bear your whoredoms, until your carcasses be wasted in the wilderness. After the number of the days in which ye searched the land, even forty days, each day for a year, shall ye bear your iniquities, even forty years, and ye shall know my breach of promise. I the LORD have said, I will surely do it unto all this evil congregation, that are gathered together against me: in this wilderness they shall be consumed, and there they shall die. (Num. 14:33–35 KJV)

According to the verse in Daniel, a person is going to come along and enter a firm covenant with many people, and Israel is on one side of that agreement for seven years. We have grown up with the "Middle East peace talks," and to date there has been no resolution. There is a time coming of Middle East peace, but it will not last. In the middle of that seven-year period, he will cause the sacrifice and offering to cease for the remaining three and a half years. Maybe part of this agreement, or covenant, comes with the provision of the Jewish nation being able to resume their religious observance of temple sacrifice.

Now the Jews in Jerusalem do not sacrifice at the temple. In 70 CE, Rome destroyed the temple, and Israel was not a nation for the next nineteen-hundred-plus years. On May 14, 1948, Israel once again became a nation and was back in Jerusalem. There are a lot of different factors why Israel does not sacrifice in the temple; however, it is now possible. There are a lot of obstacles that would have to be taken care of for Israel to resume sacrificing at the temple. According to some interpretations of biblical prophecy, Israel will one day resume sacrificing at the temple. If you had suggested two hundred years earlier that Israel could resume sacrificing at the temple, people would have called you crazy because the nation of Israel had not had a homeland in nineteen-hundred-plus years. While we are not there yet, it is within the realm of possibility that Israel could resume sacrificing at the temple if certain events fall into place. When this occurs, according to the way some interpret biblical prophecy, it will be another piece in setting the stage for the Antichrist and the abomination of desolation.

In 167 BCE, a man by the name of Antiochus Epiphanes took control of the temple in Jerusalem and committed many abominations. Among the abominations committed by this man was the sacrificing of a pig on the altar, an unclean animal according to Jewish law, and therefore, an abomination. Antiochus Epiphanes also set up an altar to Zeus over the altar in the temple in Jerusalem. When the Antichrist comes and reveals himself, the Bible says he will take a seat at the temple of God and proclaim himself to be God.

> But relative to the coming of our Lord Jesus Christ [the Messiah] and our gathering together to [meet] him, we beg you, brethren, Not to allow your minds to be quickly unsettled or disturbed or kept excited or alarmed, whether it be by some [pretended] revelation of [the] spirit or by word or by letter [alleged to be]

from us, to the effect that the day of the lord had [already] arrived and is here. Let no one deceive or beguile you in any way, *for that day will not come except the apostasy comes first* [unless the predicted great falling away of those who have professed to be Christians has come, and the man of lawlessness [sin] is revealed, who is the son of doom [of perdition] Who opposes and exalts himself so proudly and insolently against and over all that is called God or that is worshiped, [even to his actually] taken his seat in the temple of God, proclaiming that he himself is God. (2 Thess. 2:1–4) (emphasis mine)

This, then, is the abomination that makes desolate, when the Antichrist defiles the temple in Jerusalem and proclaims he is God.

If anyone says to you then, behold, here is the Christ (the Messiah)! Or, there he is!—do not believe it. For false Christs and false prophets will arise, and they will show great signs and wonders so as to deceive and lead astray, if possible, even the elect (God's chosen ones). See, I have warned you beforehand. (Matt. 24:23–25)

Jesus has stated that he is coming again, but in these verses, and in other verses in the Scriptures, Jesus tells us in what manner we will see him come again. We will not meet him in the street or in a car or out in the desert. So if anyone standing on the earth tells you he is Jesus, he is a liar, unless he is standing on the Mount of Olives and has a heavenly army behind him! One principle that is taught in interpreting Scripture in many Bible colleges is that if the passage makes common sense, look for no other interpretation. The following is an example of Scripture, not following the common-sense rule of interpretation.

For you shall go out [from the spiritual exile caused by sin and evil into the homeland] with joy and be led forth [by your leader, the Lord himself, and his word] with peace: the mountains and the hills shall break forth before you into singing, and all the trees of the field shall clap their hands. (Isa. 55:12)

Since no one has ever seen a mountain or hill sing, or a tree clap its hands, this Scripture is not to be taken literally, but it paints a picture in our minds of exuberant celebration. However, it is to be understood that when Jesus speaks in parables, the images that he paints in our minds represent real people, places, and things. Let's look at some of the Scriptures that mention Jesus's return at the end of the reign of the Antichrist.

And when he had said this, even as they were looking [at him], he was caught up, and a cloud received and carried him away out of their sight. And while they were gazing intently into heaven as he went, behold, two men [dressed] in white robes suddenly stood beside them, who said, men of Galilee, why do you stand gazing into heaven? This same Jesus, who was caught away and lifted up from among you into heaven, will return in [just] the same way in which you saw him go into heaven. (Acts 1:9–11)

Behold, he is coming with the clouds, and every eye will see him, even those who pierced him: and all the tribes of the earth shall gaze upon him and beat their breasts and mourn and lament over him. Even so [must it be]. Amen (so be it). (Rev. 1:7)

Even though no one except the apostles has seen Jesus taken up into the clouds, and this isn't a natural occurrence, I believe we can go with the literal interpretation. This is, after all, the Son of God we're talking about, and in three different places, (Dan. 7:13, Acts 1:11 and Rev. 1:7) we have seen him say that he is coming in the clouds. Miracles are part of the very nature of Jesus, so with him, we can expect miracles to occur. Also, during the Tribulation, according to Scripture, there will be miracles, signs, and wonders on both sides: good and evil.

Wherever there is a fallen body (a corpse), there the vultures (or eagles) will flock together. (Matt. 24:28)

Does this verse seem out of place to anyone else? It feels like you are following a normal chain of events, and then, Jesus plops this little gem right in the middle of the discourse, and you scratch your head, saying, "Where does this fit?"

Jesus is painting a picture here in our minds of something that is common: dead bodies and carrion birds. Recently there have been a lot of videos being posted on Facebook and other outlets about God; some good and some really off-the-wall ones. I was researching something totally unrelated about the marriage supper of the Lamb when I believe God dropped this into my spirit. My brother would send me a bunch of videos he was watching on Facebook. He is desiring to grow spiritually and asked me to provide feedback: What is wholesome in the videos, and what parts are not? While I was researching about the marriage supper of the Lamb, the verse about the carcass and vultures caught my eye from a different source entirely, and I felt God nudge me about the off-the-wall videos being posted in his name. In one video, as an example, the person was passionately exhorting that we are not going to heaven if we do not use the name of God in the original Hebrew and then misrepresented a few key Scriptures to back up his claim. This was a genuine concern for my brother, so I showed the Scriptures the person was using to make his claim and how the person was distorting the truth. Then I added that when Jesus was physically here on the earth, if this was a make-it-or-break-it kind of deal, do you not think that Jesus would have let us know? That addressing God in the original Hebrew pronunciation of his name was of paramount importance to our eternal salvation? People who are not knowledgeable about biblical content and principles, the relatively uninitiated, turn to the internet to find answers for the craziness going on in the world around them. People are more than willing to share their viewpoints. Some of them are fantastic, but some of them really stir up a lot of nonsense that works people into a frenzy and unnecessary concern. This would appear to fit. The dead body would symbolize the bad news, chaos / end-of-the-world-type calamities, the uncertainty, the fear, the ignorance of God and his ways. The vultures feeding off it would symbolize the false prophets and Messiahs. It could be something else, but this is at least plausible.

> Immediately after the tribulation of those days the sun will be darkened, and the moon will not shed its light and the stars will fall from the sky, and the powers of the heavens will be shaken. Then the sign of the Son of Man will appear in the sky, and then all the tribes of the earth will mourn and beat their breasts and lament in anguish, and they will see the Son of Man coming on the clouds of heaven with power and great glory [in brilliancy and splendor] And he will send out his angels with a loud trumpet call, and they will gather together his elect (his chosen ones) from the four winds, (even) from one end of the universe to the other. (Matt. 24:29–31)

Most of these verses appear to be straightforward. Many people would like to use a lot of symbolism, but I am not sure that is necessary.

There are other places in the Bible that speak about the heavens being shaken and the sun, the moon, and the stars not giving their light. If everything is falling apart around you, that is a pretty good sign that the world is ending as you know it.

> From the fig tree learn this lesson: as soon as its young shoots become soft and tender and it puts out its leaves, you know of a surety that summer is near. So also, when you see these signs, all taken together, come to pass, you may know of a surety that he is near at the very doors. Truly I tell you; this generation (the whole multitude of people live and at the same time, and a definite, given period) will not pass away till all these things taken together take place. (Matt. 24:32–34)

The lesson of the fig tree is exceptional; everybody who experiences seasons can relate to this. After a long, hard winter, you see the trees budding and you know that summer is coming. In the same way, when you see all the signs taken together, you know that Jesus's Second Coming is very close.

> Sky and earth will pass away, but my words will not pass away. (Matt. 24:35)

We count the sky and earth as permanent, yet the Lord states these will pass away, but his words will not. What he is saying here has more permanence than what we deem solid.

> But of that [exact] day and hour no one knows, not even the angels of heaven, nor the Son, but only the Father. (Matt. 24:36)

It never ceases to amaze how people can try to predict the date that Jesus will return; no one knows except the Father. A season, in nature, is a very general thing. Summer, for instance, has an appointed date and hour on our calendars, but really it can come days or weeks earlier, or later, for that matter. If you've ever seen fruit ripen on the tree, you know that there's no particular time or hour, but one day it's too early, and the next day it's ripe for picking. We will know the season, but we will not know the day or the hour. That is the lesson of the fig tree.

> As were the days of Noah, so will be the coming of the Son of Man. (Matt. 24:37).

We will look shortly at the climate of Noah's day. The part earlier in Jesus's discourse concerning multiplied lawlessness and iniquity is a strong parallel picture of the days of Noah.

> For just as in those days before the flood they were eating and drinking, marrying and [women] being giving in marriage until the [very] day when Noah went into the ark. (Matt. 24:38)

Life went on as normal, business as usual, until the very Day of Judgment, and then it all changed in a heartbeat, and it was too late to change.

> And they did not know or understand until the flood came and swept them all away—so will be the coming of the Son of Man. (Matt. 24:39)

The people of Noah's day saw the signs and especially the building of the ark. The Scriptures speak of this period catching people unaware, like a "thief in the night." God closed the door of the ark, and it rained.

(Gen. 7:16) The people of Noah's day probably toasted ale to Noah and his family mockingly until the water rose. They at that point could see it coming, and finally realized their danger, but at that point there was no way out. The picture here may be very similar. People are going on about their daily business and suddenly realize they are in this time and there is no escape. That sensation would be like being on the Titanic right after it has hit the iceberg. You can see the inevitable, and while it will not happen immediately, there is no escape. Let's look at what the Bible says the days of Noah were like.

> The Lord saw that the wickedness of man was great in the earth, and that every imagination and intention of all human thinking was only evil continually. And the Lord regretted that he had made man on the earth, and he was grieved at heart. So the Lord said, I will destroy, blot out, and wipe away mankind, whom I have created from the face of the ground—not only man, [but] the beast and the creeping things in the birds of the air—for it grieves me and makes me regretful that I have made them. But Noah found grace (favor) in the eyes of the Lord. (Gen. 6:5–8)

"As it was in the days of Noah, so shall it be at the coming of the Son of Man." Remember the verse that stated, "Because lawlessness will abound, the love of many will grow cold." At the end of the age, the imagination and intention of most human thinking will only be evil. Remember, in the beginning of the book, the case of Albert Fish who psychologically tormented the young girl's mother in a letter? While we are not there yet, we are well on our way. One of the most fascinating things is humankind's continued belief that humans are basically and inherently good. Do any of those who hold to the belief that we are inherently good watch the news, read the paper, or listen to the radio?

We are not basically good; we are basically evil and selfish, which is why we need a Savior. That is why we need his Holy Spirit in us to help us become more like him because, left to our own devices, we would be more like his enemy. It is tenets like that; that we are basically sinful by nature, that will not wash with the new world order.

> And they that entered, male and female of all flesh, went in as God had commanded [Noah]; and the Lord shut him in and closed [the door] round about him. (Gen. 7:16)

Now back to Matthew 24.

> At that time two men will be in the field; one will be taken and one will be left. (Matt. 24:40)

"At that time" is a reference to verse 39 about the days of Noah taking people by surprise and the coming of the Son of Man. The people of Noah's day felt the first raindrop. How long do you suppose they were outside the ark, with the rain falling, the door of the ark closed, and their deaths inevitable but not immediate? Hours? Days? Weeks? Before the water rose to such an extent that they drowned.

> Two women will be grinding at the hand mill; one will be taken and one will be left. Watch therefore [give strict attention, be cautious and active] for you do not know and what kind of a day [whether a near a remote one]. Your Lord is coming. But understand this: had the householder known in what [part of the night, whether in a night or a morning] watch the thief was coming, he would have watched and would not have allowed his house to be undermined and broken into. (Matt. 24:41–43)

There is considerable disagreement among scholars whether the wicked or the righteous get taken first. It is hard to understand what difference it makes as long as we're on the right side. It should not matter if Jesus takes us first or gets us last. There is a separation, and that we are wise if we are watchful and prepared for his return. Interpreting Scripture can be exciting; many people shy away from it because they feel it is hard, and not worth the effort. There are quite a few Christians who get deep and detailed in the symbolism. However, if we get too focused on the symbolism, we can lose sight of what is important that describes the effects in the verses. Whether the symbol is a ball or a beast, it really doesn't change what it is or what it does. It is of more importance to understand what the symbol does, and what the symbol's nature is than it is to be right on exactly what the symbol is.

Here is an example:

When He broke open the third seal, I heard the third living creature call out, Come and look! And I saw, and behold, a black horse, and in his hand the rider had a pair of scales (a balance). And I heard what seemed to be a voice from the midst of the four living creatures, saying, A quart of wheat for a denarius [a whole day's wages], and three quarts of barley for a denarius; but do not harm the oil and the wine! (Rev. 6:5–6)

In this Scripture, there is a symbol of a horse and rider. Theologians and scholars can debate until Jesus returns what exactly the horse and the rider are. Knowing ahead of time what exactly it is does not change the effect of what it does. Whether this symbol is the Antichrist, a demon, or a demented Easter Bunny, it doesn't change the fact that a person's daily wage will only be enough to buy a minimal amount of food for the day—a picture of a severe famine. Basically, it appears to be saying that a humankind's wages will provide food for one person, and that will be all. That leaves nothing for mortgages, car payments, gas, electricity, etcetera. We too often get hung up on trying to interpret what a symbol is and lose sight of what the Holy Spirit is trying to tell us through the symbolism. This is not to say that symbols are unimportant. They are important; however, Jesus chooses the symbols, and throughout the Gospels, and even in the book of Revelation, he gives the interpretation. Where he does not explain the symbolism, it is open to interpretation, and one person's sincere desire to interpret is as tenable as the next persons, but might this not be a sifting process? As previously discussed, there is a lot that is clearly revealed in prophecy, such as the horse and rider, that illustrate a great and severe famine. The sifting process may be those who focus on the symbols and get stuck on trying to get that perfected. The focus should be on what is clear. He talked to the crowds mostly in parables in his day and told the disciples that this was basically a process to sift out those with eyes to see versus those who have eyes to see and yet do not see. Those who were truly hungry and desired to see would press through until they became his disciples in truth. Those who did not played lip service and never came to a real personal understanding of the truth.

Now back to Matthew 24.

You also must be ready therefore, for the Son of Man is coming
at an hour when you do not expect Him. (Matt. 24:44)

Once again, the admonition is for preparedness. In the book of Thessalonians, we see we are not in darkness, that the day should overtake us as a thief. However, if we are in darkness, the opposite is also true that the day could overtake us as a thief. One purpose of this book is to show how there are threads or veins of thought that bear witness to each other in different places throughout the Bible that give great credence to the Holy Spirit authoring those principles. For example, in the Old Testament, we have the entire sacrificial system that is a symbol or picture of the sacrificial Lamb of God. Another vein in the New Testament includes John the Baptist saying, "Behold the Lamb of God, which takes away the sins of the world." (John 1:29) (author's paraphrase) In Isaiah 53, we have a beautiful rendition of the suffering Messiah, who was "wounded for our transgressions and bruised for our iniquities." That is a Holy Spirit–inspired theme that is woven throughout the Bible in various books separated by hundreds and sometimes thousands of years. When the Lord does this, we need to pay attention, as he is bearing witness to a truth he wants us to understand.

There is a principle in interpreting Scripture that was disclosed thousands of years ago:

> One witness shall not prevail against a man for any crime or any wrong in connection with any sin he commits; only on the testimony of two or three witnesses shall a charge be established. (Deut. 19:15)

The principle is that two to three witnesses are necessary to establish a verdict. So when the Holy Spirit uses different men and women, especially from different time periods, we need to pay particular attention. Throughout this book, we will look at what Jesus said and compare it to what Paul said. At the time Jesus was speaking these truths in Matthew 24, Paul was not a believer and was an enemy to the cross of Christ. Then the Holy Spirit spoke through Jesus to John at the close of his life while exiled on the island of Patmos. We will also cross-reference these themes with what the Holy Spirit spoke through Daniel, an Old Testament prophet who spoke centuries before the time of Jesus, as well as Isaiah and Joel. When the Holy Spirit weaves a truth, and they dovetail with each other, it is fascinating. The similarity between these passages is profound and very insightful and confirms each other. We may disagree as to the interpretation, but that the Holy Spirit authored these truths through different men of God in various time periods should be apparent to all. And that alone should cause us to stand up and take notice.

> Who then is the faithful, thoughtful, and wise servant, whom his master has put in charge of his household to give to the others the food and supplies at the proper time? (Matt. 24:45)

Remember that cross-referencing that we discussed earlier. Let's look at something the prophet Daniel had to say about the end of the age:

> And he [the angel] said, go your way, Daniel, for the words are shut up and sealed till the time of the end. Many shall purify themselves and make themselves white and be tried, smelted, and refined, but the wicked shall do wickedly. And none of the wicked shall understand, but the teachers and those who are wise shall understand. (Dan. 12:9–10)

While this is not a perfect dovetail, they have similar qualities. Those who are wise will prepare for this time and will make themselves white and purified. It would be those who made themselves white and purified that God would appoint to give to the others the food and supplies at the proper time. Preparedness is the theme in both Scriptures concerning the end of the age. This would also dovetail nicely in the book of Revelation, where he tells us to purchase from him gold refined in the fire so that we would have true riches, eye salve for our eyes so that we can see, white garments so we do not appear naked, etcetera.

Being prepared during the end of the age is of great importance to the Holy Spirit.

> Blessed (happy, fortunate, and to be envied) is that servant whom, when his master comes, he will find so doing. I solemnly declare to you, he will set him over all his possessions. But if that servant is wicked and says to himself, My master is delayed and is going to be gone a long time, And begins to beat his fellow servants and to eat and drink with the drunken, The master of that servant will come on a day when he does not expect him and at an hour, of which he is not aware, And will punish him [cut him up by scourging] and put him with the pretenders (hypocrites); there will be weeping and grinding of teeth. (Matt. 24:46–51)

This is not the time for games and pretending. There is a saying that goes, "Get right or get left." That sums it up here.

A Wise Virgin

CHAPTER 7

Matthew 25

There is coming a time in history when the stage is going to be set for the appearance of the Antichrist and the end of the age. As time continues to move forward, we are obviously getting closer to that time every day. But as we look around at the world today, we should be concerned that we are so close, it's scary.

One of the greatest signs we are nearing the end of the age is the explosion of knowledge:

> But thou, O Daniel, shut up the words, and seal the book, even to the time of the end: many shall run to and fro, and knowledge shall be increased. (Dan. 12:4 KJV)

Looking back can be a totally amazing experience as we think how much knowledge has increased in the last one-hundred-plus years. In 1908, Henry Ford started the regular production of the Model T, although he had one made in 1903. Look how far we have come in that time. Until the 1900s, for centuries, humankind got around by foot or horse. Now we travel across the ocean in six or eight hours and think nothing of it.

In the mid-1800s, the light bulb was being perfected; now we have lights in almost every home here in America. Without light and electricity, where would we be? No television, radio, cell phones, or computers. We play games on Facebook and talk to people in Asia, China, Thailand, Burma, etcetera. In just over two hundred years, we have gone from candlelight to all the technological advantages that we take for granted every day.

In the early 1900s, there were no anesthesia or injections; early films of surgery show doctors and nurses not wearing gloves. Today we have laser surgery, nanotechnology with the possibility of having microscopic robots inside the human body, and stem cell research, not to mention liposuction and many other marvelous surgical procedures.

The point is, whether you believe in evolution or creationism, for at least six thousand years—much less the millions of years that are attributed to the evolutionists' perspective—things have been relatively primitive, with no quantum leap in knowledge such as we have experienced today. We had the Renaissance, but it doesn't compare to the advancement in knowledge we have seen in the last two-hundred-plus years. Knowledge continues to compound exponentially. A computer bought today is sorely outdated just a few years down the road.

It is self-evident that knowledge has exploded in this last century, and to show more examples would be redundant.

Matthew 25 needs to be included as well, as there are two stories that illustrate how we need to respond, considering Matthew chapter 24. A section of this we will simply paraphrase.

THEN THE kingdom of heaven shall be likened to ten virgins who took their lamps and went to meet the bridegroom. (Matt. 25:1)

Immediately following Jesus's discourse on the end of the age in chapter 24, he states, "Then." So what follows next is in a direct relationship to what was just stated before.

Five of them were foolish (thoughtless, without forethought) and five were wise (sensible, intelligent, and prudent). For when the foolish took their lamps, they did not take any [extra] oil with them. (Matt. 25:2–3)

There are many places throughout this book where we are going to overlook the various possibilities of symbols and their meanings. This is not due to them not being important, because God would not have included them if that were the case. The purpose is to say, putting to the side for the moment what the various possibilities are as to the actual identity of each symbol, what could the symbols be distracting us from? We are going to look at this passage and note that many Bible scholars and theologians believe that one symbol of the Holy Spirit is oil. In the Old Testament, when a person was getting promoted to an office or position of authority, the law required that the priest pour anointing oil on the person. There are other examples as well, but those who need to study this can do so at their own leisure. This would be very important in this parable of being prepared that we have enough of the Holy Spirit operating in our lives for this time. The Bible states Jesus was "given the Holy Spirit without measure," and none of us can claim that (John 3:34, author's paraphrase) We would be wise to be prayed up and full of the Holy Spirit during the darkness of these days. We need to keep this in mind as we read this parable.

> But the wise took flasks of oil along with them [also] with their lamps. While the bridegroom lingered and was slow in coming, they all began nodding their heads, and they fell asleep. (Matt. 25:4–5)

It has been nearly two thousand years since Jesus's First Coming, and many lose heart as the wait for his return continues. God does not reckon time in the same way that we do.

> But at midnight there was a shout, Behold, the bridegroom! Go out to meet him! (Matt. 25:6)

At midnight, unless you're a night owl, most people are in bed. The picture here is that of an inconvenient and unexpected time for the bridegroom to choose to show up. And, once again, preparation is the principal theme.

> Then all those virgins got up and put their own lamps in order. And the foolish said to the wise, give us some of your oil, for our lamps are going out. (Matt. 25:7–8).

The picture here is that it is dark and there is not enough oil in the lamp to provide the light that is necessary for the journey to go meet the bridegroom at this late hour. It may be redundant for those familiar with the Scriptures to go through this step by step. However, the book is for all stages of interest and development: the novice, intermediate, and the knowledgeable. Hopefully, there is something for everyone in this approach.

But the wise replied, there will not be enough for us and for you; go instead to the dealers and buy for yourselves. But while they were going away to buy, the bridegroom came, and those who were prepared went in with him to the marriage feast; and the door was shut. (Matt. 25:9–10)

While they were going to get prepared for him, he showed up. If you have a desire to get right with God, do not wait until the last moment, as that may be too late. Being prepared is a consistent theme throughout Matthew 24 and 25.

Later the other virgins also came and said, Lord, Lord, open [the door] to us! But He replied, I solemnly declare to you, I do not know you [I am not acquainted with you]. (Matt. 25:11–12)

If you had truly known me, you would have been ready and not rushing around at the last minute trying to get ready.

Watch therefore [give strict attention and be cautious and active], for you know neither the day nor the hour when the Son of Man will come. (Matt. 25:13)

While the lesson of the fig tree would show that we will know the season, we will not know the day or the hour. However, if we are in darkness and not watching, we could even miss that we are in the season, and then our shame would be very great indeed.

In Matthew 25:14–46, there is another story to illustrate the truth of being prepared and using what God has given you to bless others, even in the darkest of times. Jesus compares the timing of his return to a man who went on a long journey and entrusted his servants with various amounts of money, each according to the individual's abilities.

Two of them doubled his investment, while one of them hid the money because he was afraid.

I was afraid. Fear can cause us probably more than any other thing to allow the gift of God that is in us to lie dormant! Fear of change, fear of failure, and fear of success paralyze the well-intentioned individual. We need to bless and honor God by using the gifts he has given us to bless others, or we run the genuine risk of Jesus taking from us and giving the gifts to another.

Upon his return, the master calls the servants together to account for their stewardship. Two that doubled his investment, he strongly commended and rewarded them accordingly. With the one who hid the money, the master was furious. The master took from the "unprofitable servant" and gave what he had to the one who had made the most. Jesus then states that when his kingdom comes, he will gather all nations before his throne and separate them. He will separate them like a shepherd separates his sheep from his goats: the righteous he depicts as sheep, and the unrighteous he depicts as goats. He tells the sheep to enter his kingdom because when he was in need, they ministered to him. They respond with, "In what way did we minister to you in need?" Jesus states that because they ministered to the less fortunate among themselves, they were doing it to him.

Once again, we are looking at those who are prepared and are actively blessing others around them. It is noteworthy that God states, "You did it for one of the 'least' of my brothers." Let's not be so quick to judge and evaluate those who are worthy of our attention. God's way of looking at things differs from ours. In 1 Samuel 16:7, God says as much, stating, "He looks at the heart while we look at the outward appearance." To the goats, he states the opposite, that they saw him in need and did nothing. They respond, "In what way have we seen you in need and did nothing?" Jesus states that because they did not minister to the less fortunate among themselves, they did not minister to him. The righteous are told to enter his kingdom, and the unrighteous do not enter. With both stories, we are told to be prepared. Preparation and using what gifts and talents we have to bless others are especially important during the darkest of times. This is to be our response to and during the time of the end.

It needs to be repeated that our actual job here on earth is not to figure this all out. We have spoken before about how Jesus spoke to the leaders of his day and told them that, with as much as you search the Scriptures, they should be able to recognize him, "because it is the Scriptures that bear witness to me." We really need to learn this lesson: he is not requiring us to get it all right. It is unnecessary to have all the t's crossed and the i's dotted. If it were, he would have required that of those he revealed himself to in his First Coming, but he did not. They only needed to get one thing out of all the Scriptures that talked about his coming to his people: that they saw enough in the Scriptures to recognize him for who he was. Most of them missed it. Coming toward the end of his ministry, Jesus had a heart cry: "Jerusalem, oh Jerusalem your people consistently murder and stone the prophets that God sends to you. I wish you could understand how I have longed to gather you together just like a hen gathers her chicks, but you have refused" (Matt. 23:37, author's paraphrase) He did not sit there and debate with them and tell them where they erred, as in the example of where his birthplace was. Why not? If getting all this stuff figured out was important to him, he had many opportunities to get their theology right and seldom did so.

If we can learn from this lesson about his First Coming, we can get it right. The requirements are simple: be prepared, watchful, and faithful. That's it. The rest is gravy. I keep coming back to this, but it is for an excellent reason. Imagine that you are alive during the time of Christ's First Coming and you are a biblical scholar. Along comes an exciting but controversial man who, many claim, is the Messiah that your nation has been waiting for. What do you do? Would you not pore through the Old Testament concerning the prophecies about the Messiah? After you have done this, what would you do next? Would you not go to the person in question and talk with him and see if the prophecies about the Messiah match up with this person's life? Many of the Bible scholars of Jesus's day did exactly that, and what is fascinating are not their questions but his responses.

Professing themselves to be wise, they became fools. (Rom. 1:22 KJV)

I do not intend to slight those that are educated. But it seems scripturally clear that God puts a lot more weight on getting the core of what he is saying, and believing it, much more than figuring out every detail in things that he has purposefully left open to interpretation. Once again, he has revealed himself to the simple people of his day and left those who were experts in the Scriptures confounded.

In that same hour He rejoiced and gloried in the Holy Spirit and said, I thank You, Father, Lord of heaven and earth, that You have concealed these things [relating to salvation] from the wise and understanding and learned, and revealed them to babes (the childish, unskilled, and untaught). Yes, Father, for such was Your gracious will and choice and good pleasure. (Luke 10:21)

That Scripture reveals the heart of God. We do not have to have it all together to be in a proper relationship with him.

In evaluating Jesus's discourse on the end of the age and his return, we need to consider some schools of thought that are prevalent on the subject. Many theologians and Bible scholars currently believe that we, as Christians, will not be around when all these dreadful events take place and that the Church or body of true believers will be raptured before the Great Tribulation. That is a distinct possibility. However, somebody is going through this period, and we need to at least consider the possibility that we might not be raptured before these dreadful events take place. So as we go through this discourse, please try to put yourself in this time frame as events that could occur in your lifetime and how you might respond to all these various pressures. There will be a group of believers going through the period of the Great Tribulation just before the end of the age, and exactly who these people are is debatable.

Jesus was not only talking to his own disciples in 33 CE. He was speaking to this group of people at the close of the age to warn and encourage them to endure to the end. So as much as possible, put aside for the moment any preconceived ideas you may have and consider the example of the narrow-mindedness of the experts in Jesus's day. They thought they had it right, and Jesus did not bother to show them how they had it wrong. Through his life and example in ministering to those the experts believed were beneath them, he showed them they were wrong. He rarely engaged them in a battle of wits to show them they were wrong. Imagine Jesus is talking to this group of believers, whoever they might be, as he knows what they are about to face. Before he returns, he is trying to equip them for what lies ahead. If it doesn't turn out that way and the Rapture occurs before this time, what have we lost by considering the possibility? So please, try to put yourself in these scenarios and consider what you would do and how you would feel. Would these pressures draw you closer to God or push you away from him?

An Angel of Light

CHAPTER 8

An Angel of Light

One of the most fascinating and polarizing figures in the Scriptures is the Antichrist. So many people see him as a monster, and he is! However, he will not appear to be so. Let's inspect what the Scriptures have to say about him. There is a tremendous difference in how the world sees him when he first arrives on the scene and how the world sees him after he has revealed his true nature.

> For false Christ and false prophets will arise, and they will show great signs and wonders so as to deceive and lead astray, if possible, even the elect (God's chosen ones) See I have warned you beforehand. (Matt. 24:24–25)

> For such men are false apostles [spurious, counterfeits], deceitful workmen, masquerading as apostles (special messengers) of Christ (the Messiah). And it is no wonder, for Satan himself masquerades as *an angel of light.* (2 Cor. 11:13–14) (emphasis mine)

The Antichrist, the man of lawlessness and sin, will not appear to be so when history first encounters him. He will be very charismatic and likable, not what you would expect. The Scripture says that the entire world will go after him.

> One of his heads seemed to have a deadly wound. But his death stroke was healed; and the whole earth went after the beast in amazement and admiration. (Rev. 13:3)

Now admittedly, someone recovering from a fatal wound would be fascinating in their own right. However, if the person who received this miracle were Charles Manson (an infamous cult leader and murderer), would we follow him?

As already discussed in Matthew 24, false Christs will appear and be so convincing they would lead astray even God's very elect, if that were possible. The Antichrist will be the master of the false Christs. Should we expect any less from him?

Keep in mind the principle of interpretation mentioned earlier: If it makes common sense, look for no other interpretation. Also remember the principle of not getting lost in the symbolism but asking yourself what the nature of the thing being symbolized is and what the result is.

As we look at prophecies that have already come to pass, let that build your faith that what the Scriptures states about the Antichrist will come to pass as well. Let us look briefly at one prophecy that is truly astounding. The prophet Isaiah is prophesying about a suffering servant who will heal God's covenant people through what he endures. There is sure to be a person this applied to during the time of the writing of Isaiah. However, there is no human being that could totally fulfill this prophecy unless that person were both God and human. So while the prophecy could have some fulfillment before Jesus, Jesus is the fullest expression of this prophecy as the Son of God and the Son of Man:

> WHO HAS believed (trusted in, relied upon, and clung to) our message [of that which was revealed to us]? And to whom has the arm of the Lord been disclosed for [the Servant of God] grew up before Him like a tender plant, and like a root out of dry ground; He has no form or comeliness [royal, kingly pomp], that we should look at Him, and no beauty that we should desire Him. He was despised and rejected and forsaken by men, a Man of sorrows and pains, and acquainted with grief and sickness; and like One from Whom men hide their faces He was despised, and we did not appreciate His worth or have any esteem for Him. Surely He has borne our griefs (sicknesses, weaknesses, and distresses) and carried our sorrows and pains [of punishment], yet we [ignorantly] considered Him stricken, smitten, and afflicted by God [as if with leprosy]. But He was wounded for our transgressions, He was bruised for our guilt and iniquities; the chastisement [needful to obtain] peace and well-being for us was upon Him, and with the stripes [that wounded] Him we are healed and made whole. All we like sheep have gone astray, we have turned everyone to his own way; and the Lord has made to light upon Him the guilt and iniquity of us all. (Isa 53:1–6)

What are the chances that the rest of God's prophecies about the end of the age will fail? A question to consider: If God is this specific and literal in all the prophecies to date, why do some of us believe the rest is allegorical? The symbols that we will look at later in the book of Daniel all deal with literal world empires: Babylonia, Mede-Persian, Greek, Roman, and finally a kingdom not made by human hands.

There are many Christians who believe the millennial reign of Christ is allegorical rather than literal. Is that possible? Of course. The way Christ came the first time took his covenant people completely by surprise. He did not come in the box they had put him in. However, the pattern to date shows all the kingdoms are literal kingdoms, so the probability is that his millennial kingdom will be literal as well. To be fair, though, God will not be in anybody's box, so he is obviously free to do it in any way he chooses.

Peace will mark the time of the Antichrist—or so it will appear. There are verses in the book of Daniel concerning the Antichrist establishing a treaty with many for seven years. It states that in the middle of that time, he is going to break faith with those he has the treaty with. It is reasonable to assume that the first part of that period is looking pretty good until he breaks his promise and reveals his true nature. Now when we cross-reference that scriptural piece of knowledge with what the Bible shows us in 1 Thessalonians, we get a clearer picture of this time of peace becoming a nightmare.

There is a man coming on the scene that will appear to be the answer to all of humankind's problems. He will appear as an angel of light. Lawlessness will be the norm then. As bad as things are today, and getting worse, it is not totally out of control yet. If everybody were afraid because that is how bad and lawless it had become, would we give up our precious personal freedom to know safety and security once again? What if things like abusive parents, or children being sold as sex slaves, rape, and violence were far more normal for our societies rather than the exception? What if our society and the world's societies were so saturated with evil men and women that our police and prisons couldn't even handle the demands placed on them?

We have been giving an example of this with some riots in London. The British prime minister David Cameron had quite a bit to say on the subject. He is a brave man and deserves credit for speaking up for the truth.

> Keeping people safe is the first duty of government. The whole country has been shocked by the most appalling scenes of people looting, violence, vandalizing, and thieving. It is criminality pure and simple. And there is absolutely no excuse for it. Finally, Mr. Speaker, let me turn to the deeper problems. Responsibility for crime always lies with the criminal. But crime has a context. And we must not shy away from it. I have said before that there is a major problem in our society with children growing up not knowing the difference between right and wrong. This is not about poverty, it's about culture. A culture that glorifies violence, shows disrespect to authority, and says everything about rights but nothing about responsibilities. In too many cases, the parents of these children—if they are still around—don't care where their children are or who they are with, let alone what they are doing. The potential consequences of neglect and immorality on this scale have been clear for too long, without enough action being taken. As I said yesterday, there is no one step that can be taken.[4]

This is a foretaste of things to come! As this trend continues, people are going to be looking for leadership. Then, from out of nowhere, someone will come who can twist order out of chaos and restore a measure of safety and security to the common person.

What would we not give to the person or persons who could bring order out of uncontrolled chaos?

As the economy gets worse, which is symbolized by one of the Four Horsemen of the Apocalypse of Revelation concerning this time, desperate people will do desperate things. Our economy in America has suffered a lot recently with high unemployment. For the first time in its history, the United States did not sustain a triple-A status credit rating. Watching the news clearly shows us that one nation's economic fortune or misfortune directly affects all the other nations' economies. We are already in a global market.

Many people would contend that there is a direct correlation between worsening economic conditions and an increase in crime rates. There have been stories of people killing others just for their sneakers in the inner city. How much more if people are starving, as depicted in Revelation? As the economy gets worse, you can expect lawlessness to go through the roof. What price is too high for safety at that point? One sure way to stop identity theft is a microchip or other mark for personal identification. A case in point would be the barcodes used to scan our groceries and other items that identify specific items for the cashiers' convenience. This microchip is probably not the item, but something similar.

We already have microchips to find our lost pets, with the information of each pet stored in a database. How far of a leap is it to implement a similar version for humans? As cybercrime becomes more prominent and lawlessness increases amid severe hardship, such as famine, how many people's bank accounts would be at risk before we would say it is worth it to take an identity chip to protect ourselves from the unscrupulous? The Antichrist does not start out leading the world. The Bible says, "He extends his authority over every tribe and nation." If it worked there, then yes, we want it too! Enter the Savior! It may not be this scenario that ushers in the reign of the Antichrist, but whatever it is, people want it bad enough to sacrifice big for it.

CHAPTER 9

The Climate of the Antichrist

"The day of the Lord" is a short chapter later in the book, but primarily it is a day of God's judgment. This day is going to catch many people napping, but not everybody. The day of the lord is a part of this period of the Tribulation and the reign of the Antichrist. As we continue to study this, we will notice patterns that are prevalent in these different places in Scripture that support each other in completing a picture of what this period looks like. There is more scriptural reference to this time of the end of the age than almost any other period in the history of humankind. If God spends this much time on this one period in humankind's history, it must be important.

"The day of the Lord" talks about a man being rarer than gold and the sun, moon, and stars not giving their light. However, we see the same themes in Zephaniah, Joel, and Isaiah about the sun, moon, and stars not given their light, as well as in Matthew 24 and the book of Revelation.

The great day of the lord is near—near and hastening fast. Hark! the voice of the day of the lord! The mighty man [unable to fight or to flee] will cry then bitterly. That day is a day of wrath, a day of distress and anguish, a day of ruin and devastation, a day of darkness and gloom, a day of clouds and thick darkness. (Zeph. 1:14–5)

The sun shall be turned to darkness and the moon to blood before the great and terrible day of the lord comes. (Joel 2:31)

For the stars of the heavens and their constellations will not give their light; the sun will be darkened at its rising and the moon will not shed its light. (Isa. 13:10)

Immediately after the tribulation of those days the sun will be darkened, and the moon will not shed its light, and the stars will fall from the sky, and the powers of the heavens will be shaken. (Matt. 24:29)

Then the fourth angel blew [his] trumpet, and a third of the sun was smitten, and a third of the moon, and a third of the stars, so that [the light of] a third of them was darkened, and a third of the daylight [itself] was withdrawn, and likewise a third [of the light] of the night was kept from shining. (Rev. 8:12)

This is the time where the Holy Spirit puts this verse in 1 Thessalonians about peace and safety and then sudden destruction right in the day of the Lord. This discourse is just after Paul's discussion of the return of the Lord and the Rapture of the people of God in chapter 4. So in 1 Thessalonians 5:1, suitable times, seasons, and dates are in direct relation to the topic he was just talking about.

Then, in 2 Thessalonians 2:3, Paul gives further insight that this day of the Lord will not come until the Antichrist is first revealed.

These verses give us glimpses of the climate and the timing of events in the ministry of the Antichrist and that all these elements are in this period:

> BUT AS to the suitable times and the precise seasons and dates, brethren, you have no necessity for anything being written to you. For you yourselves know perfectly well that the day of the [return of the] Lord will come [as unexpectedly and suddenly] as a thief in the night. When people are saying, All is well and secure, and, There is peace and safety, then in a moment unforeseen destruction (ruin and death) will come upon them as suddenly as labor pains come upon a woman with child; and they shall by no means escape, for there will be no escape. But you are not in [given up to the power of] darkness, brethren, for that day to overtake you by surprise like a thief. For you are all sons of light and sons of the day; we do not belong either to the night or to darkness. (1 Thess. 5:1–5)

I want to include these verses from a different translation of the Bible simply because the translators of the Amplified Bible state that the day of the Lord is synonymous with the return of the Lord. They may be right, but they may be wrong.

> But of the times and the seasons, brethren, ye have no need that I write unto you. For yourselves know perfectly that the day of the Lord so cometh as a thief in the night. For when they shall say,

Peace and safety; then sudden destruction cometh upon them, as travail upon a woman with child; and they shall not escape. But ye, brethren, are not in darkness, that that day should overtake you as a thief. Ye are all the children of light, and the children of the day: we are not of the night, nor of darkness. (1 Thess. 5:1–5 KJV)

As mentioned in a previous chapter, we can debate what the day of the Lord is. There are sure to be some readers who will automatically reject the Amplified Bible's attempt at translating this verse to include the return of the Lord in "the day of the Lord."

BUT RELATIVE to the coming of our Lord Jesus Christ (the Messiah) and our gathering together to [meet] Him, we beg you, brethren . . . (2 Thess. 2:1)

Many readers prefer the King James Version (KJV) of the Bible, which I adore. I have memorized extensive amounts of Scripture, almost all of it in the KJV. However, I hope to make this as understandable as possible, and I sincerely hope that the average person: truck driver, stay-at-home parent, server, taxi driver, etcetera will understand this other version easier than they would the KJV.

We have these two separate events stated in such a way that they could be the same event. One following right after the other: the coming of our Lord and our gathering together with him. Can they be separate events? Of course. He is God and can do as he likes, but both here and in 1 Corinthians 15, when Paul brings this subject up, they are together, as though it is one thought, one breath:

But each in his own rank and turn: Christ (the Messiah) [is] the firstfruits, then those who are Christ's [own will be resurrected] at His coming. After that comes the end (the completion), when He delivers over the kingdom to God the Father after rendering inoperative and abolishing every [other] rule and every authority and power (1 Cor. 15:23–24)

Not to allow your minds to be quickly unsettled or disturbed or kept excited or alarmed, whether it be by some [pretended] revelation of [the] Spirit or by word or by letter [alleged to be] from us, to the effect that the day of the lord has [already] arrived and is here. Let no one deceive or beguile you in any way, for that day will not come except the apostasy comes first [unless the predicted great falling away of those who have professed to be Christians has come], and the man of lawlessness (sin) is revealed, who is the son of doom (of perdition). (2 Thess. 2:2–3)

Sequentially, the day of the Lord will not come until after the great falling away occurs and the Antichrist reveals his true intentions. (Remember in Matthew 24, where Jesus spoke of the "great body" of believers' love growing cold and betrayal by your brothers and sisters in the Church? Could this be a dovetail?) In many places, Scripture interprets Scripture, and the picture here is similar. Some people profess to be Christians, but the pressures here will reveal that they never really knew him. Revelation gives a clearer picture of what that looks like, but for now, we have the sequence. Again, while we have two separate events, they could be two sides of the same coin: the man of lawlessness being revealed and the great falling away of Church people betraying each other. It wouldn't make much sense to turn on each other before the man of lawlessness reveals himself. But as we learn later in the book of Revelation, God allows the Antichrist to make war on God's people and prevail. It is at this point, when turning you in saves my hide, that it makes the most sense to betray my brothers and sisters in the Lord. This is especially true if I wasn't really in love with him, but I was simply giving lip service and hoping to get a little fire insurance.

CHAPTER 10

Scriptural Glimpses of the Antichrist

ere is the Scripture that Daniel spoke of concerning the seven years that he—a person many theologians would agree is the Antichrist—would break his agreement in the middle. So the first three and one-half years are going to be golden until he reveals his true nature in the second half of that seven-year period.

> And he shall enter into a strong and firm covenant with the many for one week [seven years]. And in the midst of the week he shall cause the sacrifice and offering to cease [for the remaining three and one-half years]; and upon the wings or pinnacle of abominations [shall come] one who makes desolate, until the full determined end is poured out on the desolator. (Dan. 9:27)

More scriptural insight about the beast or Antichrist follows:

AS I stood on the sandy beach, I saw a beast coming up out of the sea with ten horns and seven heads. On his horns he had ten royal crowns (diadems) and blasphemous titles (names) on his heads. And the beast that I saw resembled a leopard, but his feet were like those of a bear and his mouth was like that of a lion. And to him the dragon gave his [own] might and power and his [own] throne and great dominion. And one of his heads seemed to have a deadly wound. But his death stroke was healed; and the whole earth went after the beast in amazement and admiration. They fell down and paid homage to the dragon, because he had bestowed on the beast all his dominion and authority; they also praised and worshiped the beast, exclaiming, who is a match for the beast, and, who can make war against him? And the beast was given the power of speech, uttering boastful and blasphemous words, and he was given freedom to exert his authority and to exercise his will during forty-two months (three and a half years). And he opened his mouth to speak slanders against God, blaspheming His name and His abode, [even vilifying] those who live in heaven. He was further permitted to wage war on God's holy people (the saints) and to overcome them. And power was given him to extend his authority over every tribe and people and tongue and nation, and all the inhabitants of the earth will fall down in adoration and pay him homage, everyone whose name has not been recorded in the Book of Life of the Lamb that was slain [in sacrifice] from the foundation of the world. If anyone is able to hear, let him listen. (Rev. 13:1–9)

Regardless of your denominational or religious views, there are many things revealed here that are above reproach unless you do not take the meaning of the verses literally. There is a lot of symbolism involved here, but for the moment, put that to the side and just look at what is going to happen.

The entire world goes after the Antichrist and worships him. God gives him freedom to exert his authority for three and a half years. The Antichrist makes war on God's people and overcomes them. He extends his authority over every tribe and nation.

Remember, Paul is stating that we are not to be disturbed that the coming of our Lord and our gathering together with him, as though these events had already happened. That day will not occur until the apostasy occurs first and the man of lawlessness, the son of perdition, reveals himself.

The term apostasy or "falling away" in the KJV comes from the Greek word apostasia, "deflection from truth" or "falling away, forsake," according to Strong's Exhaustive Concordance of the Bible.[5] According to the Second College Edition of the American Heritage Dictionary, the term perdition means "the loss of the soul, eternal damnation, or hell"; its archaic meaning is "utter ruin."[6]

Paul puts these two events together—the coming of our Lord and the man of lawlessness and the Antichrist revealing himself—and tells the Thessalonians, "You guys know this stuff already." Paul gives us the sequence; the coming of our Lord will not occur until after the man of lawlessness reveals himself. This information is common knowledge between the people of Thessalonica and Paul. Fortunately for us, Paul loves to repeat himself. Notice there are certain elements in different parts of the Scriptures that paint a picture of various themes and times. We have seen in quite a few different places—Zephaniah, Isaiah, Joel, Matthew, and Revelation—about the sun and moon being darkened and the stars not giving their light. Could these different scripture passages be unique events and times? It could be, but the probability is that it is a slightly different perspective of the same event.

The time of peace and then sudden destruction found in Daniel and then here in Thessalonians appear to follow the same type of pattern. There are key elements that come up in different places that point to the same event or time. The theme of a time of peace followed by destruction, the sun, moon, and stars not giving their light, the rise of the Antichrist and the Return of the Lord, the day of the Lord, all appear to be around the same time. Revelation brings much more clarity to this time as you study it. The difference between the two groups of people and this period appears to be whether they are in darkness or light. For one group, it will take them by surprise, and not the other group. The event is the same; it is the perspective that is different.

Many believers contend that the book of Revelation is a time of God's wrath, and God did not appoint us to wrath so, we are not around during this time. It is true God did not appoint us to wrath, and this period is a time of God's wrath. However, just a casual glance at the book of Revelation shows where his wrath is being directed. God's wrath is toward the Antichrist, the false prophet, and all those who bear the mark of the beast. Unfortunately, God is not the only one who has wrath. The Bible clearly states that some of God's people will suffer persecution under the reign of the Antichrist. Martyrdom is part of the picture under the reign of the Antichrist, whether you believe that it is those who get saved during the time of the Tribulation after the Rapture of the Church or, conversely, that the Church is present, either way God's people are going to suffer.

Regardless of what any of us are called to go through, God has not appointed us to wrath. God's wrath is for his enemies. As an example, sin is an enemy of God. When Jesus went to the cross, God was not pouring out his wrath on his beloved Son (although he was there). God was pouring out his wrath on humankind's sin. God's will for Jesus was to go to the cross to pay for our sins. This was not God pouring out his wrath on his Son.

> For our sake He made Christ [virtually] to be sin Who knew no sin, so that in and through Him we might become [endued with, viewed as being in, and examples of] the righteousness of God [what we ought to be, approved and acceptable and in right relationship with Him, by His goodness]. (2 Cor. 5:21)

Because there is suffering in our lives or in the world, that is not necessarily a sign of God's wrath. Every generation has known some suffering and some generations more than others.

God's will for the early church was to spread the good news to all nations. Would it be fair to say of the early church that God did not appoint them to wrath? That they suffered persecution and were martyred is not evidence of God's wrath toward the early church, neither is it the believers, whoever they might be, who are alive and persecuted and martyred during the reign of the Antichrist.

God poured out his wrath on the sin offering—and, yes, Jesus went through the agony of that—but his wrath was on the sin and not his Son. The early church suffered severe persecution, but that is not God's wrath on his beloved children. John 10:10 says "that the thief comes to kill, steal, and destroy" (author's paraphrase) Satan has wrath on God's children and for a season, Satan unleashes his malice. However, even in that, God has established limits. Stephen, the first early church martyr in Acts 6 and 7, was a witness both in his life and probably even more so in his death. But if Satan could do exactly as he wanted, do you really believe the Christian faith would have even gotten off the ground? Christians would have all been dead before the apostles could have had one convert. Just a brief look through the book of Job shows that while

God allows Satan some wiggle room, he tells Satan: This far and no farther! Why God allows Satan this right has many answers, and none of them are exhaustive. But if you read the book to the end, Satan has an appointment with destiny that he can't escape. God revokes Satan's ability to influence God's people. Until that time, we will have to trust that the Most High God knows what he is doing.

What follows is more information about the angel of light:

> For such men are false apostles [spurious, counterfeits], deceitful workmen, masquerading as apostles (special messengers) of Christ (the Messiah). And it is no wonder, for Satan himself masquerades as an angel of light; So, it is not surprising if his servants also masquerade as ministers of righteousness. [But] their end will correspond with their deeds. (2 Cor. 11:13–15)

To the followers of David Koresh or Jim Jones (infamous cult leaders who led their followers to death), the men appeared wholesome. It is reasonable to assume that, to the Germans at the time of the reign of Hitler, he appeared good to them. However, this man will surpass them all because the Scriptures state that the entire world will go after this man.

> And one of his heads seemed to have a deadly wound. But his death stroke was healed; and the whole earth went after the beast in amazement and admiration. (Rev. 13:3)

It is an interesting thought as to who the Antichrist is and his nationality; all speculation is possible. There is a distinct possibility that he will be Jewish. After all, the nation of Israel is still waiting for its Messiah. But what a man he would have to be, as a good portion of the world is decidedly against Israel.

Many Bible scholars would say that the Antichrist will be of European nationality, as depicted in Daniel and the book of Revelation because the symbols of the ten toes or the ten heads on the beast signify a revived Roman Empire. Scripture talks of these last ten rulers as the last earthly kingdom before God himself sets up his kingdom here on earth. The Roman Empire consisted largely of European nations. However, the Roman Empire was in power during the time of Christ, so clearly the Bible depicts the empire occupying much of the Middle East. Probably the significant rulers of the occupied areas were Roman. We need to keep in mind that the Roman Empire had an eastern leg that outlasted the western by about a thousand years. When Constantine moved the capital from Rome, the new capital became Constantinople. This opens a host of other possibilities that many may have not even considered.

There are also the Muslims to consider, as they are waiting for the Twelfth Imam, which is the Muslim equivalent of the Messiah. The Bible clearly depicts beheading as the method of execution under the Antichrist, and beheading appears to be the preference for radical Muslims in driving out the infidel. Islam is also making inroads into European nations as a quick-growing religion on that continent.

There is a host of other possibilities. Time will tell.

As a point of pure speculation, I would like to paint a scenario for you. We know through Scripture many bottom-line things concerning the Antichrist; what we do not know are sequences and timelines. In the book of Revelation, we are told that the Antichrist has a deadly wound healed miraculously. Is this his rise to power? It seems to suggest that but is not definitive. President Obama was scheduled to be at Ground Zero for the tenth anniversary of 9/11 despite credible but unsubstantiated terrorists' threats. As an illustration, what if then-President Obama died and then miraculously came back to life? The point is, even if this far-fetched scenario were true, would he be in the position to increase his authority over the entire world at that point? Most probably not, but what if that was a turning point for him in his career and his popularity that started out so strong but has since diminished? And then his popularity soared? Am I suggesting President Obama is the Antichrist? Absolutely not! It is simply a case in point that while we have some key elements in place in Scripture, we will not know exactly how it is going to play out until it is the proper season. In that scenario, if President Obama were the Antichrist, he could, after reelection and the solving of America's catastrophic problems, gain influence and authority in other countries having similar catastrophic problems. We do not appear to be as bad as Scripture tells us this period will be, so I do not mind using the former president as simply an illustrative tool. The president then has three leaders in Europe, or the Middle East, assassinated and moves his seat of power over there. When we get to Daniel later, we see a scenario where the Antichrist takes out three world leaders and replaces them. The Antichrist could come from anywhere. While we know some telltale signs to identify him from Scripture, as previously mentioned, only one can say with certainty how it will play out.

Many theologians and scholars say that the nationality of the Antichrist will be Roman based on this verse:

> And after the sixty-two weeks [of years] shall the Anointed One be cut off or killed and shall have nothing [and no one] belonging to [and defending] Him. And the people of the [other] prince who will come will destroy the city and the sanctuary. Its end shall come with a flood; and even to the end there shall be war, and desolations are decreed. (Dan. 9:26)

The prince who is to come many scholars and theologians would say is from among the people who make the seven-year covenant that he then breaks in the middle, according to verse 27.

> And he shall enter into a strong and firm covenant with the many for one week [seven years]. And in the midst of the week he shall cause the sacrifice and offering to cease [for the remaining three and one-half years]; and upon the wing or pinnacle of abominations [shall come] one who makes desolate, until the full determined end is poured out on the desolator. (Dan. 9:27)

That the Romans destroyed the temple and the city in 70 CE is common knowledge. Therefore, many would say the Antichrist would be Roman. There were many Roman citizens that were not necessarily Italian, and even if this is the correct interpretation (that the Antichrist will be Italian), our bloodlines are so mixed at this point that even if the Antichrist is Italian, it is not outside the realm of possibility that he would not look like the stereotypical Italian who comes to many people's mind. My point in this is to attempt to not have a preconceived image in the mind so that when this person finally reveals himself, we do not make the same mistake that the rulers and leaders in Israel made. They were certain Jesus could not be the Messiah. Paul the apostle, who wrote about a quarter of the New Testament, was a Roman citizen, referenced in Acts 16:37–38 and Acts 22:25–28. Paul the apostle would likely not look like an Italian. What the Antichrist does, as depicted in Scripture, is a better standard of evaluation than a person's ethnicity.

CHAPTER 11

Pictures of the Antichrist in Daniel

T here are some Scriptures in Daniel that give further illumination into the personality and character of the Antichrist.

And at the latter end of their kingdom, when the transgressors [the apostate Jews] have reached the fullness [of their wickedness, taxing the limits of God's mercy], a king of fierce countenance and understanding dark trickery and craftiness shall stand up. (Dan. 8:23)

The phrase "dark trickery and craftiness" is from the Hebrew word chiydah. That word means "a puzzle"; hence, a trick, conundrum, sententious maxim: dark saying—sentence or speech—hard question, proverb, and riddle, according to Strong's Exhaustive Concordance of the Bible.[7] Would you say that our world has gotten complicated? One benefit of understanding complicated conundrums is the ability to solve those conundrums. The Bible states he will understand complex issues.

Who is better positioned to advance himself than someone who has a great understanding of complex matters?

There are many places where the Scriptures tell us that the Antichrist will be exceedingly smart, if not have genius-level intelligence, or in some other significant way stand out: Dan. 7:20, Dan. 8:23, Dan. 11:21, Dan. 8:24–25, Rev. 13:1–9. Many of those Scriptures have been written out, but some, if you desire to look more closely into this, you will need to look up. The point is most prophecy enthusiasts have a picture of the Antichrist because of these references as a slick, refined individual and the difference between the "genius" and the "big mouth" is timing. The first three and a half years he looks like goodness personified and the second half when he breaks the covenant, he reveals his true nature and boasts many things and blasphemes the god of heaven. If you are a fan of Star Wars, then Senator Palpatine would be a perfect example of this type of individual.[8] However, while we have God-given insight and criteria concerning the Antichrist, we do not actually know how this person is going to embody these qualities.

As an example, President Donald Trump would appear to have the "big mouth" part in spades. With a lot of bluster, he almost comes across like a bull in a china shop in many instances. He has no problem speaking his mind. However, he does not come across as refined and genius-level intelligence. At the same time, if you stop and look at what he is able to actually accomplish—cutting through red tape and getting the end result accomplished that he desires a goodly percentage of the time—this would suggest genius-level intelligence. Am I saying that President Trump is the Antichrist? I am not. However, this is also one of those preconceived ideas of how most picture the Antichrist because of the qualities the Scriptures tell us he is going to possess, and the truth is we do not know how he is going to "wear" those qualities, so we would be wiser to not automatically dismiss a person from consideration because of our preconceived ideas. The purpose of this observation is that we should hold loosely our preconceived ideas and be willing to adjust as events unfold.

> And his power shall be mighty, but not by his own power; and he shall corrupt and destroy astonishingly and shall prosper and do his own pleasure, and he shall corrupt and destroy the mighty men and the holy people (the people of the saints). And through his policy he shall cause trickery to prosper in his hand; he shall magnify himself in his heart and mind, and in their security he will corrupt and destroy many. He shall also stand up against the Prince of princes, but he shall be broken and that by no [human] hand. (Dan. 8:24–25)

The word security here is from the Hebrew word Shalvah, whether genuine or false, abundance, peace, prosperity, and quietness, according to Strong's Exhaustive Concordance of the Bible.[9] Securities . . . how secure are we feeling these days? That is strongly appealing in these troubled times. Security is a big part of what he is offering, and through it, destruction ensues. Do you remember that verse in 1 Thessalonians 5:3 that spoke of "when people are saying peace and safety and then in a moment unforeseen sudden destruction?" Does this look like a dovetail to anyone else?

> The vision of the evenings and the mornings which has been told you is true. But seal up the vision, for it has to do with and belongs to the [now] distant future. (Dan. 8:26)

Many theologians and Bible scholars would agree that this portion of Scripture is regarding the Antichrist. Trickery is his trademark, not military strength. The point of trickery is that what you see is not what you get. Here, in a different place in Daniel, is another glimpse into the personality and character of the Antichrist.

> And armed forces of his shall appear [in the holy land] and they shall pollute the sanctuary, the [spiritual] stronghold, and shall take away the continual [daily burnt offering]; and they shall set up [in the sanctuary] the abomination that astonishes and makes desolate [probably an altar to a pagan god]. (Dan. 11:31)

That Scripture is another biblical reference to the abomination of desolation.

> And such as violate the covenant he shall pervert and seduce with flatteries, but the people who know their God shall prove themselves strong and shall stand firm and do exploits [for God]. And they who are wise and understanding among the people shall instruct many and make them understand, though some [of them and their followers] shall fall by the sword and flame, by captivity and plunder, for many days. Now when they fall, they shall receive a little help. Many shall join themselves to them with flatteries and hypocrisies. And some of those who are wise, prudent, and understanding shall be weakened and fall, [thus, then, the insincere among the people will lose courage and become deserters. It will be a test] to refine, to purify, and to make those among [God's people] white, even to the time of the end, because it is yet for the time [God] appointed. (Dan. 11:32–35)

Does that sound like a great falling away to anyone else? The people who are here during this time need to be prepared. Some of the strong are going to fall, and it is a test for God's people. Are our eyes focused on "Him who sits on the throne," or on the adverse circumstances? Many people's faith will not stand because some leaders die, and doubt will set in. God has warned us in advance. Also, notice that the enemy infiltrates with flatteries and hypocrisies. If you are chosen by God to be among those who know their God and do exploits. . . keep an eye out for those who join you and ask God for discernment because some are going to be wolves in sheep's clothing. We do not hear of exploits very often in our day and age. An exploit would be a deed that is heroic in nature. God will call some of us to do exploits in the time of the end. Like the three Hebrew children in the fiery furnace, or Daniel in the lion's den.

> And the king shall do according to his will; he shall exalt himself and magnify himself above every god and shall speak astonishing things against the God of gods and shall prosper till the indignation be accomplished, for that which is determined [by God] shall be done. He shall not regard the gods of his fathers or Him [to Whom] women desire [to give birth—the Messiah] or any other god, for he shall magnify himself above all. But in their place he shall honor the god of fortresses; a god whom his father's knew not shall he honor with gold and silver, with precious stones, and with pleasant and expensive things. And he shall deal with the strongest fortresses by the help of a foreign god. Those who acknowledge him he shall magnify with glory and honor, and he shall cause them to rule over many and shall divide the land for a price. (Dan. 11:36–39)

Many theologians and Bible scholars would agree that this Scripture also has references to the Antichrist. The Antichrist, once again, is seducing with flatteries and exalts himself above God.

CHAPTER 12

The Church and Israel

Many theologians and Bible scholars make a distinction in biblical prophecy between God's dealings with Israel and God's dealings with the Church. This is important because what you believe concerning this distinction determines the perspective you have in attempting to interpret prophecy. When Jesus was talking to the disciples, who were they? In speaking to his disciples, was he talking to Jewish men or the formation of his Church? According to Scripture, he made the Jewish believers into the formation of the Church, and created one people of the kingdom of God, comprising both Jewish and Gentile believers.

Scripturally speaking, God has included us (Gentiles or non-Jewish people) who believe in Christ in his gift of salvation, and Israel (mostly) rejected its Savior, which is the door that let us in.

Therefore, remember that at one time you were Gentiles (heathens) in the flesh, called Uncircumcision by those who called themselves Circumcision, [itself a mere mark] in the flesh made by human hands. [Remember] that you were at that time separated (living apart) from Christ [excluded from all part in Him], utterly estranged and outlawed from the rights of Israel as a nation, and strangers with no share in the sacred compacts of the [Messianic] promise [with no knowledge of or right in God's agreements, His covenants]. And you had no hope (no promise); you were in the world without God. But now in Christ Jesus, you who once were [so] far away, through (by, in) the blood of Christ have been brought near. For He is [Himself] our peace (our bond of unity and harmony). He has made us both [Jew and Gentile] one [body], and has broken down (destroyed, abolished) the hostile dividing wall between us. (Eph. 2:11–14)

But God did not reject Israel; Israel, with a few exceptions, rejected him. Paul has quite a bit to say concerning what are their losses and are our gains. There are again more verses included in this than are necessary to establish this point, but for those unfamiliar with this topic, the context is illuminating:

I ASK then: Has God totally rejected and disowned His people? Of course not! Why, I myself am an Israelite, a descendant of Abraham, a member of the tribe of Benjamin! No, God has not rejected and disowned His people [whose destiny] He had marked out and appointed and foreknown from the beginning. Do you not know what the Scripture says of Elijah, how he pleads with God against Israel? Lord, they have killed Your prophets; they have demolished Your altars, and I alone am left, and they seek my life. But what is God's reply to him? I have kept for Myself seven thousand men who have not bowed the knee to Baal! So too at the present time there is a remnant (a small believing minority), selected (chosen) by grace (by God's unmerited favor and graciousness). But if it is by grace (His unmerited favor and graciousness), it is no longer conditioned on works or anything men have done. Otherwise, grace would no longer be grace [it would be meaningless]. What then [shall we conclude]? Israel failed to obtain what it sought [God's favor by obedience to the Law]. Only the elect (those chosen few) obtained it, while the rest of them became callously indifferent (blinded, hardened, and made insensible to it). As it is written, God gave them a spirit (an attitude) of stupor, eyes that should not see and ears that should not hear, [that has continued] down to this very day. And David says, let their table (their feasting, banqueting) become a snare and a trap, a pitfall and a just retribution [rebounding like a boomerang upon them]. Let their eyes be darkened (dimmed) so that they cannot see, and make them bend their back [stooping beneath their burden] forever. So, I ask, have they stumbled so as to fall [to their utter spiritual ruin, irretrievably]? By no means! But through their false step and transgression salvation [has come] to the Gentiles, so as to arouse Israel [to see and feel what they forfeited] and so to make them jealous. Now if their stumbling (their lapse, their transgression) has so enriched the world [at large], and if [Israel's] failure means such riches for the Gentiles, think what an enrichment and greater advantage will follow their full reinstatement! But now I am speaking to you who are Gentiles. Inasmuch then as I am an apostle to the Gentiles, I lay great stress on my ministry and magnify my office, In the hope of making my fellow Jews jealous [in order to stir them up to imitate, copy, and appropriate], and thus managing to save some of them. For if their rejection and exclusion from the benefits of salvation were [overruled] for the reconciliation of a world to God, what will their acceptance and admission mean? [It will be nothing short of] life from the dead! Now if the first handful of dough offered as the firstfruits [Abraham and the patriarchs] is consecrated (holy), so is the whole mass [the nation of Israel]; and if the root [Abraham] is consecrated (holy), so are the branches. But if some of the branches were broken off, while you, a wild olive shoot, were grafted in among them to share the richness [of the root and sap] of the olive tree, do not boast over the branches and pride yourself at their expense. If you do boast and feel superior, remember it is not you that support the root, but the root [that supports] you. You will say then, Branches were broken (pruned) off so that I might be grafted in! That is true. But they were broken (pruned) off because of their unbelief (their lack of real faith), and you are established through faith [because you do believe]. So, do not become proud and conceited, but rather stand in awe and be reverently afraid. For if God did not spare the natural branches [because of unbelief], neither will He spare you [if you are guilty of the same offense]. Then note and appreciate the gracious kindness and the severity of God: severity toward those who have fallen, but God's gracious kindness to you—provided you continue in His grace and abide in His kindness; otherwise you too will be cut off (pruned away). And even those others [the fallen branches, Jews], if they do not persist in [clinging to] their unbelief, will be grafted in, for God has the power to graft them in again. For if you have been cut from what is by nature a wild olive tree, and against nature grafted into a cultivated olive tree, how much easier will it be to graft these natural [branches] back on [the original parent stock of] their own olive tree. Lest you be self-opinionated (wise in your own conceits), I do not want you to miss this hidden truth and mystery, brethren: a hardening (insensibility) has [temporarily] befallen a part of

Israel [to last] until the full number of the ingathering of the Gentiles has come in, and so all Israel will be saved. As it is written, The Deliverer will come from Zion, He will banish ungodliness from Jacob. And this will be My covenant (My agreement) with them when I shall take away their sins. From the point of view of the Gospel (good news), they [the Jews, at present] are enemies [of God], which is for your advantage and benefit. But from the point of view of God's choice (of election, of divine selection), they are still the beloved (dear to Him) for the sake of their forefathers. For God's gifts and His call are irrevocable. [He never withdraws them when once they are given, and He does not change His mind about those to whom He gives His grace or to whom He sends His call.] Just as you were once disobedient and rebellious toward God but now have obtained [His] mercy, through their disobedience, So they also now are being disobedient [when you are receiving mercy], that they in turn may one day, through the mercy you are enjoying, also receive mercy [that they may share the mercy which has been shown to you—through you as messengers of the Gospel to them]. For God has consigned (penned up) all men to disobedience, only that He may have mercy on them all [alike]. Oh, the depth of the riches and wisdom and knowledge of God! How unfathomable (inscrutable, unsearchable) are His judgments (His decisions)! And how untraceable (mysterious, undiscoverable) are His ways (His methods, His paths)! For who has known the mind of the Lord and who has understood His thoughts, or who has [ever] been His counselor? Or who has first given God anything that he might be paid back or that he could claim a recompense? For from Him and through Him and to Him are all things. [For all things originate with Him and come from Him; all things live through Him, and all things center in and tend to consummate and to end in Him.] To Him be glory forever! Amen (so be it). (Rom. 11:1–36)

If we are God's people through faith and they become restored to their natural place through faith in Jesus Christ as their Messiah, doesn't the Bible teach we become one? Not that God would not deal differently sometimes, just as a father will differ in response from one child to another. But end-time events do not clearly state that God would deal drastically differently with one group in comparison to another. It would be tough to believe that we as the Church, as God's light in the world, have done any better in our behavior than ancient Israel. There have been times, yes, but if we are honest with ourselves, there are many times we have missed the mark. In Jesus, the two have become one, and as we go further, we will see various theories for very different outcomes for these two groups. Keep in mind that these are interpretations of Scripture, and while they are honest attempts at interpretation, they are humankind's attempt to interpret and may or may not be accurate.

Would the following Scripture passage apply in principle to both Israel and the Church?

> I call heaven and earth to witness against you this day that you shall soon utterly perish from the land which you are going over the Jordan to possess. You will not live long upon it but will be utterly destroyed. And the Lord will scatter you among the peoples, and you will be left few in number among the nations to which the Lord will drive you. There you will serve gods, the work of men's hands, wood and stone, which neither see nor hear nor eat nor smell. But if from there you will seek (inquire for and require as necessity) the Lord your God, you will find Him if you [truly] seek Him with all your heart [and

mind] and soul and life. When you are in tribulation and all these things come upon you, in the latter days you will turn to the Lord your God and be obedient to His voice. For the Lord your God is a merciful God; He will not fail you or destroy you or forget the covenant of your fathers, which He swore to them. (Deut. 4:26–31)

While applying specifically to Israel in the latter days especially, are the principals not universal? If we fall away from the Lord, repent, and turn again to him, is he not merciful to us as his Church? The principles are entirely universal and apply to all of God's people in all periods of time. Would we not apply the truth of the prodigal son to ourselves as the Church . . . even though written by and spoken to the people of Israel?

For he is not a [real] Jew who is only one outwardly and publicly, nor is [true] circumcision something external and physical. But he is a Jew who is one inwardly, and [true] circumcision is of the heart, a spiritual and not a literal [matter]. His praise is not from men but from God. (Rom. 2:28–29)

Know and understand that it is [really] the people [who live] by faith who are [the true] sons of Abraham. (Gal. 3:7)

There is [now no distinction] neither Jew nor Greek, there is neither slave nor free, there is not male and female; for you are all one in Christ Jesus. And if you belong to Christ [are in Him Who is Abraham's Seed], then you are Abraham's offspring and [spiritual] heirs according to promise. (Gal. 3:28–29)

And I have other sheep [beside these] that are not of this fold.
I must bring and [impel those also]; and they will listen to My
voice and heed My call, and so there will be [they will become]
one flock under one Shepherd. (John 10:16)

Israel was the chosen people of the Old Covenant, and the Church
is God's chosen people of the New Covenant, including believing or
messianic Jewish people.

If we are the people of the New Covenant, then do not all the
promises and prophecies of the Old Testament revert by default to the
New Covenant? We also need to look at God's severity in dealing with
his Old Covenant people. He did not adjust to their thinking regarding
his kingdom's agenda. He expected them to keep pace with the agenda as
it came to pass in actuality, regardless of their preconceived ideas. Would
it not be to our advantage to realize this as we head into the end of the
age? Everybody gets it right with hindsight. "We know God was with
Moses, but we do not know that about this man." (John 9:29, author's
paraphrase) Anybody remember all the trouble the nation of Israel
gave Moses while the Exodus was happening? The people of Jesus's day
said, "If we had been alive during the time of the prophets, we would
not have killed them like our forefathers did." (Matt. 23:30, author's
paraphrase) Of course, then they turned around and killed the actual
Son of God. In every generation in which events/prophecies come to
pass, most people of that time are wrong. They think things are going
to happen a certain way, and they usually don't. History and Scripture
give us profound evidence that God does as he wills and does not adjust
to our preconceived ideas but expects us to adjust to him.

CHAPTER 13

The Day of the Lord

Behold, the day of the lord is coming!—fierce, with wrath and raging anger—to make the land and the [whole] earth a desolation and to destroy out of it its sinners. For the stars of the heavens and their constellations will not give their light; the sun will be darkened at its rising and the moon will not shed its light. And I, the Lord, will punish the world for its evil, and the wicked for their guilt and iniquity; I will cause the arrogance of the proud to cease and will lay low the haughtiness of the terrible and the boasting of the violent and ruthless. I will make a man more rare than fine gold, and humankind scarcer than the pure gold of Ophir. Therefore, I will make the heavens tremble; and the earth shall be shaken out of its place at the wrath of the Lord of hosts in the day of His fierce anger. And like the chased roe or gazelle, and like sheep that no man gathers, each [foreign resident] will turn to his own people, and each will flee to his own land. Everyone who is found will be thrust through, and everyone who is connected with the slain and is caught will fall by the sword. Their infants also will be dashed to pieces before their eyes; their houses will be plundered and their wives ravished. (Isa. 13:9–16)

That does not sound like a pleasant day, does it? Remember, we have looked at the day of the Lord in 1 Thess. as well. That the day will come as a thief in the night, while people are saying everything is fine, and we have peace and safety, and then sudden destruction.

But the day of the lord will come like a thief, and then the heavens will vanish (pass away) with a thunderous crash, and the [material] elements [of the universe] will be dissolved with fire, and the earth and the works that are upon it will be burned up. (2 Pet. 3:10)

So, call to mind the lessons you received and heard; continually lay them to heart and obey them, and repent. In case you will not rouse yourselves and keep awake and watch, I will come upon you like a thief, and you will not know or suspect at what hour I will come. (Rev. 3:3)

Behold, I am going to come like a thief! Blessed (happy, to be envied) is he who stays awake (alert) and who guards his clothes, so that he may not be naked and [have the shame of being] seen exposed! (Rev. 16:15)

One problem that theologians and Bible scholars have is that one "coming of the Lord" seems to be secret, like a "thief in the night." And in other Scriptures, his coming is visible to all. This is one of the primary reasons dispensational premillennial adherents believe there must be two separate events that take place.

> Behold, He is coming with the clouds, and every eye will see Him, even those who pierced Him; and all the tribes of the earth shall gaze upon Him and beat their breasts and mourn and lament over Him. Even so [must it be]. Amen (so be it). (Rev. 1:7)

Now the day of the Lord and the return of the Lord are not necessarily the same; however, they could connect closely. What if it is not the event that is so different, but two different perspectives of the same event? It would seem putting aside the return of the Lord for a minute that, with just the day of the Lord, one group is going to be taken by surprise, and the other group is not. The return of the Lord follows the day of the Lord. From the description of the day of the Lord, it does not sound like there is an awful lot left that could come after.

CHAPTER 14

More Insight from the Book of Daniel

T here is a prophecy in the book of Daniel that, while not dealing with the day of the Lord, sheds some light on last events. The wonderful thing about divinely inspired prophecy is that it is completely accurate. We may not fully understand all that is in there, but what we can understand and see the fulfillment of is utterly amazing. Some suggest that prophecy by God Almighty himself is nothing more than history written in advance. Listen to Daniel's prophecies; their fulfillment in our history will amaze you! Will the rest of the vision be any less accurate? The story takes place in Daniel chapter 2. The king of Babylon, Nebuchadnezzar, has had a dream that really troubles him. He gathers a lot of the wise men of the realm. He then informs them he needs them to interpret his dream, but there is a catch: he cannot remember it. When they tell him that what he is asking is impossible, he is furious and commands all the wise men in his realm to be executed. This included the four Hebrew children: Daniel, Shadrach, Meshach, and Abednego. Daniel petitions the king to give him and his three companions time to fast and pray, and they will perform the king's request. This is where we are going to drop into the narrative.

But there is a God in heaven Who reveals secrets, and He has made known to King Nebuchadnezzar what it is that shall be in the latter days (at the end of days). Your dream and the visions in your head upon your bed are these: As for you, O king, as you were lying upon your bed thoughts came into your mind about what should come to pass hereafter, and He Who reveals secrets was making known to you what shall come to pass. But as for me, this secret is not revealed to me for any wisdom that I have more than anyone else living, but in order that the interpretation may be made known to the king and that you may know the thoughts of your heart and mind. You, O king, saw, and behold, [there was] a great image. This image which was mighty and of exceedingly great brightness stood before you, and the appearance of it was frightening and terrible. As for this image, its head was of fine gold, its breast and its arms of silver, its belly and its thighs of bronze, Its legs of iron, its feet partly of iron and partly of clay [the baked clay of the potter]. As you looked, a Stone was cut out without human hands, which smote the image on its feet of iron and [baked] clay [of the potter] and broke them to pieces. Then the iron, the [baked] clay [of the potter], the bronze, the silver, and the gold were broken and crushed together and became like the chaff of the summer threshing floors, and the wind carried them away so that not a trace of them could be found. And the Stone that smote the image became a great mountain or rock and filled the whole earth. This was the dream, and we will tell the interpretation of it to the king. You, O king, are king of the [earthly] kings to whom the God of heaven has given the kingdom, the power, the might, and the glory. And wherever the children of men dwell, and the beasts of the field, and the birds of the heavens—He has given them into your hand and has made you to rule over them all. You [king of Babylon] are the head of gold. And after you shall arise another kingdom [the Medo-Persian], inferior to you, and still a third kingdom of bronze [Greece under Alexander the Great] which shall bear rule over all the earth. (Dan. 2:28–39)

The translators of the Amplified Bible included in brackets the fulfillment of the prophecies for the reader's convenience in chapter 2. In Daniel chapter 8 we have the angel Gabriel name to Daniel the Media-Persian Empire and Greece. This foretells the rise of two world empires before they came to power. History records only three world empires since the time of Babylonian domination: Mede-Persian, Grecian, and Roman. There has not been a world empire since Rome. Germany tried, and they came close, but ultimately failed. There are only two empires left: the kingdom of the final ten kings out of the revived Roman Empire which is the Antichrist's kingdom and the kingdom of the millennium. After that we enter the eternal state.

And the fourth kingdom [Rome] shall be strong as iron, since iron breaks to pieces and subdues all things; and like iron which crushes, it shall break and crush all these. And as you saw the feet and toes, partly of [baked] clay [of the potter] and partly of iron, it shall be a divided kingdom; but there shall be in it some of the firmness and strength of iron, just as you saw the iron mixed with miry [earthen] clay. And as the toes of the feet were partly of iron and partly of [baked] clay [of the potter], so the kingdom shall be partly strong and partly brittle and broken. And as you saw the iron mixed with miry and earthen clay, so they shall mingle themselves in the seed of men [in marriage bonds]; but they will not hold together [for two such elements or ideologies can never harmonize], even as iron does not mingle itself with clay. And in the days of these [final ten] kings shall the God of heaven set up a kingdom which shall never be destroyed, nor shall its sovereignty be left to another people; but it shall break and crush and consume all these kingdoms and it shall stand forever. (Dan. 2:40–44)

Compare this to the ten rulers in the book of Revelation, which we will get to a little later.

Just as you saw that the Stone was cut out of the mountain without hands and that it broke in pieces the iron, the bronze, the clay, the silver, and the gold, the great God has made known to the king what shall come to pass hereafter. The dream is certain and the interpretation of it is sure. (Dan. 2:45)

God cuts the stone out without human hands and consumes all the other kingdoms. There are Bible scholars today that suggest we are to usher in the kingdom of God, one heart at a time. Does this Scripture passage not suggest that the setting up of the kingdom of God is not through human effort? While we are to proclaim the kingdom of God is at hand like John the Baptist and Jesus did, are we not looking at two separate contexts? This passage is clearly talking about literal world empires.

That is a particular type of prophecy—history written in advance! When we get to the time of the final ten kings, the end of humankind is upon us, and the kingdom of God in the millennial reign is about to begin. Jesus talked to us about the time of the Gentiles. Does it not make sense that this image would capture the time of the Gentiles in Nebuchadnezzar's dream that God gave him? We are only looking at when unbelievers control the kingdoms of the world until the kingdom of God comes that shall never know destruction. According to these verses in Daniel, it is in the time of these last ten kings that God sets up his kingdom. When you cross-reference that with the book of Revelation, you get a more complete picture. Since all the kingdoms that God showed Nebuchadnezzar have been literal so far, should the kingdom of the last ten kings and the millennial reign be any different?

CHAPTER 15

The Faithfulness of God in Hard Times

What is the end of the age going to look like? If you dovetail Matthew 24 with the book of Revelation, it is hard to see anything but dark times ahead—not that God has abandoned his people; as we look through the Bible, we see there have been dark times before. God has always been there for those who call on him. Actually, it has been during the darkest of times that God's people have always shone the brightest. In the time of Moses, we have some of the greatest threats by the rulers of the day and the greatest miracles of God on behalf of his people. In the Church's birthing, there was some of the greatest persecution by the leaders and rulers of that day and again some of the greatest moves of God on behalf of his people. Hard times tend to bring out the very best and the very worst in people. We only need to determine which side of that fence we are going to be on.

> Because of multiplied lawlessness and iniquity, the love of many will grow cold. (Matt. 24:12, author's paraphrase)

This is probably one of the key verses about the end of the age. As bad as things are today, we can look for things to get much worse. The Church may shine brighter and brighter, but the climate is going to be dark outside. There are some Christians who believe things are going to get much better, that we as Christians are going to rise to the top in all areas of life: government, science, police enforcement, environmentalism, etcetera. It is hard to understand, considering Matthew 24 and the book of Revelation, how they believe this. We will arise individually sometimes to the forefront, as God gives promotion to who he wants when he wants. The Scriptures seem clear that the time of the end is a time of darkness and iniquity. Discouragement is not the goal, as we want Christians to excel in what God has given into their hands as faithful stewards. The purpose is to encourage people to be steadfast in hard times.

God told Abraham, "I want you to know that your people will be strangers in a land and there they will be enslaved for four hundred years but afterwards I will bring them out with great riches." (Gen. 15:13–14, author's paraphrase) Does that sound like a good word to anyone? God is very interested in the journey of his people, both during good times and bad, but he always has his eye on the finished product. What we go through changes us, and if we allow him, it makes us more Christlike. There are seasons when we are to endure and honor God during the hard times. The example of Job's life is one of exceptional inspiration. We need to remember that there was no Scripture written when Job was alive. He had no written Word to rest on, only the character of the God that he knew. We can look back now and say without a doubt that God was in that. Can you imagine being Job and stripped of everything? You have just lost your children, your wealth, and finally your health, and amid all these tragedies, you give God praise and worship? Was God the thief in this scenario? No, but God allowed the thief to test Job, and this made Job incredibly rich eternally. This shows us that trusting God in the darkest of times is wise.

Jesus himself speaks of the climate at the end of the age. He says plainly that multiplied lawlessness and iniquity will abound, as it had in the days of Noah. As we look at our culture today, things are getting terrible. We have already talked about the pornographic industry and the virulent increase of murder. We are rapidly becoming desensitized to all the wickedness that is around us. This is setting the stage for the rise of the Antichrist, as it is in this climate that he comes along and restores order out of chaos.

There is a story about a frog that slowly gets killed while not realizing his dilemma. He is swimming in a pot of water on a stove, and slowly the heat turns the water to boiling, and the frog dies in the pot. Now the reality is, the frog would not stay in the pot. The analogy is prudent for us. If someone dropped the frog in a pot of boiling water, the frog would immediately jump out. However, if the heat increased slowly, the frog could boil to death, not realizing its danger until it was too late. This is a myth and false from all I could find on the subject. But it is an outstanding metaphor about gradual change taking us to a place we would never go to immediately. We are in a pot of water that is slowly coming to a boil.

There will be quite a few who will say that I am attempting to scare people, and it is unwarranted. That is not accurate. I am simply looking at the facts of our society and its ills and cross-referencing that with biblical prophecy and affirming that we are probably closer than we think to our Lord's return. Before his return, the Bible shows us that there will be a time of great darkness, and it is their moment—evil men and women. Is that scary? Without a doubt, that is scary! Our God is faithful to his character and his people even in the darkest of times. It does not do to close our eyes to the truth, and it is Jesus himself who depicts the time of the end in such dire straits. No matter what your understanding of the timing of the Rapture and God gathering his people to himself is, there will be some of God's people who go through this period known as the Great Tribulation. If it is not the Church, then there will be those who get saved during this period, and in that case, this book is for them.

In Luke 22:53, Jesus is talking to those who have arrested him, the religious leaders, how he was "daily in the temple and now you come out with clubs like I am a common criminal." He states, "But this is your hour and the hour of darkness." Jesus had to trust his Father. Jesus recognized that in his Father's plan, he allowed "the hour of darkness." There are seasons, and we do not understand them, when God gives the powers of darkness their time on the world stage.

The close of human history will be fraught with peril and trouble. It will also be a time of some coming into their fullness and doing great exploits for God. The darkness of human history is where heroes and heroines rise to the top. There are many generations that do not have many prominent men or women rising to the top to draw attention to the King of kings and Lord of lords. During Israel's captivity in Egypt for four hundred years, there was no mention of anyone doing great things for God until Moses. Have you ever wondered what it would have been like to be a child in Israel during this period? You are going from sunup to sundown, enslaved your whole life to taskmasters who mistreat you. And this is God's will for your life? This was a necessary part of the plan of God for his people. In the end, he brought them out into a land flowing with milk and honey. For those who were in the in-between, it was a life of drudgery and enslavement.

What if your lot in life was one of those in-between generations? "I love you, Lord, for this life of slavery and degradation!" It does not seem fair, does it? How about the period theologians describe as the silent years? There were four hundred years when not much was going on in the nation of Israel between the last recorded prophet of the Old Testament, Malachi, and the Messiah. What if it was your lot to have been born during this time? The period known as the Dark Ages in our history appears to be an inglorious time, when not much happened among the people of God. It is during perilous times that heroes emerge. God is faithful, regardless of what period you have been born in, but he shines most brightly in the darkness, and so do his people.

Have you ever considered the mothers and fathers who lost their children during the time of Herod? Herod inquired of the wise men about the birth of the new king. When he discovered they would not give away where he was born, he sent men and killed all the male children two years old and younger. Put yourself in their place and hear their heart's anguish.

> A voice was heard in Ramah, wailing and loud lamentation,
> Rachel weeping for her children; she refused to be comforted,
> because they were no more. (Matt. 2:18)

Did God spare his covenant people because he was breaking into time and history to rescue them? Or did he call them to adjust and trust him in their anguish? Did he ask them to trust, even though they could not see immediately, that salvation came to the entire world because of the plan he was enacting? That the enemy, Satan, seized this opportunity and caused more anguish to God's people is in keeping with his nature. Our real problem is with a loving, compassionate, and all-powerful God that allows pain and suffering. That does not compute in our human reasoning. Two things to consider in that equation: (1) God alone knows the end from the beginning and sees the other side of this equation, and (2) "He who did not spare his own Son but freely gave him for us all." (Rom. 8:32, author's paraphrase) If we are talking about what is fair and unfair; how fair is it that a sinless, holy, all-powerful God should choose to suffer and die for our mistakes? He does not ask of us anymore than he required of himself.

The end of the age is a perilous time, and while it is fraught with many difficulties, it is also a time for heroes and heroines in the faith. The book of Hebrews chapter 11 talks about the heroes and heroines of faith, but that chapter is waiting for us to be completed. As we approach the end of the age, there will be others with faith, like Abraham, Isaac, Jacob, Deborah, Samuel, Ruth, Esther, David, Peter, Paul, John, Priscilla, and the like. It says in the latter part of one verse in Daniel, concerning the end of the age, "The people who know their God shall be strong and do great exploits for God." (Dan. 11:32, author's paraphrase)

Yes, it is a horrible time and one of dire straits and tribulations, the likes of which the world has never seen before. But it is also a time of action and for heroes and heroines to rise out of the darkness and be a light. When you read to the end of the book, God wins! But it does us no good to close our eyes to the fact that dark days are coming. God will be faithful to himself and to his people through those dark times. The question that really remains is this: Who are the people who go through the Great Tribulation period and the rise of the Antichrist? Nobody in their right mind wants to go through this period. The Bible articulates it as being the worst humankind has ever seen, the likes of which we shall never see again. The Bible tells us in Psalm 103:8 that God is full of mercy and slow to anger. We see God as loving and forgiving, and he is! We see so much of that side of him we struggle when he shows us the harder truth of his anger. The truth is God is slow to anger . . . but you do not want to get him there.

If you are familiar with the story of Daniel and the lions' den or the three Hebrew children and the fiery furnace, then you are probably applauding and affirming their faithfulness. For those who are unfamiliar, we will look at these examples, as they show a striking point.

The Babylonian Empire has risen to power. God has allowed his people to be captured and taken captive from their homeland. He has judged his people and their consistent sin of idolatry and given his people to the enemies' hands for a season. It is our pattern that we fall away from him, and then God allows adversity in our lives to point us back to him and remember his goodness and faithfulness. Amid this climate of captivity and adversity, four Hebrew children rise to prominence because of their faithfulness to God. Their names are Daniel, Shadrach, Meshach, and Abednego, and their stand for God is about to be tested.

The king of Babylon made a statue of gold and ordered all his subjects to bow down and worship this image when the music played. It omits Daniel in this narrative, but Shadrach, Meshach, and Abednego refused to worship this image. It clearly violated their love relationship with God. They refused, even though they knew the decree was whoever did not bow down and worship this image was subject to death by being thrown into a fiery furnace. The other leaders in Babylon took note that these three did not bow down and worship the image. They went straightway to the king and made sure he was aware of their refusal. The king liked these guys and gave them another chance. He said, "When the music starts up again, if you bow down and worship, then all is well. But if you do not, then the consequences are going to be severe and who is that god who can deliver you from me?"

The three Hebrew children responded to the king, "We do not need to be careful in this matter, O king, as our God can deliver us from the fiery furnace. Even if he chooses not to, we still will not bow down to the image because it is more important to obey God than man." At this response, the king was furious and had the furnace heated seven times hotter than normal and had them thrown in. However, when the king investigated the fiery furnace, he saw not three but four men walking in the furnace, and the fourth looked like the Son of Man. The king called them out and declared to his entire nation, "Anyone who speaks badly about the God of Shadrach, Meshach, and Abednego will die and their entire house be destroyed." He made this declaration because he said, "There is no god who can deliver and do miracles like we just saw with these guys."

Shadrach, Meshach, and Abednego did not choose the time that they were born in any more than we have. They were faithful in the time God gave them to live their lives. In this example, we see God showing himself strong on behalf of his children by delivering them out of the trouble the enemy had set for them. (Dan. 3)

In the story of Daniel, we see another example of steadfast perseverance in the face of great adversity. Some rulers came to the king of Babylon, Darius, and said, "We want you to make a rule that no man can make a petition of any god or man except you for thirty days." These rulers had tried to trip up Daniel in other ways and could find nothing they could use against him. They said, "Only regarding his allegiance to God can we use something to hurt him." These were probably the same troublemakers who came to Nebuchadnezzar about the three Hebrew children, trying to get them in trouble, as it seemed that great jealousy motivated them against them. They knew Daniel had made a lifestyle of prayer and petitioned God three times a day. Quickly, these leaders came back to Darius and reported on Daniel petitioning God three times a day. They reminded him of his decree that the perpetrator bear the penalty of the lions' den. Darius had a lot of respect for Daniel and sought diligently to have him delivered. However, he was bound by his own oath and ordered Daniel to be cast into the lions' den. Darius said, "May the God whom you serve continually deliver you." Darius sealed the den with his own insignia. When Darius came back to the den of lions in the early morning, he cried out to Daniel to see if his God could deliver him. Daniel responded that God had sent an angel to stop the mouths of the lions. The king was thrilled and got Daniel out of the lions' den. He then ordered those who had accused Daniel thrown into the lions' den, along with their wives and children. Before they even hit the floor, the lions ate them. Then Darius made a decree that "everyone everywhere needed to revere Daniel's God." (Dan. 6)

Would you or I choose to be born during this time? There were a lot of bad feelings going around about the God of Israel and his people. People everywhere were trying their best to trip up God's bond servants and, in these examples, were unsuccessful. That was because the bond servants stuck to their guns and remained faithful under enormous pressure. These are two examples of God miraculously delivering his people out of danger and the traps set by their enemies.

The religious leaders and government officials sawed Isaiah the prophet in half, according to history. Samson killed more enemies of God in his death than he did during his life. Jesus stated to the rulers of his day that they "be held responsible for all the righteous blood spilled from righteous Abel through Zechariah, son of Barachiah." (Matt. 23:35, author's paraphrase) It is apparent that even in the Old Testament, some were called to be martyrs of their generation. God was faithful to all, whether his plan was deliverance through or deliverance from evil men. Martyrdom was the fate of most of the Apostles for their faith in Jesus. Peter, by himself, shows God delivering him from evil men and then later in life; Peter died as a martyr at the hands of evil men. The rulers cast Peter into prison after Herod had martyred James, the brother of John, with a sword. Herod saw that "the death of James pleased the people." An angel of the Lord miraculously broke Peter out of jail and restored him to the Church. (Acts 12) Peter the apostle died by crucifixion upside down, as he felt unworthy of being crucified as his Lord and Savior was. God sometimes delivers men and women out of trouble and sometimes through trouble, and he is just as trustworthy in either case.

There is a quote from the book Experiencing God that I would like to include because it illustrates powerfully our goal to trust God when things make little sense:

> Your confidence in the love nature of God is crucial. This has been a powerful influence in my life. I always view my circumstances against the backdrop of the cross, where God clearly showed once and for all his deep love for me. I may not always understand my current situation or how things will eventually turn out, but I can trust in the love Christ proved to me when he laid down his life for me on the cross. In the death and resurrection of Jesus Christ, God forever convinced me he loves me. I choose to base my trust in God on what I know—his love for me—and I choose to trust that in time, he will help me understand the confusing circumstances I may be experiencing.[1]

---

1   Henry T. Blackaby & Claude V. King, *Experiencing God: Knowing and Doing the Will of God*, rev. ed. (Nashville, Tenn.: B&H Books, 2008), 21.

Whoever goes through this period, whether it is the Church or those who get saved after the Rapture of the Church, needs to guard this in their heart. The Bible clearly states that the saints, whoever they are, are going to be given over to the Antichrist and suffer under his reign. Why does God allow this? Why not just allow the mortal wound the Antichrist is going to suffer to run its natural course and spare the world the Antichrist's reign? The Scriptures foretell the Antichrist recovers from a wound that, in the natural, should cause death, but does not, and the world follows him. Why not take out Hitler at birth or during early childhood? God knew what Hitler would become. If he died from a childhood disease, none of us would have been the wiser. We do not know. There is only one with the position of the Most High God. There is sure to be a reason, but our part is not to understand ahead of time why God allows the pain and suffering to continue to be a part of the mix of human experience. Our part is to trust that in the pain and suffering we go through, our heavenly Father loves us and somehow this works out for our good—that, as my brother so eloquently pointed out, the love of God on the cross of Calvary forever solidified God's love for us, to not allow contrary circumstances to suggest otherwise.

I do not say this lightly: I am guiltier than most of doubt and fear when what is going on in the natural does not match what God has spoken to me. This is difficult to learn, especially if abuse and betrayal have impaired your ability to trust. But whoever goes through this period is going to need to trust and hold fast because it will not make sense in the natural.

The Bible states that "our times are in God's hands." (Psalm 31:15, author's paraphrase) God chose us to be born in the time we are at. It is not an accident that this is our period. We need to do what we can in the time we are in. God says:

Declaring the end and the result from the beginning, and from ancient times the things that are not yet done, saying, My counsel shall stand, and I will do all My pleasure and purpose. (Isa. 46:10)

God alone knows the end from the beginning, and our stewardship is to be faithful in whatever time God has called us to. Not that it is this generation that will see the return of the Lord, but with all the prophetic signs that abound in our generation, you would be hard-pressed to suggest that it would be a long way from this generation.

It is not a message that many are going to gravitate toward, as it is a time of trouble, and we would just as soon avoid trouble. However, it is the plain reading of the text in Matthew 24 and the book of Revelation—not that the book of Revelation is plain, because symbolism and imagery are abundant throughout the book, but what is plain in the book of Revelation is that it is a time of great peril.

It may be more tempting to believe that these dire straits are for another group of people and not for us as believers. It is painfully obvious that some group of believers is going through this time—why should we assume we are exempt? The plain reading of Matthew 24 says then "they will hand you over, all men will hate you, death will come to many of you," etcetera. Now, few people want to hear that. These are not pleasant words, but who was Jesus talking to at the time? He was talking to his disciples, and the plain inference would be that if we are his disciples, then he is talking to us by extension. Not for nothing, but we sure are quick to claim all the good promises that Jesus spoke of as belonging to us by extension. It may not be a nice truth, and it certainly is not one to give people the happy feeling that we enjoy in the presence of the Lord, but it is the truth. Any suggestion outside of that is reading between the lines. It is possible that those theories of God rapturing his covenant people out before the Tribulation begins are correct. Time will tell, but we need to see them for what they are and that is a theory, not the plain reading of the text. What if that theory turns out to be incorrect? There are going to be an awful lot of disillusioned believers out there with their hearts ripped out and their faith stunned.

We have talked previously about the theory that God is going to wrap up his dealings with the Church and conclude his dealings with the nation of Israel. This is one of the largest reasons believers all over the world believe that the Church does not partake in the time of Jacob's trouble, that we rise in the Rapture before the Great Tribulation. Apparently, it's Jacob's trouble and not ours, and before we get into the time of Jacob's trouble, let's ask ourselves another penetrating question. Earlier, we explored that God grafted us into the natural olive tree, or Israel, in the imagery that Paul talked about. Then God grafted Israel out because of their unbelief. Is it fair that we can partake of all Israel's blessings but expect none of Israel's troubles? How fair is that? Now I am not saying that those who believe in God dealing separately regarding the Church—and in another regard, to Israel—are wrong, but they could be. It is a plausible hypothesis, but that is what it is: a hypothesis. We have seen in many places in the Bible that he has made the two entities one. The Bible says that "he is our peace, and he has made us both Jew and Gentile alike to be one body and he has broken down the dividing wall between and made of the two one new man and in that way establishing peace." (Eph. 2:14, author's paraphrase)

It is okay to theorize and hypothesize. God gave us these brains, and he knows we are going to explore. One thing that the body of Christ needs is the humility to say that this is a theory and not a fact. The Church comes off, especially to unbelievers—this is my belief—as having the one Word of Truth, yet few of us agree with the next person. What does that say to the unbeliever? Did Jesus say they, the unbelievers, would know we are Christians because we agree on doctrinal issues? No, we can give each other the room to explore the vast possibilities in Scripture and in this area take a lesson from the world and be tolerant of different points of view. We should not be tolerant in deviations to areas that are bedrock to the Christian faith: Jesus is Lord, he died for our sins; we are sinners in need of salvation, etcetera. But in areas such as prophecy, we need to be tolerant of other points of view, as the truth is we do not know it all.

I could be wrong in my interpretation of end-time events. I do not think that I am wrong, but that is the point. Nobody thinks they are wrong. We would not put it into print if we seriously thought it was wrong. But that is what we think, and the Bible says that "they" (unbelievers) will know we are Christians by our love for one another." (John 13:35, author's paraphrase), not by our theological points of view. Prophecy is going to come to pass the way the Lord has stated. We need to be ready for it in whatever way it comes to pass in actuality. If it comes to pass that God separates the Church from the nation of Israel in end-time events and that we rise in the Rapture before the Great Tribulation. What harm has it done to the body of Christ to explore the possibility that we may go through it? The danger is that our preconceived ideas will keep us from recognizing the events until it is too late. Some people's faith will fail. That could be a part of the great falling away.

CHAPTER 16

The Harvest

I have entitled this chapter "The Harvest" because I want the chapters to build upon each other. It would be advantageous to have the process and the Scriptures to understand the various theories on the timing of the Rapture. If I simply titled this chapter "The Rapture," many people would skip some of the process and foundation found in the earlier chapters and go directly to this chapter. Many would make up their minds whether they wanted to continue reading the book or stop at that point. Viewing the context should make a dramatic difference. There are only a few places in the Scriptures that use the word harpazo, which is the original Greek word that means "to be seized or caught up" and, in English, became the Rapture. The concentration in this study is on the words "caught up" (because it is in this framework we derive the word rapture), there are a few other instances of the word harpazo in the New Testament but they are not in direct relationship to this study.

1. Acts 8:39, where the Spirit *caught* up Phillip.

2.   2 Corinthians 12:2 and 4, where Paul was *caught* up to the third heaven or paradise.

3.   1 Thessalonians 4:17, which is the only direct reference to the Rapture; everything else is indirect. Those who are alive and remain shall be *caught* up to meet the Lord in the air.

4.   Revelation 12:5, where the Child is *caught* up to God.

There is much exploration that we need to do concerning the Rapture, as it is a pivotal point in end-time events.

> Then we, the living ones who remain [on the earth], shall simultaneously be caught up along with [the resurrected dead] in the clouds to meet the Lord in the air; and so always (through the eternity of the eternities) we shall be with the Lord! (1 Thess. 4:17)

The word translated caught in this verse in Strong's Exhaustive Concordance of the Bible is harpazo, which means "to seize: catch (away, up), pluck, pull, and take by force." Translated into Latin, it became the word raptus, and then raptus became the English word rapture, which many biblical scholars and theologians believe is the secret coming of Christ for his Church. Why is this important? Because according to how you believe, it will largely determine how you respond.

There are three dominant views concerning the Rapture:

1.   Pre-Tribulation is the school of thought that there is a secret rapture where Christ comes to take his Church before the Great Tribulation starts. We then return with him at the end

of the Tribulation as he destroys the Antichrist and sets up his kingdom on earth.

2. Mid-Tribulation is the school of thought that there is a secret rapture where Christ comes to take his Church halfway through the Great Tribulation. Then we return with him at the end of the Tribulation as he destroys the Antichrist and sets up his kingdom on earth.

3. Post-Tribulation is the school of thought that we as believers go through the Great Tribulation. The rapture occurs just before he returns to earth. He destroys the Antichrist and sets up his kingdom on earth.

The last one is obviously the least popular currently, as who wants to go through the time the Bible describes as the worst in human history? Also, with all the signs abounding in our generation, it is becoming more real than in previous generations.

Pre-Tribulation thinkers base their belief mostly on the following verses:

BUT AS to the suitable times and the precise seasons and dates, brethren, you have no necessity for anything being written to you. For you yourselves know perfectly well that *the day of the [return of the] Lord will come [as unexpectedly and suddenly] as a thief in the night.* When people are saying, all is well and secure, and, there is peace and safety, then in a moment unforeseen destruction (ruin and death) will come upon them as suddenly as labor pains come upon a woman with child; and they shall by no means escape, for there will be no escape. (1 Thess. 5:1–3) (emphasis mine)

So in the pre-Tribulation point of view, he comes like a thief secretly to rapture his people before the proverbial crap hits the fan. That he comes like a thief suggests that the world at large is unaware, and we are caught up with Jesus. We stay with him until the Great Tribulation is over. If he came and every eye saw him, even "those who pierced him," that would not be like a thief because the goal of the thief is to remain undetected. Therefore, the pre-Tribulation view is that there must be two raptures: one for his Church, which is done secretly, and then again at the end of the Tribulation for those who get saved during the time of the Tribulation.

> *For God has not appointed us to [incur His] wrath* [He did not select us to condemn us], but [that we might] obtain [His] salvation through our Lord Jesus Christ (the Messiah). (1 Thess. 5:9) (emphasis mine)

Another main point is that God did not appoint us to suffer wrath. If we are here during this period of the Great Tribulation, we are going to suffer wrath, and God has not called us to that.

> *But the day of the lord will come like a thief,* and then the heavens will vanish (pass away) with a thunderous crash, and the [material] elements [of the universe] will be dissolved with fire, and the earth and the works that are upon it will be burned up. (2 Pet. 3:10) (emphasis mine)

Behold, He is coming with the clouds, and every eye will see Him, even those who pierced Him; and all the tribes of the earth shall gaze upon Him and beat their breasts and mourn

and lament over Him. Even so [must it be]. Amen (so be it).
(Rev. 1:7)

One picture of his coming is open, and everybody sees him, while
other Scriptures portray his return like a thief catching people unaware,
which we have already established. This would suggest to many two
distinct events: one in secret and one in plain sight.

And [how you] look forward to and await the coming of His
Son from heaven, Whom He raised from the dead—*Jesus,
Who personally rescues and delivers us out of and from the wrath*
[bringing punishment] which is coming [upon the impenitent]
and [draws us to Himself, investing us with all the privileges
and rewards of the new life in Christ, the Messiah]. (1 Thess.
1:10) (emphasis mine)

Here, Jesus rescues us from the wrath to come on the unbelievers.
Jesus specifically rescues us, in this view, from the wrath, which is the
Great Tribulation period spoken of in the book of Revelation and
Matthew 24.

So that He may strengthen and confirm and establish your
hearts faultlessly pure and unblameable in holiness in the sight
of our God and Father, at the coming of our Lord Jesus Christ
(the Messiah) *with all His saints* (the holy and glorified people
of God)! Amen, (so be it)! (1 Thess. 3:13) (emphasis mine).

The reasoning here would be that this verse clearly states that when
Jesus returns, his saints are with him. In the pre-Tribulation point of
view, it makes very little sense to have Jesus returning and us on the earth
raptured to him just as he comes to destroy the Antichrist. We would

just be doing a U-turn, and what kind of sense does that make? It makes better sense that we have been enjoying the marriage feast of the Lamb and then return with him as he vanquishes the Antichrist.

> AFTER THIS I looked, and behold, *a door standing open in heaven!* And the first voice which I had heard addressing me like [the calling of] a war trumpet said, *come up here,* and I will show you what must take place in the future. (Rev. 4:1) (emphasis mine)

Regarding Revelation 4:1, we see the reasoning is something like this: There is no mention of the Church after this point until Revelation 19:7–9. Therefore, the Church must be gone, as God's Church is the center of his attention in the affairs of men. Christ opened a door in heaven, and the reasoning is that John's call to come up here and the door being opened is a prophetic picture of the Church being raptured into heaven.

The reasoning goes something like this: The day of the Lord will come quietly and unexpectedly, like a thief in the night who is trying to avoid being noticed. The Jews of Jesus's day did not understand how their Messiah would come in two separate periods: one as the suffering Savior and again as the conquering King. They were looking for a king to take the oppression of Rome off their necks. They could not fathom that the prophetic Scriptures, which foretold of their Messiah, could be the same person in two different periods of time. We don't want to repeat that mistake. So even though he stated he was coming again a second time, we cannot rule out the possibility that he comes secretly like a thief in the night to gather his Church before the Great Tribulation. Then he returns at the end of the Tribulation to destroy the Antichrist and set up his kingdom on earth.

Watch therefore [give strict attention and be cautious and active], *for you know neither the day nor the hour when the Son of Man will come.* (Matt. 25:13) (emphasis mine)

We will not know the day or the hour, and in Revelation, it talks about a place prepared for God's people that they will have provided for them to endure for three and a half years. Starting from the time, the Antichrist stands in the temple and declares that he is God.

And the woman [herself] fled into the desert (wilderness), where she has a retreat prepared [for her] by God, in which she is to be fed and kept safe for 1,260 days (42 months; three and one-half years). (Rev. 12:6)

So if we don't know the day and the hour, how is that even possible when all we need to do is start counting from the day the Antichrist reveals himself in the temple for 1,260 days? This is, in some ways, the strongest support for the pre-Tribulation point of view. As previously mentioned, we will not know the exact day or hour, but we will know the season. The 1,260 days puts us right in the ballpark, and they could be right. At the time Jesus was speaking in Matthew 24, he declares no one knows the day or the hour, not even the angels, but only the Father. However, some things have changed since then. Jesus has ascended back to his Father's throne. Where Jesus was not omniscient while physically on earth, that is not the case any longer. Can anyone believe that after ascending to the fullness of what he was before that he no longer knows the day of his return? He is once again omniscient. Of course he knows. If—and, agreed, this is a big if—he wanted to share this secret with his servant John, and therefore to the rest of his people, is it not now his to reveal? It is, after all, called the book of Revelation.

In Revelation 5, there is a scene where the Ancient of Days seals a scroll or a book with seven seals. And no one is worthy of opening the seals and reading the scroll. So John weeps. Then one elder in heaven tells him to stop weeping because the Lion of Judah has overcome. He is worthy of breaking open the seals and revealing what is in the book. This could imply insight that was never available before. Is this a strong possibility? Probably not, but the proposition serves to illustrate the point that we can rule nothing out.

> So do not make any hasty or premature judgments before the time when the Lord comes [again], for He will both bring to light the secret things that are [now hidden] in darkness and disclose and expose the [secret] aims (motives and purposes) of hearts. Then every man will receive his [due] commendation from God. (1 Cor. 4:5)

One problem with dealing with an all-knowing and all-powerful God is that you can't box him in. There is always an angle we haven't considered. Is this to imply that God is devious? No, not at all, but he discloses what he chooses and keeps to himself what he also chooses. His reasons for doing this are his own. This is an example—and bears repeating—he never disclosed to the prominent people of his day that he was their Messiah. That the prophecies concerning him, while accurate, entailed two separate appearances. Why do you suppose he did that? Jesus could have set the record straight and chose not to. Going back to the illustration of the owner of a company and his employees, what we choose to focus on says much more about us than it does about him. In all these views, there is scriptural evidence for and scriptural evidence against each view. So who is right? Good question. The truth? Nobody knows for sure except one, and he has already stated what he wanted to say on the subject. It's kind of frustrating, isn't it? He could just spell it out in simple terms, but even in the Old Testament, prophecy was seldom simple. There is sure to be a reason; God does not do things arbitrarily. The Bible says, "The secret things belong to God." (Deut. 29:29, author's paraphrase) There are many things, however, that are not in dispute among all three points of view:

Jesus is coming again.

1. We, as his people, are going to be caught up in the air to be with him.
2. There is a Great Tribulation period.
3. The Antichrist reveals himself.

Part of God's glory is to conceal things, as noted in the verse below. However, if God wanted to make something hidden no amount of effort on our part would uncover it—he is God! So a distinct part of the glory of God is hiding something and then engaging us, his children, in the discovery of what God hid, in the proper season.

It is the glory of God to conceal a thing, but the glory of kings is to search out a thing. (Prov. 25:2)

God can handle different points of views, and it doesn't slow him down one bit. We might want to view it as a sifting process, like when he spoke to the people in parables. Why do that? Why not just speak plainly? As you read the Gospels and Jesus's interaction with the "crowds," Jesus wasn't after their heads but their hearts. This sifting process brought people who really wanted to know closer to him. Those who did not want to grow closer probably felt very good about themselves. "Good word, Pastor!" However, there was no genuine change.

> And be like men who are waiting for their master to return home from the marriage feast, so that when he returns from the wedding and comes and knocks, they may open to him immediately. (Luke 12:36)

Another key verse for the pre-Tribulation point of view is in Luke 12:36. This verse states to be like men waiting for their master to return from a marriage. Revelation has a scene called the marriage feast of the Lamb. We will get to that book shortly. Basically, though, it says to be like men awaiting their master's return from a wedding, and the picture here is once again one of preparedness. This may or may not be a specific reference to the marriage feast of the Lamb. However, when we get to the wedding feast of the Lamb in Revelation, we should note that this event of the marriage feast of the Lamb occurs after the fall of Babylon, which is at the end of the Great Tribulation. The pre-Tribulation point of view adheres to the imminent return of Christ. This basically means Jesus can come back at any second to gather his people and take them with him. This view believes that there is no prophecy that needs to be fulfilled before God raptures his Church to himself. However, they base this belief on referencing scripture verses about Jesus's unexpected arrival like a thief in the night. Jesus's admonition to be watchful and alert doesn't necessitate that no other prophecies need fulfillment before this event. That is how they are interpreting what those verses are saying. Jesus could be simply saying to be watchful and alert, so it doesn't take you by surprise, like the illustration with the Titanic. You have turned a corner and realized you have hit the iceberg. While the end is not immediate, you know there is no way you are getting out of this situation—you are now in it. Basically, they say that this doctrine of imminence helps them keep in the practice of holiness. Because he may come at any moment, you walk through your day with that awareness. Most pre-Tribulation believers would say that this would happen just before the Great Tribulation. Part of that belief is from another key verse.

> For the mystery of lawlessness (that hidden principle of rebellion against constituted authority) is already at work in the world, [but it is] restrained *only until he who restrains is taken out of the way*. (2 Thess. 2:7) (emphasis mine)

He who is restraining needs to be taken out of the way before the Antichrist reveals himself. God's Spirit lives inside of us as Christians. When we rise in the Rapture, the restraining presence of the Holy Spirit inside of us is gone from the world, clearing the way for the Antichrist to come into power. From the mid-Tribulation point of view, the secret rapture occurs somewhere in the middle of the seven-year period of the reign of the Antichrist. This is close to the pre-Tribulation point of view, except they believe that the Rapture occurs in the middle, as the first half of the reign of the Antichrist is relatively peaceful—until the Antichrist shows his true colors and breaks the covenant. Their viewpoint is that God did not appoint us to suffer wrath.

CHAPTER 17

Our Glorified Eternal Bodies

Post-Tribulation is the view that we, as God's people, will go through the entire Tribulation until Christ's return. This is based on the following Scriptures.

> For this we declare to you by the Lord's [own] word, *that we who are alive and remain until the coming of the Lord* shall in no way precede [into His presence] or have any advantage at all over those who have previously fallen asleep [in Him in death]. (1 Thess. 4:15–17) (emphasis mine)

The Scriptures only plainly speak of Christ coming again. The natural inference is a second time. Any inference of multiple phases of his coming are sincere attempts at interpretation, but not the natural reading of the verses. The plain reading of the verse says we, the believers, are alive and remain until he comes. Notice that we do not get raptured before those who have died in Christ. This gives us a fixed position of timing in God's prophetic timetable.

For the Lord Himself will descend from heaven with a loud cry of summons, with the shout of an archangel, and with the blast of the trumpet of God. *And those who have departed this life in Christ will rise first. Then we, the living ones who remain [on the earth], shall simultaneously be caught up along with [the resurrected dead] in the clouds to meet the Lord in the air;* and so always (through the eternity of the eternities) we shall be with the Lord! (1 Thess. 4:16–17) (emphasis mine)

Since Paul the apostle was writing this epistle, can we safely assume that he included himself in the "we" who were to be caught up to meet the Lord in the air? God could have not shared everything with Paul on this subject. Each prophet or apostle received their own piece of the puzzle from God. What Isaiah saw about the Messiah was not the same viewpoint God showed Moses about the Messiah. However, it is reasonable to think that Paul fully expected that he could be alive at the coming of the Lord. The following are more Scriptures that support the post-Tribulation view.

But he who endures to the end will be saved. (Matt. 24:13)

And if those days had not been shortened, no human being would endure and survive, but for the sake of the elect (God's chosen ones) those days will be shortened. (Matt. 24:22)

Who are the elect Jesus is referring to? Many theologians and Bible scholars would say that these are the Jewish people saved during the Tribulation after God has raptured the Church out of here. However, we, as the Church, are called the elect:

Therefore I [am ready to] persevere and stand my ground with patience and endure everything for the sake of the elect [God's chosen], so that they too may obtain [the] salvation which is in Christ Jesus, with [the reward of] eternal glory. (2 Tim. 2:10–13)

The rapture will probably not happen without believers having resurrected bodies. It is possible that God, being who he is, could, but it makes more logical and scriptural sense that we have our resurrected bodies when we "meet him in the air." If we are going to meet Jesus in the air, as the Scriptures foretell, how far up do you suppose these bodies of ours that we have right now would make it? "In a moment, in the twinkling of an eye, we shall be changed." (1 Cor. 15:52, author's paraphrase) Here are some Scriptures that speak about that change and our resurrected bodies:

But now if Christ (the Messiah) is preached as raised from the dead, how is it that some of you say that there is no resurrection of the dead? But if there is no resurrection of the dead, then Christ has not risen; And if Christ has not risen, then our preaching is in vain [it amounts to nothing] and your faith is devoid of truth and is fruitless (without effect, empty, imaginary, and unfounded). We are even discovered to be misrepresenting God, for we testified of Him that He raised Christ, Whom He did not raise in case it is true that the dead are not raised. For if the dead are not raised, then Christ has not been raised; And if Christ has not been raised, your faith is mere delusion [futile, fruitless], and you are still in your sins [under the control and penalty of sin]; And further, those who have died in [spiritual fellowship and union with] Christ have perished (are lost)! If we who are [abiding] in Christ have hope only in this life and that is all, then we are of all people most miserable and to be pitied. But the fact is that Christ (the Messiah) has been raised from the dead, and He became the firstfruits of those who have fallen asleep [in death]. For since [it was] through a man that death [came into the world, it is] also through a Man that the resurrection of the dead [has come]. For just as [because of their union of nature] in Adam all people die, so also [by virtue of their union of nature] shall all in Christ be made alive. But each in his own rank and turn: Christ (the Messiah) [is] the firstfruits, then those who are Christ's [own will be resurrected/ *at His coming*. <u>After that comes the end</u> (the completion), when He delivers over the kingdom to God the Father after rendering inoperative and abolishing every [other] rule and every authority and power. (1 Cor. 15:12–24) (emphasis mine)

Notice again that his coming is scripturally when the end comes. Also, notice that the dead rise at his coming. If we do not presuppose multiple comings, since it only clearly states he is coming again, this is another fixed position in the timing of God's prophetic timetable.

But someone will say, how can the dead be raised? With what [kind of] body will they come forth? You foolish man! Every time you plant seed, you sow something that does not come to life [germinating, springing up, and growing] unless it dies first. Nor is the seed you sow then the body which it is going to have [later], but it is a naked kernel, perhaps of wheat or some of the rest of the grains. But God gives to it the body that He plans and sees fit, and to each kind of seed a body of its own. (1 Cor. 15:35–38)

Isn't this incredible? We see this principle in nature. The seed must first die before it can grow, and the seed doesn't represent the full potential of the mature body (or plant).

For all flesh is not the same, but there is one kind for humans, another for beasts, another for birds, and another for fish. There are heavenly bodies (sun, moon, and stars) and there are earthly bodies (men, animals, and plants), but the beauty and glory of the heavenly bodies is of one kind, while the beauty and glory of earthly bodies is a different kind. The sun is glorious in one way, the moon is glorious in another way, and the stars are glorious in their own [distinctive] way; for one star differs from and surpasses another in its beauty and brilliance. So it is with the resurrection of the dead. [The body] that is sown is perishable and decays, but [the body] that is resurrected is imperishable (immune to decay, immortal). It is sown in dishonor and humiliation; it is raised in honor and glory. It is sown in infirmity and weakness; it is resurrected in strength and endued with power. It is sown a natural (physical) body; it is raised a supernatural (a spiritual) body. [As surely as] there is a physical body, there is also a spiritual body. Thus it is written, The first man Adam became a living being (an individual personality); the last Adam (Christ) became a life-giving Spirit [restoring the dead to life]. But it is not the spiritual life which came first, but the physical and then the spiritual. The first man [was] from out of earth, made of dust (earthly-minded); the second Man [is] the Lord from out of heaven. Now those who are made of the dust are like him who was first made of the dust (earthly-minded); and as is [the Man] from heaven, so also [are those] who are of heaven (heavenly-minded). And just as we have borne the image [of the man] of dust, so shall we and so let us also bear the image [of the Man] of heaven. But I tell you this, brethren, flesh and blood cannot [become partakers of eternal salvation and] inherit or share in the kingdom of God; nor does the perishable (that which is decaying) inherit or share in the imperishable (the immortal). Take notice! I tell you a mystery (a secret truth, an event decreed by the hidden purpose or counsel of God). We shall not all fall asleep [in death], but we shall all be changed (transformed) In a moment, in the twinkling of an eye, at the [sound of the] *last trumpet call. For a trumpet will sound, and the dead [in Christ] will be raised imperishable (free and immune from decay), and we shall be changed (transformed).* (1 Cor. 15:39–52) (emphasis mine)

Remember that Scripture in 1 Thessalonians 4:15–17 about "we who are alive and remain have no advantage over those who have died in Christ, for the Lord shall descend and the trumpet shall sound and the dead in Christ shall rise first." The last trumpet appears to be found in the book of Revelation. When we get there, see what you think. If the dead in Christ rise at the last trumpet found in Revelation and that trumpet ushers in the millennial reign of Christ, what makes the most sense for the timing of the Rapture? The Scripture says, "We who are alive and well at his coming do not go before the dead in Christ rise." If they do not get raised until the last trumpet, and after the last trumpet, the kingdoms of this world become the kingdoms of our Christ and of his God, what is the natural reading for when the Rapture occurs? Would it not be that the Rapture occurs at the end of the Tribulation, when the kingdoms of this world become the kingdoms of our God and of his Christ? Keep "the last trumpet call" in mind when we look at the book of Revelation. We will see the last trumpet call a few times in the book as God keeps taking us from some point in the Tribulation period up to this momentous period.

> For this perishable [part of us] must put on the imperishable [nature], and this mortal [part of us, this nature that is capable of dying] must put on immortality (freedom from death). And when this perishable puts on the imperishable and this that was capable of dying puts on freedom from death, then shall be fulfilled the Scripture that says, Death is swallowed up (utterly vanquished forever) in and unto victory. O death, where is your victory? O death, where is your sting? (1 Cor. 15:53–55)

In these verses we have just looked at we see our glorified eternal bodies that we receive from God at the time of the Rapture.

CHAPTER 18

The Resurrection of the Just

Now concerning the resurrection, when does this take place?

Jesus said to her, "Your brother shall rise again. Martha replied, I know that he will rise again in the resurrection at *the last day.*" (John 11:23–24) (emphasis mine)

We have mentioned this thought before: that Jesus speaks one way to the crowds and plainly to his disciples and friends. Martha is both a disciple and a friend. It is a good bet that Martha and Jesus have talked about this subject before, and she is giving back to him what Jesus has previously told her.

No one is able to come to Me unless the Father Who sent Me attracts and draws him and gives him the desire to come to Me, and [then] I will raise him up [from the dead] at *the last day.* (John 6:44) (emphasis mine)

A thought to consider: If we do not get taken until the dead in Christ rise first, and they do not get resurrected until the last day, how do we get up to heaven seven years earlier? Remember those verses in 1 Thessalonians 4:15–17? We who are alive and remain until his return do not go ahead of those who have already died knowing Jesus as their Savior. The only definitive mention of his returning is at the end when he destroys the Antichrist.

> And then the lawless one (the antichrist) will be revealed and the Lord Jesus will slay him with the breath of His mouth and bring him to an end *by His appearing at His coming.* (2 Thess. 2:8) (emphasis mine)

This is another fixed point in the timing of God's prophetic timetable. Jesus destroys the Antichrist at his coming. If you do not presuppose multiple phases of his return, all of this is at the end of the prophesied history of humankind.

> For I know that my redeemer liveth, and that he shall stand at the latter day upon the earth: And though after my skin worms destroy this body, *yet in my flesh shall I see God:* Whom I shall see for myself, and mine eyes shall behold, and not another; though my reins be consumed within me. (Job 19:25–27 KJV) (emphasis mine)

So we do not meet the Lord in the air until the dead in Christ rise first, and they do not get resurrected until the last day. If we take "the last day" literally, then it would be the day before "the kingdoms of this world become the kingdoms of our Christ and of his God." After the millennial reign and the releasing of Satan for a short period to instigate a rebellion, we have a new heaven and a new earth.

Let us look at what we have as prophetic landmarks if we take the text at face value.

1. Believers who are alive and remain are here at his coming.
2. We do not get raptured ahead of those who have died knowing Jesus as their Savior.
3. The dead rise at his coming.
4. The dead who knew Jesus as Savior rise on the last day.
5. The dead who have Jesus as Savior rise at the last trumpet. The last trumpet in Revelation is the seventh and ushers in the kingdoms of this world being transferred to God.
6. The only definitive mention of his coming is when he destroys the Antichrist.
7. This would have to be at the end of the Tribulation. Jesus will not destroy him in the middle of the peace treaty.

Another thing to consider is that this came not from Paul as inspired as he was. He starts out with "This we declare to you by the Lord's own word." So Paul was saying, "This is not coming from my authority but from the Lord himself."

In the post-Tribulation point of view, both Jesus and Paul assume that God's people will be here on earth when he returns. Neither Jesus nor Paul explicitly states that he is passing the baton from the Church to Israel. Jesus instituted the Church Age and stated the gates of hell would not prevail against his Church. In every place that the Scriptures plainly speak of the Great Tribulation or his return, his covenant people are in the middle of the events taking place. If you do not presuppose that the Church gets raptured out before the actual pressure starts, then the plain reading says that we will be here.

In all the sections that show that Jesus is speaking, how many times do we, as the Church, believe Jesus is talking to us: the Church? As far as I have been able to ascertain, Christians believe that when Jesus is speaking, he is speaking to us Christians. As an example, let me list some topics of the Scriptures: the beatitudes (God forgives your sin); the parables (Jesus loves sinners); the kingdom of heaven; the Great Commission; etcetera. As far as I have been able to find out, there is only one exception to this principle. The principle is that since Jesus is talking to his disciples, he is talking to us, as we are his disciples. The only exception that I have heard of is the end of the age. Does it not seem strange to you that everything else Jesus had to say applied to us as his believers, but we can skip the end of the age?

There are some believers who say that this is because of the people who get saved during the Great Tribulation period after the Church has risen to meet Christ in the air. While this is possible, there are some serious drawbacks to the theory. First, you have brand-new baby Christians who must endure the greatest Tribulation the world has ever seen before and will never see again and not lose faith. This would be an impressive feat for the most mature and seasoned Christian believer among us. Could God do this? Of course. He is God, and miracles are a part of his nature, but those newborn believers would need a lot of Miracle-Gro.

Where are the sermons of Jesus concerning giving to the people food and supplies at the proper time during the end of the age? I have never heard even one. Jesus warns us repeatedly to be prepared. Where are the preachers that are preaching this topic? They are absent. Is this not because many of us believe we will rise in the Rapture before these terrible events take place? Since it does not apply to us, as we are not here during that time in that perspective. Then there is no point in teaching and preaching it. Those sermons, in that perspective, rightly belong to the Jews who get saved during the Tribulation. What are we expecting? That God will take brand-new baby Christians who have little or no knowledge of the Scriptures and supernaturally impart the Scriptures into their minds and spirits? Could God do that? Of course he could, but there is no plain teaching that this is what will happen. That is a mighty big jump in faith because, to some extent, he would have to do that. You have newly saved believers who are blank slates. They have just gotten saved, so how much Scripture do they know? How many can lead in prayer? Who can effectively deliver an evangelistic sermon and handle the altar call? They have no one to show them, as all the trained Spirit-filled people are in heaven, according to the pre-Tribulation perspective. There are those who believe that God would use a lot of the secular Jews and professing Christians for this task. A lot of these people would not be blank slates, and some would be very knowledgeable. That is a distinct possibility, but that is all it is—a possibility. We cannot say for certain that this will happen.

The signing of the covenant leaves humankind with only seven years. If the Church goes up in the Rapture at the beginning of the Antichrist's reign, that is not an awful lot of time to grow spiritually. Now God could supernaturally impart the entire Bible to them and pour out his Spirit on them to such a degree that they can do all that is required of them. However, the text doesn't explicitly say that. In the natural order of things, scripturally, God takes the time that is necessary to produce a Joseph, Moses, Esther, Ruth, David, Peter, Paul, Priscilla, and the like. Character development normally takes many years and trial and error to produce a mature man or woman of God. One pastor suggests that the pressures of this time will produce the rapid growth necessary to produce these amazing children of the Most High God. This is clearly plausible, but it is not stated it would happen that way. It is an enormous gamble because in all the generations of recorded history, God produced godly character over many years. Actually, the greater the pressure of the time, the longer God took to prepare his men and women of action and faith. The Church had better be right, or there are going to be a lot of disillusioned believers wondering what is going on during this period. The verses that follow are regarding who goes through the time of the Great Tribulation, which has a direct bearing on all views.

> For false Christs and false prophets will arise, and they will show great signs and wonders so as to deceive and lead astray, if possible, even the elect (God's chosen ones). (Matt. 24:24)

Jesus is talking plainly to his disciples, God's covenant people, not to the crowds in parables, as already discussed. These signs and wonders will be so convincing; they would lead astray even the elect of God, if that were possible. Is that a test for new Christians or for seasoned? Instant maturity is a contradiction in terms.

> For in Christ Jesus you are all sons of God through faith. For as many [of you] as were baptized into Christ [into a spiritual union and communion with Christ, the Anointed One, the Messiah] have put on (clothed yourselves with) Christ. There is [now no distinction] neither Jew nor Greek, there is neither slave nor free, there is not male and female; for you are all one in Christ Jesus. (Gal. 3:26–28)

Many theologians would say that this period—the Great Tribulation—is for Israel and not for the Church. However, the Jews who come to believe in Christ are now part of the Church. He currently has no other institution. While he will certainly save the Jewish people, they are now messianic Jews and have come into a relationship with their Messiah. Jesus is building his Church, and while he is faithful to his covenant with the nation of Israel, they are no longer the instrument through which he blesses the world spiritually. The concept that he will rapture the Church and resume where he left off in his dealings with Israel remains a concept. He certainly does not come right out and say so. You must conjecture because it is not the plain reading of the text. Is it possible? Of course it is. The Jews of Jesus's day were looking for a kingly Messiah and not a suffering servant. They could not conceive of these two pictures of their Messiah being fulfilled in one person in two totally different places in time. In this example, he fulfilled his prophecy unexpectedly by splitting his coming into two time periods and two distinct personas, the suffering Messiah and the conquering King. Because we have this as an example, many believe that he is going to follow a similar pattern and have two or more phases of his return. The face value of the Scripture only clearly states he is returning, the natural reading would assume once. He does not always share the fullness of his plan, so all speculation is possible, but being possible does not mean it is probable.

Let us consider that those who hold to the pre-Tribulation view concerning the Rapture do so because they legitimately understand scripture that way. However, along with believing the word of God along this trajectory, there is also an element of love involved. In what particular manner is an element of love involved? That they love their children, and their grandchildren, their wives and husbands. Is it not easier to believe we, as the Church, rise in the Rapture before these terrible events take place? That it is someone else's loved ones who must go through this period? In that view, does God love these other children, grandchildren, wives, and husbands less than he loves us?

Regarding our resurrection body, as Jesus is the first fruit, we should look at his resurrected body. Jesus appeared to his disciples shortly after his resurrection and said, "Peace" to them. Startled, the disciples thought they were seeing a ghost. Jesus asked them, "Why are you so startled and full of questions?" He told them to see his hands and his feet and touch him to verify that he was real. He said, "A ghost does not have a body, as you see that I have." Then, to take it a step further and prove even more that it was really him physically among them and that he had risen from the dead, he asked them for something to eat. They gave him some broiled fish, and he ate with them. Then he showed them in the Scriptures all the prophecies regarding his First Coming and how he had to die and rise to life on the third day. (Luke 24:36–46, author's paraphrase)

Another quick question: As Jesus was with the disciples for three years, why did he wait to explain the prophecies about his First Coming after his resurrection? Why not before he died? If he waited until after he accomplished his purposes before really explaining them, what precedent does that establish for us as we await his return?

Who will transform and fashion anew the body of our humiliation to conform to and be like the body of His glory and majesty, by exerting that power which enables Him even to subject everything to Himself. (Phil. 3:21)

So in our resurrected state, we will be like him in our glorified bodies.

CHAPTER 19

Science or the Supernatural?

O ne reason pre-Tribulation and mid-Tribulation believers believe the Church will not be here is also because of these verses:

And now you know what is restraining him [from being revealed at this time]; it is so that he may be manifested (revealed) in his own [appointed] time. For the mystery of lawlessness (that hidden principle of rebellion against constituted authority) is already at work in the world, [but it is] restrained only until he who restrains is taken out of the way And then the lawless one (the antichrist) will be revealed and the Lord Jesus will slay him with the breath of His mouth and bring him to an *end by His appearing at His coming.* The coming [of the lawless one, the antichrist] is through the activity and working of Satan and will be attended by great power and *with all sorts of [pretended] miracles and signs and delusive marvels—[all of them] lying wonders.* (2 Thess. 2:6–9) (emphasis mine)

The book of Revelation also portrays this. What of these "lying wonders"? As a point of speculation, what if these miracles, signs, and wonders come in the guise of science? What if scientists isolate a particular gene and state that this gene is the source of humankind's inherent untapped potential? We already have cloning and stem cell research and many other things that are extraordinary currently; it is not really that far-fetched. What they have isolated, whether a gene or some other discovery, is the next step in humankind's evolution. It is that new discovery and not God that explains the miraculous, that this gene is the reason some people operate in the paranormal: ESP, clairvoyance, telekinesis, levitation, miraculous healings, etcetera, and God is not the origin of these apparent abilities. Certain genes determine our eye color, height, weight, etcetera. Why can't there be a gene that has been there all along that could explain the supernatural, but we never knew how to avail ourselves of it consciously? That is a much more palatable proposition to seduce the world at large than actual miracles. It would be very easy for them to say about Christians that these are not miracles manifested by their God. They unwittingly have tapped into the miracle gene and are using their own human potential and falsely giving God the credit. As a result, we disillusioned Christians, and our rigid beliefs, act as obstacles to progress and human evolution. It would then be a service to all humankind to remove us, as we would resist and challenge this hypothesis, stating that miracles have their source of power in one of two places: either God or Satan. It does not need to be this; there are many scenarios that could usher in these lying signs and wonders. Many theologians and Bible scholars believe that the he that is restraining the coming of the lawless one or the Antichrist is the Holy Spirit. The reasoning goes something like this: When a person is born again or saved, the Holy Spirit of God indwells them.

Do you not discern and understand that you [the whole church at Corinth] are God's temple (His sanctuary), and that God's Spirit has His permanent dwelling in you [to be at home in you, collectively as a church and also individually]? (1 Cor. 3:16)

In Him you also who have heard the Word of Truth, the glad tidings (Gospel) of your salvation, and have believed in and adhered to and relied on Him, were stamped with the seal of the long-promised Holy Spirit. That [Spirit] is the guarantee of our inheritance [the firstfruits, the pledge and foretaste, the down payment on our heritage], in anticipation of its full redemption and our acquiring [complete] possession of it—to the praise of His glory. (Eph. 1:13–14)

Since the spirit of the living God indwells the believer, if the Church ascends to join Jesus, the Holy Spirit's presence in us and our call to be light in this darkened world will no longer exist. Therefore, the restraining presence of the Holy Spirit has left the world, and the Antichrist is free to come into his own. However, the Bible clearly states:

Then they will hand you over to suffer affliction and tribulation and put you to death, and you will be hated by all nations for My name's sake. (Matt. 24:9)

He was speaking to his disciples.

And if those days had not been shortened, no human being would endure and survive, but for the sake of the elect (God's chosen ones) those days will be shortened. (Matt. 24:22)

So who are these people who are being persecuted and for whom God shortens the days? Many theologians and Bible scholars suggest that these are the Jews who get saved during the Great Tribulation. But how do they get saved? If all the Holy Spirit–led preachers have gone to heaven, who preaches to the unsaved?

> But how are people to call upon Him Whom they have not believed [in Whom they have no faith, on Whom they have no reliance]? And how are they to believe in Him [adhere to, trust in, and rely upon Him] of Whom they have never heard? And how are they to hear without a preacher? (Rom. 10:14)

Could the Holy Spirit save men without preachers? It's possible. He is God and can do as he wills, but this is the pattern that he set up. Even if the unsaved Jews get saved without the help of a preacher, we will then have Holy Spirit–filled believers, so the restrainer is back in keeping with this theory.

CHAPTER 20

The Ministry of the Holy Spirit

There is an alternate possibility to be considered, yet it is the same in a way. There are even more possibilities than this. It is a theory that the Holy Spirit leaving the world restrains the Antichrist. While the idea is totally possible, it is not conclusive. God knows exactly who the restrainer is, but the time is coming when the restraint against the Antichrist will no longer be there, and then the Antichrist will have his time for a brief season.

> Then the Lord said, My Spirit shall not forever dwell and strive with man, for he also is flesh; but his days shall yet be 120 years. (Gen. 6:3)

One of the many jobs of the Holy Spirit is to convince humankind of their need for Christ, to woo the hearts of rebellious men and women back to the heart of God. However, the Lord has said his spirit will not always strive with humankind. (Gen. 6:3) What if he simply stops restraining the unsaved person after his Gospel has gone throughout the world? What if he simply stops contesting with men's and women's hearts and wills to get saved? The Scriptures tell us that there is a point where God says, "You who are righteous remain that way, and you who are unrighteous remain that way." (Rev. 22:11, author's paraphrase) Have we had a time when the Spirit of God was not striving with humankind? There has been no record of such a time. It would make little sense to stop striving with humankind after the Second Coming of Christ. God would then eternally save us or eternally separate us from him, unless it occurs during the millennial reign of Christ before he lets Satan loose for a brief season. We do not know who populates the millennial kingdom, but at the end of the millennial reign, some will choose to follow Satan. Because the Bible does not clearly address a topic to our satisfaction, that does not mean one does not exist. Such is the case of who populates the millennial kingdom. God could start over with a new Adam and Eve for us to rule over, or millions of them. It could be many things; our God is an infinitely creative God. This would be the only other period when the Spirit of God could conceivably stop striving with humankind. After the millennial reign, we enter the eternal state, where everything remains fixed for all eternity.

> He who is unrighteous (unjust, wicked), let him be unrighteous still; and he who is filthy (vile, impure), let him be filthy still; and he who is righteous (just, upright, in right standing with God), let him do right still; and he who is holy, let him be holy still. (Rev. 22:11)

> And this good news of the kingdom (the Gospel) will be preached throughout the whole world as a testimony to all the nations, and then will come the end. (Matt. 24:14)

This verse deals with the working of the Holy Spirit in people's lives:

However, I am telling you nothing but the truth when I say it is profitable (good, expedient, advantageous) for you that I go away. Because if I do not go away, the Comforter (Counselor, Helper, Advocate, Intercessor, Strengthener, Standby) will not come to you [into close fellowship with you]; but if I go away, I will send Him to you [to be in close fellowship with you]. *And when He comes, He will convict and convince the world and bring demonstration to it about sin and about righteousness (uprightness of heart and right standing with God) and about judgment:* About sin, because they do not believe in Me [trust in, rely on, and adhere to Me]; About righteousness (uprightness of heart and right standing with God), because I go to My Father, and you will see Me no longer; About judgment, because the ruler (evil genius, prince) of this world [Satan] is judged and condemned and sentence already is passed upon him. (John 16:7–11) (emphasis mine)

Currently, the Holy Spirit continues his job to convince the world of sin, righteousness, and judgment. (John 16:8) God has stated that his spirit would not always strive with humankind. At what point will he stop? After the Tribulation and everyone has come into their eternal states of being, either in heaven or hell? No, once we have died (or been raptured) and come into our eternal destiny—either good or bad—it is too late, except for those born during the millennial reign of Christ; these will need to decide for or against Christ. Some will choose to follow Satan in a last-ditch revolt at the end of the millennial reign to overthrow the government of God. We cover that in the book of Revelation. Here's a thought to consider about the different points of views concerning the Rapture: Of the three, which would be most helpful from Satan's point of view, for men to believe and be wrong about it? If pre- and mid-Tribulation points of view are correct, we go home to heaven before things get nasty. If that's the case, how much preparation do we need? However, if the post-Tribulation view is correct, will those who believe differently become discouraged, confused, and disillusioned because no one prepared them for it?

CHAPTER 21

The Gog Magog War

We need to look at a couple of chapters in Ezekiel that describe a war that takes place in Israel that has not happened yet. Trying to figure out where this fits in God's timeline has had many scholars scratching their heads.

We will look at two chapters in Ezekiel: 38 and 39. The reason this is important is that the war described here has not taken place in the past. So it is still a piece of the end-time timeline that needs to occur in the future. Most scholars believe it must happen before Jesus returns.

And the word of the Lord came to me, saying, Son of man, set your face against Gog, of the land of Magog, the prince of Rosh, of Meshech, and of Tubal, and prophesy against *him,* And say, Thus says the Lord God: Behold, I am against you, *O Gog, chief prince (ruler) of Rosh, of Meshech, and of Tubal. (*Ezek. 38:1–3) (emphasis mine)

The first part we need to focus on is that Gog is a person. This is not a common name in our day and age and sounds an awful lot like the geographical area that he is from, which is Magog.

> And I will turn you back and put hooks into your jaws, and I will bring you forth and all your army, horses and horsemen, all of them clothed in full armor, a great company with buckler and shield, all of them handling swords—Persia, Cush, and Put or Libya with them, all of them with shield and helmet, Gomer and all his hordes, the house of Togarmah in the uttermost parts of the north and all his hordes—many people are with you. You [Gog] be prepared; yes, prepare yourself, you and all your companies that are assembled about you, and you be a guard and a commander for them. After many days you shall be visited and mustered [for service]; in the latter years you shall go against the land that is restored from the ravages of the sword, where people are gathered out of many nations upon the mountains of Israel, which had been a continual waste; but its [people] are brought forth out of the nations and they shall dwell securely, all of them. (Ezek. 38:4–8)

God, according to this prophecy, is going to draw Gog as the leader of Magog and a coalition of nations against Israel. Israel, at the time of this war, is dwelling securely. There has never been a recorded time of Israel dwelling securely, so this is in the future.

> You shall ascend and come like a storm; you shall be like a cloud to cover the land, you and all your hosts and many people with you. Thus says the Lord God: At the same time thoughts shall come into your mind, and you will devise an evil plan. And you will say, I will go up against an open country [the land of

unwalled villages]; I will fall upon those who are at rest, who dwell securely, all of them dwelling without walls and having neither bars nor gates, To take spoil and prey, to turn your hand upon the desolate places now inhabited and assail the people gathered out of the nations, who have obtained livestock and goods, who dwell at the center of the earth [Palestine]. Sheba and Dedan and the merchants of Tarshish, with all their lionlike cubs [or satellite areas], shall say to you, have you come to take spoil? Have you gathered your hosts to take the prey? To carry away silver and gold, to take away livestock and goods, to take a great spoil? (Ezek. 38:9–13)

In this prophecy, Israel is dwelling so securely that it has no defenses: no walls, no Iron Dome, no David's Sling, which enhanced Israel's missile defense, etcetera. For many people, the thought that Israel could be relaxed enough to say, "We do not need the Iron Dome, or any of the rest of our defenses" is an inconceivable thought! What could transpire to make these conditions possible? You can see the dilemma. Not that it could not happen. Let us consider this verse:

Who has heard of such a thing? Who has seen such things? Shall a land be born in one day? Or shall a nation be brought forth in a moment? For as soon as Zion was in labor, she brought forth her children. (Isa. 66:8)

We had never seen it before, and probably will never see it again, but the nation of Israel was born in a day. On May 14, 1948, Israel once again became a nation. On May 13, 1948, it was not a nation, and the next day, it was. Many would argue that the horrors of the Holocaust and the resulting sympathy from the nations took many years to prepare, so it wasn't technically a one-day birth for the nation. However, we can debate semantics later. The point is an incredibly unlikely prophecy came true. So we cannot rule out something we cannot comprehend coming to pass to make these conditions viable. In the natural Israel, feeling secure enough to not have any defenses is an outlandish thought.

Now let us continue:

Therefore, son of man, prophesy and say to Gog, thus says the Lord God: In that day when My people Israel dwell securely, will you not know it and be aroused? And you will come from your place out of the uttermost parts of the north, you and many peoples with you, all of them riding on horses, a great host, a mighty army. And you shall come up against My people Israel like a cloud to cover the land. In the latter days I will bring you against My land, that the nations may know, understand, and realize Me when My holiness shall be vindicated through you [vindicated and honored in your overwhelming destruction], O Gog, before their eyes. Thus says the Lord God: Are you he of whom I have spoken in olden times by My servants the prophets of Israel, who prophesied in those days for years that I would bring you [Gog] against them? But in that day when Gog shall come against the land of Israel, says the Lord God, my wrath shall come up into My nostrils. For in My jealousy and in the fire of My wrath have I said, Surely in that day there shall be a great shaking or cosmic catastrophe in the land of Israel, So that the fishes of the sea and the birds of the heavens, the beasts of the field and all creeping things that creep upon the earth, and all the men that are upon the face of the earth, shall tremble and shake at My presence; and the mountains shall be thrown down and the steep places shall fall and every wall [natural or artificial] shall fall to the ground. And I will call for a sword against [Gog] throughout all My mountains, says the Lord

God, every man's sword shall be against his brother [over the dividing of booty]. And with pestilence and with bloodshed will I enter into judgment with [Gog], and I will rain upon him and upon his hordes and upon the many peoples that are with him torrents of rain and great hailstones, fire and brimstone. Thus will I demonstrate My greatness and My holiness, and I will be recognized, understood, and known in the eyes of many nations; yes, they shall know that I am the Lord [the Sovereign Ruler, Who calls forth loyalty and obedient service]. (Ezek. 38:14–23)

Israel's secure and safe dwelling arouses Gog. Gog (remember, this is a person) leads a vast multitude in the latter days to attack Israel as the prophets foretold, but in that day, God gets angry and destroys Gog and all the people he is leading, some through natural causes and some through supernatural causes. Many nations will acknowledge God and give him glory and honor, thus vindicating him among the nations. Now let's turn our attention to the next chapter.

AND YOU, son of man, prophesy against Gog, thus says the Lord God: Behold, I am against you, O Gog, chief prince (ruler) of Rosh, of Meshech, and of Tubal. And I will turn you about and will lead you on and will cause you to come up from the uttermost parts of the north and will lead you against the mountains of Israel; and I will smite your bow from your left hand and will cause your arrows to fall out of your right hand. You shall fall [dead] upon the mountains of Israel, you and all your hosts and the peoples who are with you. I will give you to the ravenous birds of every sort and to the beasts of the field to be devoured. You shall fall in the open field, for I have spoken [it], says the Lord God. I will send fire on Magog and upon those who dwell securely in the coastlands, and they shall know, understand, and realize that I am the Lord [the Sovereign Ruler, who calls forth loyalty and obedient service]. And I will make My holy name known in the midst of My people Israel, and I will not let them profane My holy name anymore; and the nations shall know, understand, and realize that I am the Lord, the Holy One of Israel. Behold, it is coming, and it will be done, says the Lord God; that is the day of which I have spoken. (Ezek. 39:1–8)

Gog comes from the uttermost parts of the north, which most would say, if it were today, Russia. Birds of prey feast on Gog and his army, slain on the mountains of Israel. God will visit the far north and the coastlands with judgment, and people will recognize the sovereignty of God. Israel and all nations will revere the Lord. There is recognition that paraphrasing can seem redundant, but there are points being brought out that at the end will make better sense after the paraphrasing. God will accomplish this prophecy. God is not man that he should lie, which for many is part of the puzzle. Where can these events fit, especially as Israel has never had a time when the nations were not attacking it? Let us continue:

And [when you, Gog, are no longer] they who dwell in the cities of Israel shall go forth and shall set on fire and burn the battle gear, the shields and the bucklers, the bows and the arrows, the handspikes or riding whips and the spears; and they shall burn them as fuel for seven years, So that My people shall take no firewood out of the field or cut down any out of the forests, for they shall make their fires of the weapons. And they shall despoil those who despoiled them and plunder those who plundered them, says the Lord God. And in that day, I will give to Gog a place for burial there in Israel, the valley of those who pass through on the east side in front of the [Dead] Sea [the highway between Syria, Petra, and Egypt], and it will delay and stop those who pass through. And there shall they bury Gog and all his multitude, and they shall call it the Valley of Hamon-gog [multitude of Gog]. For seven months the house of Israel will be burying them, that they may cleanse the land. Yes, all the people of the land will bury them, and it shall bring them renown in the day that I shall be glorified, says the Lord God. And they shall set apart men to work continually who shall pass through the land, men commissioned to bury, with the help of those who are passing by, those bodies that lie unburied on the face of the ground, in order to cleanse the land. After the end of seven months, they shall make their search. And when these pass through the land and anyone sees a human bone, he shall set up a marker by it as a sign to the buriers, until they have buried it in the Valley of Hamon-gog or of Gog's multitude. And Hamonah [multitude] shall also be the name of the city [of the dead]. Thus shall they cleanse the land. (Ezek. 39: 9–16)

In this war, Israel burns the battle gear of its enemies for seven years. We are in a time when we have tanks, Humvees, jeeps, rocket launchers, etcetera. How does this fit? Not much of our modern warfare is flammable, yet there is no mention of this war having taken place back in the days when the battle gear was flammable. What are we supposed to do with that? God has a massive grave for Gog and his host. It will take Israel seven months to bury the host of Gog. To cleanse the land, they have people place markers where bone is. This process is to have the dead army properly buried and be able to cleanse the land. Let us continue:

And you, son of man, thus says the Lord God: Say to the birds of prey of every sort and to every beast of the field, Assemble yourselves and come, gather from every side to the sacrificial feast that I am preparing for you, even a great sacrificial feast on the mountains of Israel at which you may eat flesh and drink blood. You shall eat the flesh of the mighty and drink the blood of the princes of the earth, of rams, of lambs, of goats, and of bullocks, all of them fatlings of Bashan [east of the Jordan]. And you shall eat fat till you are filled and drink blood till you are drunk at the sacrificial feast which I am preparing for you. And you shall be filled at My table with horses and riders, with mighty men, and with soldiers of every kind, says the Lord God. And I will manifest My honor and glory among the nations, and all the nations shall see My judgment and justice [in the punishment] which I have executed and My hand which I have laid on them. So the house of Israel shall know, understand, and realize beyond all question that I am the Lord their God from that day forward. And the nations shall know, understand, and realize positively that the house of Israel went into captivity for their iniquity, because they trespassed against Me; and I hid My face from them. So I gave them into the hand of their enemies and they all fell [into captivity or were slain] by the power of the sword. According to their uncleanness and according to their transgressions I dealt with them and hid My face from them. Therefore, thus says the Lord God: Now will I reverse the captivity of Jacob and have mercy upon the whole house of Israel and will be jealous for My holy name. They shall forget their shame and self-reproach and all their treachery and unfaithfulness in which they have transgressed against Me, when they dwell securely in their land and there is none who makes them afraid. When I have brought them again from the peoples and gathered them out of their enemies' lands, and My justice and holiness are set apart and vindicated through them in the sight of many nations, Then shall they know, understand, and realize positively that I am the Lord their God, because I sent them into captivity and exile among the nations and then gathered them to their own land. I will leave none of them remaining among the nations any more [in the latter days]. Neither will I hide My face any more then from them, when I have poured out My Spirit upon the house of Israel, says the Lord God. (Ezek. 39:17–29)

As discussed in the previous chapter, God calls the birds of prey to feast on the host of Gog. God will win reverence and renown among the nations, and maybe even more so in Israel. The nations will know in that day that Israel went into captivity because of its transgressions. Israel will know positively that the Lord is their God on that day. On that day, the Lord pours out his Spirit upon Israel. Okay, so where in the world, with all these distinct elements, can this war take place?

Let us look at a unique book for a solution:

And when the thousand years are completed, Satan will be released from his place of confinement, and he will go forth to deceive and seduce and lead astray the nations which are in the four quarters of the earth—*Gog and Magog*—to muster them for war; their number is like the sand of the sea. And they swarmed up over the broad plain of the earth and encircled the fortress (camp) of God's people (the saints) and the beloved city; but fire descended from heaven and consumed them. Then the devil who had led them astray [deceiving and seducing them] was hurled into the fiery lake of burning brimstone, where the beast and false prophet were; and they will be tormented day and night forever and ever (through the ages of the ages). (Rev. 20:7–10) (emphasis mine)

In remembering that Gog is a person and not a nation, it is striking that Jesus mentions him here at the end of the millennial reign of Christ. After being bound for a thousand years, Satan is released by God from the bottomless pit, and he deceives the nations once more.

In thinking about Gog here at the end of the millennial reign of Christ, would it not be like Hitler in Germany during the height of his power in the 1940s? He is a person in a particular place and time in history, and so is Gog. Jesus, who is dictating this revelation, puts the person Gog here at the end of the millennial reign of Christ. In this context, it is much easier to imagine Israel being relaxed enough to not feel the need for defenses. God has put the New Jerusalem in place. We are reigning with God in this world as kings and priests. It is a time of peace and prosperity while Satan is bound in the bottomless pit for a thousand years.

There is actually very little known about this period people call the millennial reign of Christ. There are fragments. We know a few things: the lion will lie down with the lamb. Anyone born during this time who dies at a hundred will be the exception rather than the rule during this time, most people will live many hundreds of years. The people in the millennium now have the tree of life restored, and its leaves bring healing for the nations. We know a few more details, but we lack a clear picture of what this looks like.

God could take away our modern instruments of war and revert us back to the basics. In this way, Israel could use its battle gear for fire for seven years. The plain truth is we do not know; God knows. What we know is Jesus places this person Gog here at the end of the millennium.

Why is the Gog Magog war important to the understanding of end-time prophecy? Because most scholars and theologians are trying to factor in where this war takes place before Jesus's return. Allowing for the events that would have to occur naturally, such as Israel feeling secure enough to drop its defenses, adds a considerable amount of time before the war could even begin. If the understanding presented here is correct, we are not waiting for this war to happen before Jesus's return.

CHAPTER 22

The Seventy Weeks of Daniel

Here is a thought to consider regarding the Rapture and the Tribulation: Many theologians and Bible scholars who believe in the Church's rapture before the Tribulation say this because of the seventy weeks of Daniel. God has yet to complete his dealings with the nation of Israel. We will look briefly at the seventy weeks of Daniel just to have a background of understanding what they are talking about. The thought to consider is this: Are the dealings of God with his covenant people, the Church, and his covenant people the nation of Israel, including the last week, mutually exclusive? We'll only touch on this briefly, as it's a complicated subject with different opinions on Daniel's seventy weeks. The purpose here is to make some key points and not dwell on what is in dispute between various theories among theologians. We trust that those who need to study this further will do so.

Seventy weeks [of years, or 490 years] are decreed upon your people and upon your holy city [Jerusalem], to finish and put an end to transgression, to seal up and make full the measure of sin, to purge away and make expiation and reconciliation for sin, to bring in everlasting righteousness (permanent moral and spiritual rectitude in every area and relation) to seal up vision and prophecy and prophet, and to anoint a Holy of Holies. Know therefore and understand that from the going forth of the commandment to restore and to build Jerusalem until [the coming of] the Anointed One, a Prince, shall be seven weeks [of years] and sixty-two weeks [of years]; it shall be built again with [city] square and moat, but in troublous times. And after the sixty-two weeks [of years] shall the Anointed One be cut off or killed and shall have nothing [and no one] belonging to [and defending] Him. And the people of the [other] prince who will come will destroy the city and the sanctuary. Its end shall come with a flood; and even to the end there shall be war, and desolations are decreed. And he shall enter into a strong and firm covenant with the many for one week [seven years]. And in the midst of the week he shall cause the sacrifice and offering to cease [for the remaining three and one-half years]; and upon the wing or pinnacle of abominations [shall come] one who makes desolate, until the full determined end is poured out on the desolator. (Dan. 9:24–27)

In the simplest way possible, this is a very brief understanding, from one point of view of these verses. Counting from the decree to rebuild Jerusalem until the birth of Christ, we find seven plus sixty-two weeks—of years—which totals sixty-nine. While there's debate about which decree is the decree (since there were three), one decree marks the beginning of a 483-year period that ends with Christ's triumphant entry.

The equation of sixty-nine weeks of years—or 69 x 7 = 483 years—is the timeline between the decree and the death of the Messiah, or Jesus, as we looking back through history now know him. This is roughly accurate, depending upon which decree you believe is the correct one. The debate is long and complicated, as Israel in ancient times used a lunar year instead of the solar year that we now work with. Those interested can find more than enough information on this subject online.

There is a lot more to this, but it is unnecessary for our study. However, there are seventy weeks of years decreed upon God's covenant people, not sixty-nine. We have one more week of years left of this prophecy. Many theologians and Bible scholars agree that this is the last week referenced in verse 27: "He shall enter a covenant with many for one week (or seven years) and in the middle or approximately three and one-half years into the covenant he will cause the sacrifice and offering to cease." He will commit the abomination of desolation that we have already discussed. When we look at the book of Revelation, we will see this seven-year period again, as well as the three and one-half years. So there is a separation of time between the 483 years and the seven years that God had decreed upon his covenant people for 490 years total in his dealings with them.

This shows that there are scriptural examples of God splitting a prophecy with a gap of many years in between. Therefore, a prophecy can have parts that occur at one time and find fulfillment in completely different periods, like Jesus coming as a Savior in one time and a conquering King in another. This is one of the scriptural principles that pre-Tribulation believers base their beliefs on. It has definite scriptural support. However, that may be true concerning the rapture coming in two distinct phases or it may not. The fact that God did so here and in other places does not guarantee that he is going to continue this pattern about the Rapture and his Second Coming. There are still seven years that have yet to be fulfilled in this prophecy in Daniel. This period, which many theologians agree upon, comprises the seven years of the Great Tribulation in which the Antichrist is reigning.

The Thinker

This is going to require some careful thought.

CHAPTER 23

The Book of Revelation, Chapters 1-2

A look at the end of the age would not be complete without the book of Revelation. We will not be getting deep into the symbolism that is prevalent throughout the book, as previously stated. It is more about what is being symbolized and the result of what the symbol accomplishes than in trying to identify beforehand exactly what the symbol is. Keep in mind that the book is a revelation and not a book of mysteries. God is revealing to his people what will happen at the end of human history, according to this paradigm. God is looking to reveal, not confuse. And that is why it's okay not to get hung up on all the symbolism but to look at what the symbol does and what its nature is. This is one reason we looked at the people that understood prophecy the first time around. It was not the religious leaders, the scholars, and the prominent people in positions of power who understood that prophecy was being fulfilled right in front of them. It was the common women and men who understood, not the elite. This is the heart of God:

At that time Jesus began to say, I thank You, Father, Lord of heaven and earth [and I acknowledge openly and joyfully to Your honor], that You have hidden these things from the wise and clever and learned, and revealed them to babies [to the childish, untaught, and unskilled]. Yes, Father, [I praise You that] such was Your gracious will and good pleasure. (Matt. 11:25–26)

Because of that, it's okay if we read the book of Revelation like the average Joe and Jolene on the street, because who is Jesus's target audience? If we look at his First Coming, it was to the average Joe and Jolene on the street, not the religious leaders, scholars, and experts of the law. Jesus revealed himself to those who the elite thought was beneath them.

Other individuals gifted in this area can also provide further explanations about the symbolism. God alone knows what the true symbols are in each case, and we get too bogged down trying to figure out beforehand what the identity of each symbol is. For example, many people—even those who have not read the Bible—have heard of the mark of the beast and the number 666. Does it really make any difference to know his name beforehand? Is it not enough to know that he will stand in the temple and proclaim himself to be God? That he will make war with the saints and will prevail? A miracle heals the Antichrist's deadly wound. We have never had in one person all these unique events occur. I am not saying that we should not speculate; God calls us specifically to use wisdom to know his identity.

Here is [room for] discernment [a call for the wisdom of interpretation]. Let anyone who has intelligence (penetration and insight enough) calculate the number of the beast, for it is a human number [the number of a certain man]; his number is 666. (Rev. 13:18)

However, knowing his name beforehand is not as important as not taking his mark or following him. Wouldn't it be helpful to know his name in advance to not take his mark? Sure, that would be helpful, but according to Scripture, there will be a one-world government, one-world religion, and one-world currency, which has not happened yet. When these things come to pass, as they must (because God cannot lie), it will quickly become apparent when someone states that you must receive his mark, or you cannot buy or sell.

Now let us begin the revelation of Jesus Christ as given to his bond servant, John the apostle. There is a lot to this book, and we will cover it in its entirety. However, let me state unequivocally that I am no expert in symbolism and imagery. Where the Word of God interprets the symbols, we are obviously safe, and it shows us a pattern. This pattern is consistent with the symbolism prevalent in the Gospels, where Jesus speaks to the crowds in parables, and his interpretation of those symbols while talking privately to his disciples. We also find this pattern in the images given to Daniel, which we have interpreted. I unequivocally state that I do not understand this book fully. However, full understanding is not actually necessary to obey the truths found within. Cross-referencing this book of Revelation with many previously introduced verses reveals a picture of this period. The Bible spends an awful lot of time speaking about the end of the age, so it is of great importance. Repeatedly, the theme that runs through this narrative, both here in the book of Revelation and in the aforementioned Scriptures, is preparedness. When the Holy Spirit states the same thing repeatedly, it is to our advantage to hear him.

The approach to interpretation differs from most. I see the book of Revelation as both sequential and nonsequential. It starts out sequential with one event following another event in chronological order, but at some point, in the narrative, it becomes apparent that you are coming in and out of different time frames that are not in chronological order.

The easiest way to spot this is the phrase "the kingdoms of this world have become the kingdom of our God and of his Christ." Starting in Revelation 11:16, that is the climax, the conclusion. Revelation 12 summarizes God's people and their history from Genesis to Revelation. Chapter 13 then depicts the beast, its deadly wound healed, and the beast's war against the saints, thus returning the narrative to the Tribulation period. It is obvious at this point that we have gone back in time.

On a side note, it is also interesting to observe that the book of Daniel is out of chronological order. I read this in one of the many books I have read on this subject. I cannot remember which one, or I would give the author credit for it, but I do not appear to have it now. Chapter 1 in Daniel starts out with King Jehoiakim of Judah, and then Nebuchadnezzar comes and captures Jerusalem. The second chapter starts with the second year of the reign of Nebuchadnezzar—so far, so good. Chapters 3 and 4 are also dealing with Nebuchadnezzar. Chapter 5, however, deals with the last year of Belshazzar and the reign of King Darius the Mede. Then chapter 6 is another chapter involving Darius, but in chapter 7, we go back to the first year of the reign of Belshazzar. Chapter 8 is the third year of Belshazzar, and chapter 9 flips back to the first year of King Darius. Chapter 10 starts in the third year of King Cyrus, and chapter 11 takes us back to the first year of king Darius. I'm simply noting that the text sometimes deviates from a chronological order for a reason. But we won't explore that here.

Chronologically speaking, the chapters should follow in succession: Nebuchadnezzar, followed by Belshazzar—although there is much debate about him being a ruler of Babylon as stated in the book of Daniel. However, some Bible scholars believe that the king of Babylon made Belshazzar co-regent, which would explain why Belshazzar offered Daniel to be the third ruler in Babylon instead of the second, because Belshazzar was only in the second position himself. Next in the line of succession should be Cyrus, followed by Darius. When you look at who is ruling at the beginning of each chapter, it becomes apparent that the chapters are not in chronological order.

There are many who say that John put the book of Revelation in code so that the ruling powers of his day would not know that God was prophesying against them. While this is plausible, the probability is low. It does not say anywhere that he had the liberty to reinterpret what he saw in code, so this is a theory. It seems much more likely that, as a scribe, he wrote exactly what he saw, and that would make Jesus the selector of the symbols and visions that John recorded.

Now let's begin our look into the book of the Revelation.

[THIS IS] the revelation of Jesus Christ [His unveiling of the divine mysteries]. God gave it to Him *to disclose and make known to His bond servants certain things which must shortly and speedily come to pass in their entirety.* And He sent and communicated it *through* His angel (messenger) *to* His bond servant John. (Rev. 1:1) (emphasis mine)

Notice—and some of this is going to seem painfully obvious—that the revelation is from Jesus and not John. Some call this the revelation of John, but verse one reveals it is Jesus's revelation and God gave it to him. This is important as the inspiration for the book came from "the word made flesh" (John 1:14) or Jesus, not from any man, no matter how Spirit-led he was. It also is important to note the purpose of the revelation is to show his bond servants what must come to pass. God wrote the book of Revelation for his bond servants, even more so than for the Church or Israel. This revelation appears to be focused for this last generation of bond servants who are alive at the time of the Great Tribulation and the reign of the Antichrist. Let us recognize bond servants are a subset of the Church and messianic Jews—specifically, the bond servants in the Church.

The Bondservant

I would like to give a word on bond servants, as there will doubtless be some who are unfamiliar with this term. A bond servant was someone who started out as a slave, and in Jewish custom, when the slave had served for a certain number of years, they were to be set free. However, if that freed servant declared, "I do not wish to leave your service," they remained a bond servant. Basically, they loved their master and did not want to be parted from their master. Instead of compulsion, it was love that was the driving force in their life. The authorities took this servant and pierced their ear, signifying lifelong devotion to their master—a servant bound by love (Exod. 21:1–6).

Now let's look into the future, shall we?

Who has testified to and vouched for all that he saw [in his visions], the word of God and the testimony of Jesus Christ. (Rev. 1:2)

John the apostle bears witness that this is the truth of all the things that he saw.

Blessed (happy, to be envied) is the man who reads aloud [in the assemblies] the word of this prophecy; and blessed (happy, to be envied) are those who hear [it read] and who keep themselves true to the things which are written in it [heeding them and laying them to heart], for the time [for them to be fulfilled] is near. (Rev. 1:3)

There is a special blessing given to all those who read and even those who just hear, but the blessing does not stop there. It is not enough just to read and hear; obedience is required to get the blessing that God promises. About two thousand years ago, someone wrote this book, and some people will undoubtedly find it strange that God says, "The time is near."

> Nevertheless, do not let this one fact escape you, beloved, that with the Lord one day is as a thousand years and a thousand years as one day. (2 Pet. 3:8)

So from Jesus's perspective, it has only been a weekend since he returned to his Father. Now let's continue our look at Revelation.

> John to the seven assemblies (churches) that are in Asia: May grace (God's unmerited favor) be granted to you and spiritual peace (the peace of Christ's kingdom) from Him Who is and Who was and Who is to come, and from the seven Spirits [the sevenfold Holy Spirit] before His throne. (Rev. 1:4)

John penned the visions that he saw to seven churches in Asia as his intended audience. He probably didn't realize that his writing would become part of the Bible's canon, accessible to Christians throughout history.

Why God chose these specific seven churches is quite interesting. Some suggest that there are semblances of each individual church throughout the entire Church age. Basically, if you are in a church, your church would fit roughly into one of these seven types of churches. We will get more specific about what that means, as Jesus does something of a character study on each of them shortly. There are also dispensationalists' doctrines, which are that God administers different methods of revealing his grace and will during different periods in humankind's history. They relate that theory to these seven churches as different periods of church ages and that each church represents a different Church age. We need to briefly visit this theory, which is quite popular these days, as it affects a lot concerning a person's view of end-time events. The theory is called dispensational theology.

Systemized dispensational theology is associated with John Nelson Darby. He came to believe in a future dispensation for national Israel that would hold earthly blessings that differed from the church's spiritual blessings. The basic understanding of dispensationalist theology is that God required a certain test of obedience from humankind during different seasons or dispensations of time, according to the revelation of God, and these were:

1. From the time of creation to the fall of humankind was an age of innocence.
2. From the fall of humankind to the flood was an age of conscience.
3. From the flood to Abraham was an age of human government.
4. From Abraham to Moses was an age of promise.
5. From Moses to Christ was an age of law.
6. From Christ to the millennial kingdom is an age of the Church.
7. Finally, the millennial kingdom is an age of the kingdom.

During all these ages, what God requires of humankind is a little different. It is a unique dispensation in God's dealing with humankind. John Nelson Darby came to believe in a clear distinction between God's dealings with the Church and the nation of Israel, especially regarding prophetic Scriptures made to national Israel. This was a part of the process that prompted him to believe in the any-moment rapture of the Church at the beginning of Daniel's seventieth week. Then Israel would once again be front and center. At the end of the seventieth week,

God would set up his millennial kingdom and fulfill his unconditional promises to national Israel. He believed that in each dispensation, God had a requirement placed upon humankind in response to his revelation in that dispensation and in each dispensation, humankind failed.

Dispensationalism is belief in a literal fulfillment of all Old Testament prophecies about national Israel. This signifies a separation between the Church and Israel; God will deal with each consecutively. It means that the seventy weeks in Daniel, or 490 years, apply solely and exclusively to the nation of Israel and have no bearing on the Church. The nonexistence of the Church during the prophecy's first 483 years prevented its inclusion. However, as Israel was his covenant people, then, so we are now his covenant people. Let's see if this part of the covenant includes the Church, since we apply everything else belonging to God's covenant people to ourselves. According to this theory, the Rapture will occur in two phases at the beginning of the seventieth week of Daniel. The second phase will occur at the Second Coming of Christ at the end of the Great Tribulation. According to this interpretation of Scripture and the application of dispensational theology, the Church will not be here during the Great Tribulation. Because God has finished, the dispensation of the Church age and is now going to resume his interaction with the nation of Israel.

I had been an adherent of dispensationalism for many years, and regarding its basic tenets, I still am. I agree that the history of humankind has different dispensations and God's requirements of humankind differ in the revelation God gives to that age. However, regarding the separation of the Church and Israel, while it is a plausible theory, it is just a theory. It is easy enough with hindsight to look back and say this was one dispensation, and the way God interacted with humankind differed from this other dispensation. What dispensational theology does in this instance is to project two different dispensations that have not occurred yet. While they may be right, they may also be wrong. It is a lot more complicated to predict into the future what types of dispensations God is going to enact. There have been those that suggest that the seven churches of Asia are a distinct Church age within the entire history of the Church. As we have looked at the seven dispensations espoused by Darby, these would be similar. The Church of Ephesus would symbolize the time of the apostles as one distinct dispensation. The Laodicean Church would be the last Church age, etcetera. There may be some truth in that, but after that, dispensationalists take the Church out of the book of Revelation. They theorize that, since there is no mention of the Church from Revelation 3:22 until Revelation 19:7–9, this is the end of the Church dispensation. Everything then between Revelation 3 and Revelation 19:7–9 is the beginning of the new—new because it picks up from the unfinished seventieth week of Daniel—Jewish dispensation. This theory makes most of Revelation irrelevant to the Church; we are not present during the events described. The book's intended audience was the Church, not Israel. Is this theory possible? Of course, it's possible, but possibility does not equate to probability. That Jesus gave this revelation to the Church suggests that he intended it for us. He will be faithful to his promises to Israel, and exactly how that is going to pan out only he knows. But God never said that he would treat Israel and the Church entirely differently; theologians and scholars did. Time will tell.

Now let us return to the book of Revelation.

And from Jesus Christ the faithful and trustworthy Witness, the Firstborn of the dead [first to be brought back to life] and the Prince (Ruler) of the kings of the earth. To Him Who ever loves us and has once [for all] loosed and freed us from our sins by His own blood. (Rev. 1:5)

John goes back to his original point that this letter, although penned by his hand, has its inspiration and substance in Jesus himself. John is a scribe in simply reporting what he is being told or taking dictation. Notice the attributes ascribed to Jesus: a faithful witness, the firstborn among the dead, and the Prince of the kings of the earth. We think that we have control; but he who laughs last laughs best. The rulers of the world think they are in control and momentarily they are, but throughout eternity, Jesus is the prince and ultimate sovereign of all.

And formed us into a kingdom (a royal race), priests to His God and Father—to Him be the glory and the power and the majesty and the dominion throughout the ages and forever and ever. Amen (so be it). (Rev. 1:6)

God is building his kingdom, and it is not a place but a people. He has redeemed all those who comprise his kingdom from the beginning of time until his return.

Jesus Coming in the Clouds with his Angels

Behold, He is coming with the clouds, and every eye will see Him, even those who pierced Him; and all the tribes of the earth shall gaze upon Him and beat their breasts and mourn and lament over Him. Even so [must it be]. Amen (so be it). (Rev. 1:7)

Once again, he is coming in the clouds. We repeatedly emphasize this truth to prevent false prophets and Antichrists claiming to be him from misleading us. When he returns, he has specifically told us in what manner his return will be. The return of Jesus will dismay the Jewish nation, who, with a few exceptions, rejected him.

I am the Alpha and the Omega, the Beginning and the End, says the Lord God, He Who is and Who was and Who is to come, the Almighty (the Ruler of all). I, John, your brother and companion (sharer and participator) with you in the tribulation and kingdom and patient endurance [which are] in Jesus Christ, was on the isle called Patmos, [banished] on account of [my witnessing to] the Word of God and the testimony (the proof, the evidence) for Jesus Christ. (Rev. 1:8–9)

John declares his affiliation; he is one of us. Jesus tells us, "In this life we will have tribulation but be encouraged. I have overcome the world!" (John 16:33, author's paraphrase) As part of his kingdom, one attribute that is so necessary is patient endurance. Nobody enjoys tribulation and trouble, requiring patient endurance, but it is one of our Lord's chief attributes, and the Bible says we are to be like him.

I was in the Spirit [rapt in His power] on the Lord's Day, and I heard behind me a great voice like the calling of a war trumpet. (Rev. 1:10)

Many have stated that John was in the Spirit on the Lord's Day, by which they mean Sunday. Given the context, it's very possible that God transported John to the future "day of the lord," frequently mentioned in the Old Testament and in this book. Not bodily, mind you, but in the Spirit, and shown what the "day of the Lord" was going to look like when the proper season came. You could get the picture here of someone playing reveille with a bugle or, in this case, a trumpet call to war.

> Saying, I am the Alpha and the Omega, the First and the Last. Write promptly what you see (your vision) in a book and send it to the seven churches which are in Asia—to Ephesus and to Smyrna and to Pergamum and to Thyatira and to Sardis and to Philadelphia and to Laodicea. (Rev. 1:11)

Again, John is not the one directing who this book is being written for or being sent to. He is a bond servant of the Most High God. Now we see the names of the seven churches, and just a little later, God is going to give a character assessment of each of these churches. When he does so, it will become clearer why people of many generations have stated that each of these churches captures a picture of a particular Church, which we as churches and individuals fall into one of these seven categories.

Jesus Walking Among the Seven Candlesticks

Then I turned to see [whose was] the voice that was speaking to me, and on turning I saw seven golden lampstands, and in the midst of the lampstands [One] like a Son of Man, clothed with a robe which reached to His feet and with a girdle of gold about His breast. (Rev. 1:12–13)

Gold often denotes royalty, and later in this book, he is called the King of kings and the Lord of lords. I have already confessed that I am not one whom God has gifted with great insight into symbolism and imagery. Where nothing comes to mind, I will not attempt to make something up just to have something to say. However, there are some things that come to mind, and I will share what I see and ask forgiveness and tolerance for those with greater insight. Why am I doing this type of book if symbolism and imagery are not part of my gifting? Because what I believe my gifts are in this area are sequences and patterns. A look at the end of the age would not be nearly as complete without utilizing the truths, sequences, and patterns found here, along with those found in the Gospels and major and minor prophets. I see dovetails where one Scripture ties in with another, much like a carpenter or furniture maker fashions so that unique pieces of wood dovetail together to make an exquisite piece of furniture or project.

> His head and His hair were white like white wool, [as white] as snow, and His eyes [flashed] like a flame of fire. (Rev. 1:14)

This image is reminiscent of wisdom in the white hair and the fire as passion in his eyes.

> His feet glowed like burnished (bright) bronze as it is refined in a furnace, and His voice was like the sound of many waters. In His right hand He held seven stars, and from His mouth there came forth a sharp two-edged sword, and His face was like the sun shining in full power at midday. (Rev. 1:15–16)

Jesus himself reveals the interpretation of these images.

When I saw Him, I fell at His feet as if dead. But He laid His right hand on me and said, do not be afraid! I am the First and the Last, And the Ever-living One [I am living in the eternity of the eternities]. I died, but see, I am alive forevermore; and I possess the keys of death and Hades (the realm of the dead). (Rev. 1:17–18)

There is a Scripture that talks about when he "triumphed over the forces of darkness that he led captivity captive and gave gifts to men." (Eph. 4:8, author's paraphrase) This is a picture of him: descending into hell, confronting the devil, taking back from him the keys of death and Hades, and saying something like, "Thank you very much. I'll take those!" Although the picture is not explicit, I'm kind of reading between the lines.

Write therefore the things you see, what they are [and signify] and what is to take place hereafter. (Rev. 1:19)

Many see this as an outline of the entire book of Revelation, write about the things that were, are, and shall be. This is easier to see in the King James Version:

Write the things which thou hast seen, and the things which are, and the things which shall be hereafter. (Rev. 1:19 KJV)

They would say that everything John wrote before would be the things that were. What John is going to write about the seven churches would be the things that are. Everything from chapter 4 to the end would be the things that will be (past, present, and future). For this study, that works well (with some exceptions, and we will get into those as we explore further).

"Record your observations of the future, for I will reveal my plans to my servants so they can prepare" would be an over-arching theme for the book of Revelation even within the aforementioned paradigm. As within that paradigm, past and present only account for the first three chapters of the book and the remaining chapters are for the future. Whoever these bond servants are, this book is for them, so that makes them especially important. I believe God has had bond servants in every generation. As we look through the Scriptures at every age, God has had bond servants. In the Old Testament, we have had Abraham, Isaac, Jacob, Sarah, Daniel, Job, Ruth, and many others as bond servants for their generation. In the New Testament, we have had Jesus, Peter, Paul, Mary, James, John, and Priscilla, with many others as bond servants for their generation. During our generation, can anyone believe that Mother Teresa, Billy Graham, Bill Bright, Sylvia Evans, Henry and Richard Blackaby, Tamara Lowe, Ruth Veach, David Wilkerson, George Veach, and many more were not bond servants? Some of these names you will recognize, and others you will not, but all bear the mark of surrender. We make it more mystical than it is. These men and women completely dedicate themselves to the Lord without reservation; they are love slaves.

> As to the hidden meaning (the mystery) of the seven stars which you saw on My right hand and the seven lampstands of gold: the seven stars are the seven angels (messengers) of the seven assemblies (churches) and the seven lampstands are the seven churches. (Rev. 1:20)

Now we are sure that there were more than just these seven churches around at the time of John. History suggests that he was the last apostle to die. It is likely that these seven churches symbolized all the churches around and in no way suggest that Jesus didn't walk among the rest of the churches. These seven represented all the churches of that time and, as mentioned earlier, probably all the churches throughout all the ages. Right here, Jesus gives us great insight into symbols and symbolism. We see that Jesus interprets the seven lampstands of gold as the seven churches in Asia. Let's see how that dovetails with a Scripture in Matthew.

> You are the light of the world. A city set on a hill cannot be hidden. Nor do men light a lamp and put it under a peck measure, but on a lampstand, and it gives light to all in the house. Let your light so shine before men that they may see your moral excellence and your praiseworthy, noble, and good deeds and recognize and honor and praise and glorify your Father Who is in heaven. (Matt. 5:14–16)

We, as the body of believers, are the Church of God. God calls us light in this dark world. A candlestick symbolizes the Church's light-giving nature. Giving this interpretation by Jesus himself, you see, he uses symbols to capture the essence or nature of the thing being symbolized. In the Gospels, he uses symbols a lot. In his parables, as you study the symbols that he chooses, you notice the symbols capture the nature or essence of what he is talking about. However, it is not all that straightforward and easy to interpret in every case. There is a symbol of "many waters being races, multitudes, nations, and languages" in Revelation 17:15. Honestly, if Jesus had not given the interpretation, how many of us would have figured that one out? Therefore, we need to be much more concerned with what the nature of the thing being symbolized is rather than a dogmatic declaration that this particular object is being symbolized.

Different theologians have different interpretations of what each symbol represents and confuse the sincere person trying to make sense of it all. If the experts cannot agree, how are we to know what the truth is? These events must come to pass, as God has said they will. We do not need to know exactly what each symbol represents to be prepared for what lies ahead in these last days. There is more than enough basic truth to equip us for what lies ahead without getting bogged down with agreeing on what each symbol represents. Let us follow the flow of the Word and not get hung up in trying to figure out every definitive thing. It will happen as God has stated, and he alone knows the beginning from the end and all the elements in between.

> TO THE angel (messenger) of the assembly (church) in Ephesus write: These are the words of Him Who holds the seven stars [which are the messengers of the seven churches] in His right hand, Who goes about among the seven golden lampstands [which are the seven churches]: I know your industry and activities, laborious toil and trouble, and your patient endurance, and how you cannot tolerate wicked [men] and have tested and critically appraised those who call [themselves] apostles (special messengers of Christ) and yet are not, and have found them to be impostors and liars. (Rev. 2:1–2)

The people of this church are industrious, endure patiently, and test those who try to lead in the church to make sure of their sincerity and Christlikeness.

> I know you are enduring patiently and are bearing up for My name's sake, and you have not fainted or become exhausted or grown weary. (Rev. 2:3)

He again praises this church for their patient endurance. When he says something twice about something that is positive, that is something we should emulate.

> But I have this [one charge to make] against you: that you have left (abandoned) the love that you had at first [you have deserted Me, your first love]. (Rev. 2:4)

This church is doing well. God loves most of what they are doing; however, this one thing he has against them is critical. God's word says that what is essential is "faith, hope, and love, and the greatest of these is love." (1 Cor. 13:13, author's paraphrase) In another place, he states to "love the Lord God with all your heart, mind, soul, and strength is the greatest commandment and the second greatest is like the first: to love your neighbor as you love yourself." (Matt. 22:37–40, author's paraphrase) We can do a lot of great things, but if love does not motivate them, we are missing the point, and God finds this grievous.

> Remember then from what heights you have fallen. Repent (change the inner man to meet God's will) and do the works you did previously [when first you knew the Lord], or else I will visit you and remove your lampstand from its place, unless you change your mind and repent. (Rev. 2:5)

This seems rather severe; after all, they had an awful lot of good things going on in their church. It gives us quite a sense of how high on God's priority list love really is.

> Yet you have this [in your favor and to your credit]: you hate the works of the Nicolaitans [what they are doing as corrupters of the people], which I Myself also detest. (Rev. 2:6)

Here, God gives another affirmation to this church of something that he finds commendable. They share his hate of the practices of the Nicolaitans. The Nicolaitans, according to most of the information that is out there, practiced the doctrine of "fleshly indulgences" because faith alone saves us and not "works." This reasoning argues that salvation removes the consequences of sexual immorality and other sins because Jesus paid the penalty for sin. Though it's true that we are free and forgiven, God doesn't allow us to act however we want. Jesus stated, "if you love me keep my commandments." (John 15:14, author's paraphrase) The exhortation in Romans asks: What shall we say, considering all these wondrous things God has done for us?

> WHAT SHALL we say [to all this]? Are we to remain in sin in order that God's grace (favor and mercy) may multiply and overflow? Certainly not! How can we who died to sin live in it any longer? (Rom. 6:1–2)

According to Eerdmans Dictionary of the Bible, the word "Nicolaitan" means, in Greek, "to conquer or have victory over the people."[10] Some scholars suggest that the Nicolaitans and the followers of Balaam were the same, a theory based on the similar etymology "to conquer the people" ascribed to both names.

In the Old Testament, a king wanted a prophet to curse the people of Israel and called on Balaam to do this. The prophet ended up blessing the people of God, despite the king's desire. However, the king had promised the prophet money and honor for cursing Israel. Only God would not allow the man to do that but commanded a blessing instead. (Num. 22–24:25) Greed motivated the prophet, as Numbers 31:16 states that Balaam's advice seduced and overcame God's people. Balaam got his gold by going against the wishes of God. Balaam taught the king of

Moab how to be victorious over the people of God. He did this through sexual seduction, which led to worshipping other gods. Balaam achieved victory over the people of God through subtlety and deception. We might want to keep this in mind, as later there are symbols in Revelation of someone coming to conquer the people. And the Antichrist conquers not through strength of arms but subtlety and deception.

> He who is able to hear, let him listen to and give heed to what the Spirit says to the assemblies (churches). To him who overcomes (is victorious), I will grant to eat [of the fruit] of the tree of life, which is in the paradise of God. (Rev. 2:7)

He who has ears to hear—this example praises several things. This church deserves commendation for its industriousness, patient endurance, its testing of those falsely claiming apostleship, its steadfastness under pressure, and its hatred of God's enemies—the false Nicolaitan doctrine. What God does not like about this church is that they have left their first love: him. He treats this as a very critical element in their walk before him. It would be to our advantage to take this as seriously as God does.

As we look at each church, we will see what God likes about them and what he does not. Many times, God tries to give the church a praise sandwich. By that I mean he will say something positive about them and then something he sees as a deficiency and finally more about what he likes about them. There is probably more, but at the very least, what the Spirit of God is saying to each church is, "This is what I like, and this is what I dislike." However, some churches do not give the Lord enough to work with, so he cannot offer them a praise sandwich. In our individual lives and our various churches, we should take notice and do our best to emulate what God likes and run from what he does not—very simple indeed, but sometimes the truth is not all that deep, and we make it more complicated than it is.

> And to the angel (messenger) of the assembly (church) in Smyrna write: These are the words of the First and the Last, Who died and came to life again: I know your affliction and distress and pressing trouble and your poverty—but you are rich! and how you are abused and reviled and slandered by those who say they are Jews and are not, but are a synagogue of Satan. (Rev. 2:8–9)

God calls this church rich! They have a lot of pressure on them but remain steadfast to the Lord. The world would call this church poor, and God calls them rich. We judge by the outside, and God looks on the inside. Our way of looking and evaluating something is often diametrically opposed to the way God sees them.

> Fear nothing that you are about to suffer. [Dismiss your dread and your fears!] Behold, the devil is indeed about to throw some of you into prison, that you may be tested and proved and critically appraised, and for ten days you will have affliction. Be loyally faithful unto death [even if you must die for it], and I will give you the crown of life. (Rev. 2:10)

God says of this rich church, "You are going to suffer but remain steadfast." If we go through hard times, it does not mean that God does not love us. We often discover our true character and loyalties during these pressures. Notice that God says Satan is going to put some of them in prison; it is not God who beats up his kids but our enemy. Why does God allow the enemy the ability to put pressure into our lives? Here is one answer given by Jesus himself in one of his many conversations with Peter.

Jesus and Peter are having a discussion, and Jesus informs Peter, "Satan has asked permission to test you. I am going to allow this. I have prayed for you that your faith will not fail. This will be painful, but after your restoration, strengthen your brothers." (Luke 22:31-34) (authors paraphrase) This experience taught him humility. Peter's experience enhanced his empathy, making him far better able to restore others who had fallen. It was in this discussion that Jesus told Peter that he was going to deny him three times. Peter declared, "I am ready to die for you," but as we know, he ended up doing just that and denied the Lord. (Luke 22:31–34)

Pressure reveals character, and we grow from these lessons. It is not God who is evil and looks to harm us, but allows various pressures to try our faith, including Satan. In 1 Peter 1:7, it states that "our troubles have come in order to show that our faith is real and the trying of our faith is much more precious than fine gold." (author's paraphrase) Romans 8:18 states that "our present circumstances, whether good or evil, do not even compare to the glory that awaits us." (author's paraphrase) In 1 Corinthians 2:9, it states that our "eye has not seen, and our ear has not heard, and it has not even been imagined the things that God has prepared for those who love him." (author's paraphrase)

What we go through here cannot compare to what awaits us on the God side of the equation. First, we cannot compare the time. Our brief life compared to eternity is like taking a drop of water and throwing it into the ocean, and even that does not do it justice. We love this world and cling to it so ferociously. We cannot imagine much better, if everything was in perfect condition. However, what awaits us in eternity is like a baby in the womb. The baby, we can imagine, is quite content inside the womb; it is warm, comfortable, fed, and at peace. Imagine trying to relay to the child inside the womb the wonders that await the child once outside the womb. The child has nothing to compare their reality to the wonders outside. How can the child imagine a waterfall, the top of Mount Everest, and the wonders of a rainbow? Like the child inside the womb, we cannot imagine what awaits us on the other side of the God equation. We need not hold on so tightly. What we are leaving does not compare to what awaits us.

This life is just the beginning; eternity stretches before us. What we do here and now has a ripple effect across all eternity. We will not always understand why God allows certain events into our lives, but we can learn to trust that he has always our best interests at heart. More important than the here and now is what we are giving him to work with for all of eternity.

The following is a story to illustrate this principle:

There was a man who was exceedingly rich, and he died in a head-on car crash with a poor man who also died that day. Both were believers in the Lord. They both appeared before Jesus, and he said, "Come, I have prepared a place for you." They went with him, and Jesus brought the poor man to a mansion whose grandeur was unlike anything seen on earth. Jesus told the poor man, "Behold, your new home." The poor man delightedly and promptly went into his new home. The rich man and Jesus went past these magnificent mansions, and the rich man's heart fell, as he supposed that he also would have gotten one of the magnificent mansions. As they went on, they came to mansions that were like those found on earth. He said to himself, "Surely one of these is mine." But they continued walking, passing sections of magnificent homes, regular houses, and beaten-down shacks. Finally, they came to a hole in the ground where a foundation had been dug. Jesus turned to the rich man and said, "Behold, your new home!" The man looked at Jesus and said, "There must be some kind of mistake. This is nothing but a hole in the ground." And Jesus said, "I am sorry, my friend, but that is all the material you gave us to work with." While the story is fictional and no one is getting a hole in the ground, it illustrates a biblical truth: what we choose to do here has a direct impact on what awaits us in eternity.

> For no other foundation can anyone lay than that which is [already] laid, which is Jesus Christ (the Messiah, the Anointed One). But if anyone builds upon the Foundation, whether it be with gold, silver, precious stones, wood, hay, straw, The work of each [one] will become [plainly, openly] known (shown for what it is); for the day [of Christ] will disclose and declare it, because it will be revealed with fire, and the fire will test and critically appraise the character and worth of the work each person has done. If the work which any person has built on this Foundation [any product of his efforts whatever] survives [this test], he will get his reward. But if any person's work is burned up [under the test], he will suffer the loss [of it all, losing his reward], though he himself will be saved, but only as [one who has passed] through fire. (1 Cor. 3:11–15)

> He who is able to hear, let him listen to and heed what the Spirit says to the assemblies (churches). He who overcomes (is victorious) shall in no way be injured by the second death. (Rev. 2:11)

Let us hear what the Spirit is saying. In these messages to the churches, God's spirit tells us to listen closely, and then he follows with a reward for listening: "To him, who overcomes will I give!" In every scenario, it's a little different, but they are all wonderful. Here is a truth about overcoming: You need obstacles to be an overcomer. In almost all the churches, there is a deficiency that the spirit points out. We need to look in our own lives and ask God if any of those deficiencies are in our lives and ask for his help to overcome these obstacles.

> Then to the angel (messenger) of the assembly (church) in Pergamum write: These are the words of Him Who has and wields the sharp two-edged sword. (Rev. 2:12)

This image appears to point us to Jesus as the Word of God.

> For the Word that God speaks is alive and full of power [making it active, operative, energizing, and effective]; it is sharper than any two-edged sword, penetrating to the dividing line of the breath of life (soul) and [the immortal] spirit, and of joints and marrow [of the deepest parts of our nature], exposing and sifting and analyzing and judging the very thoughts and purposes of the heart. (Heb. 4:12)

> I know where you live—a place where Satan sits enthroned. [Yet] you are clinging to and holding fast My name, and you did not deny My faith, even in the days of Antipas, my witness, my faithful one, who was killed (martyred) in your midst—where Satan dwells. (Rev. 2:13)

This church is situated right where Satan lives, so the opposition must be fierce, yet they are clinging to and holding on to their Savior.

Nevertheless, I have a few things against you: you have some people there who are clinging to the teaching of Balaam, who taught Balak to set a trap and a stumbling block before the sons of Israel, [to entice them] to eat food that had been sacrificed to idols and to practice lewdness [giving themselves up to sexual vice]. You also have some who in a similar way are clinging to the teaching of the Nicolaitans [those corrupters of the people] which thing I hate. (Rev. 2:14–15)

Remember the previous passage where the Spirit of God talked about the Nicolaitans? Here we see them tied together and the teachings of both are similar.

Repent [then]! Or else I will come to you quickly and fight against them with the sword of My mouth. (Rev. 2:16)

Notice that the Spirit of God distinguishes between those who are clinging to him, even though they live in the seat of Satan, and those who are holding on to a false teaching or doctrine. He will fight against those who hold on to a false teaching and not those who are doing their best to just hold on to him.

He who is able to hear, let him listen to and heed what the Spirit says to the assemblies (churches). To him who overcomes (conquers), I will give to eat of the manna that is hidden, and I will give him a white stone with a new name engraved on the stone, which no one knows or understands except he who receives it. (Rev. 2:17)

The manna was a supernatural manifestation of God for the Jews when they were in the wilderness, escaping from Egypt and before entering the Promised Land. (Exodus 16) It was bread from heaven, and Jesus referred to himself as "the Bread of Life." (John 6:35) We may not know exactly where God is going with this illustration, but it bears mention. The Lord will give each of us a new name, and our actions in this life may directly influence the name he chooses. Let us then endeavor to build upon our given foundation using excellent materials.

> And to the angel (messenger) of the assembly (church) in Thyatira write: These are the words of the Son of God, who has eyes that flash like a flame of fire, and Whose feet glow like bright and burnished and white-hot bronze. (Rev. 2:18)

God's passion is for his people. While there may be other reasons for his eyes to flash like a flame of fire, we are precious to him. There was a nation that plundered the people of God and God said, "he who touches you touches the apple of my eye." (Zech. 2:8, author's paraphrase)

> I know your record and what you are doing, your love and faith and service and patient endurance, and that your recent works are more numerous and greater than your first ones. (Rev. 2:19)

This church is doing well. God sees what they are doing, and it would appear mostly he approves. They are working even harder now than when they first began. Sprinkled into those works are very favorable attributes: love, faith, service, and patient endurance, which are highly prized by God.

> But I have this against you: that you tolerate the woman Jezebel, who calls herself a prophetess [claiming to be inspired], and who is teaching and leading astray my servants and beguiling

them into practicing sexual vice and eating food sacrificed to idols. (Rev. 2:20)

This may be another reason for his eyes to flash like fire. He is angry with Jezebel and her followers and how they are negatively affecting his people.

Where have we heard this before? This is now the third time we are looking at a doctrine or teaching that leads the people of God astray through sexual immorality and idol worship. While we no longer worship idols as they did in the Old Testament, there are no doubts that we have our idols in this modern age. How much time do we spend with the TV, our children, our spouses, our video games, etcetera? None of those things are bad in themselves, depending on context. If any of them have taken first place in our lives, that is idol worship. There is a place reserved for the number-one spot in our lives for our affection and time, and that is the Most High God. If anything else is there in the number-one spot, we are guilty of spiritual idolatry. Each person has their own unique personality with likes and dislikes. What may vie for your attention may not appeal to me in the least, and vice versa. But idol worship is no respecter of persons. Whatever takes the place of the Most High God in your life is an idol. What we have here and in those two other churches are teachings of immorality and idol worship. Few currently preach this from the pulpit: "Jesus forgave your sins, so you may do as you please." It is not based on your performance but on what Christ did for you, so sin.

However, we don't always teach from the pulpit. Some of our strongest teachings come from the examples of our lives. The Church today is unfortunately notorious for its affairs and sexual immorality, both within the Church and among the leadership. However, it also needs to be stated that there are many who are operating in their respective spheres of influence who are highly commendable and are faithful servants. Unfortunately, we do not hear about these men and women as much as we should. God has given us forgiveness, and we have the liberty to sin or not to sin, but we are not to abuse this freedom. We are "called to freedom, only we should not use this freedom to indulge our immoral nature." (Gal. 5:13, author's paraphrase) Paul the apostle states,

> Everything is permissible (allowable and lawful) for me; but not all things are helpful (good for me to do, expedient and profitable when considered with other things). Everything is lawful for me, but I will not become the slave of anything or be brought under its power. (1 Cor. 6:12)

Teachers of this doctrine, who claim freedom to do whatever we want because Jesus paid the price for our sin, miss the point. While there is truth in that teaching, that is not the whole truth. Remember the illustration of the bond servants? We are free to do as we please, but what we choose will reverberate throughout all eternity. As free men and women, shouldn't we choose to give up our freedom? Bond servants who will never leave Jesus! Should we not give him our ear so he can pierce it, and everyone can know that we are bond servants of the Most High God?

What we choose to build upon the foundation of our salvation follows us into all of eternity. Let's throw away the wood, hay, and stubble and instead build with gold, silver, and precious stone. We have been called to freedom, and with that freedom is the possibility of abusing that freedom. God already knows that there have been, and there will be, those who choose to abuse his gift, and he gave it anyway without our input. However, he has also clarified that he hates the abuse of his gift and will not leave unscathed those who choose this abuse. That he states he hates the teachings of the Nicolaitans gives abundant testimony to that.

> I gave her time to repent, but she has no desire to repent of her immorality [symbolic of idolatry] and refuses to do so. Take note: I will throw her on a bed [of anguish], and those who commit adultery with her [her paramours] I will bring down to pressing distress and severe affliction, unless they turn away their minds from conduct [such as] hers and repent of their doings. And I will strike her children (her proper followers) dead [thoroughly exterminating them]. And all the assemblies (churches) shall recognize and understand that I am He Who searches minds (the thoughts, feelings, and purposes) and the [inmost] hearts, and I will give to each of you [the reward for what you have done] as your work deserves. (Rev. 2:21–23)

This was an actual church during the time of John the apostle, but the warnings persist to this day. If anybody relates to this church and its false teaching, wisdom advises us to run and repent. There are places where God takes things seriously. We can never know when he might forbear or when he might be severe, so let's not take the chance.

> But to the rest of you in Thyatira, who do not hold this teaching, who have not explored and known the depths of Satan, as they say—I tell you that I do not lay upon you any other [fresh] burden: Only hold fast to what you have until I come. (Rev. 2:24–25)

Sometimes God knows the stress we are under, and he will not add any more to your burdens, as he knows you are doing all you can as it is. That is the situation with this church.

> And he who overcomes (is victorious) and who obeys My commands to the [very] end [doing the works that please Me], I will give him authority and power over the nations. (Rev. 2:26)

Many think this symbolic, but later in Revelation, we see we are called to be kings and priests before God. In the new millennium, would it be so far-fetched that God appointed various people to govern different parts of his kingdom? Yes, he is the King of kings and Lord of lords, but he delights in blessing his children and giving us additional responsibilities. Remember the parable of the talents? He said, "You have been faithful in the little I have given you and I will put you in charge of much." (Matt. 25, author's paraphrase)

> And he shall rule them with a sceptre (rod) of iron, as when earthen pots are broken in pieces, and [his power over them shall be] like that which I Myself have received from My Father. (Rev. 2:27)

Jesus says that we rule even as he has ruled and received it from his Father.

> And I will give him the Morning Star. He who is able to hear, let him listen to and heed what the [Holy] Spirit says to the assemblies (churches)." (Rev. 2:28–29)

So let us hear and look at this church. What are the things commended by God, and what are the things he hates? God commends their love, faith, service, and patient endurance, and that their current works are more and greater than when they first started. However, he hates that they tolerate Jezebel and, by doing so, tolerate her teachings.

CHAPTER 24

The Book of Revelation, Chapters 3-4

AND TO the angel (messenger) of the assembly (church) in Sardis write: These are the words of Him Who has the seven Spirits of God [the sevenfold Holy Spirit] and the seven stars: I know your record and what you are doing; you are supposed to be alive, but [in reality] you are dead. (Rev. 3:1)

Wow, not a nice way to start a letter! There is no praise sandwich here. This church looks alive, but God says it is dead.

Rouse yourselves and keep awake, and strengthen and invigorate what remains and is on the point of dying; for I have not found a thing that you have done [any work of yours] meeting the requirements of My God or perfect in His sight. (Rev. 3:2)

Nothing that they are doing is pleasing to God, and God says, "Wake up!" There is hardly any life here. It is close to being dead. It is like a fire in the fireplace, and there is a little ember still glowing, and this church needs to blow on that ember and feed it with new wood, so the fire burns again.

> So call to mind the lessons you received and heard; continually lay them to heart and obey them, and repent. In case you will not rouse yourselves and keep awake and watch, I will come upon you like a thief, and you will not know or suspect at what hour I will come. (Rev. 3:3)

This church has had teaching in the past, but they are not doing anything with it. They are "hearers of the Word but not doers." (James 1:22, author's paraphrase) God admonishes them to review their past teachings and obey. If they do not, they will be unprepared for the time of his return.

> Yet you still have a few [persons'] names in Sardis who have not soiled their clothes, and they shall walk with Me in white, because they are worthy and deserving. (Rev. 3:4)

Not everyone in this church is dead. There is a remnant, and those who walk with him will be prepared for the time of his return. It is hard enough to stand and walk when the people surrounding you are alive and vital. It takes a special focus of faith to do so when those around you are dead and unfocused. God commends these few believers.

> Thus shall he who conquers (is victorious) be clad in white garments, and I will not erase or blot out his name from the Book of Life; I will acknowledge him [as Mine] and I will confess his name openly before My Father and before His angels. (Rev. 3:5)

Jesus will clothe the overcomers with his righteousness, and their names remain in the Book of Life. God wrote our names in, and he has the power to erase our names. It is unwise to play games when so much is on the line.

> He who is able to hear, let him listen to and heed what the [Holy] Spirit says to the assemblies (churches). (Rev. 3:6)

What have we heard here? If we are close to being spiritually dead, wake up! Remember the lessons that we knew before and start to obey and put those things into practice, or we will be unprepared for his coming. It does not need to be his coming in the clouds, which is only going to occur once—or in other points of view a few times. What about his coming when you die? Regardless of your point of view about what happens immediately after you die, there are no reset buttons. Once it's over, that's it. What we want to do for him and to be a blessing to others needs to be done now.

> And to the angel (messenger) of the assembly (church) in Philadelphia write: These are the words of the Holy One, the True One, He Who has the key of David, Who opens and no one shall shut, Who shuts and no one shall open. (Rev. 3:7)

It is a comforting thought that our God can open doors for us so that no man can close, and he can close doors for us that no man can open.

> I know your [record of] works and what you are doing. See! I have set before you a door wide open which no one is able to shut; I know that you have but little power, and yet you have kept My Word and guarded My message and have not renounced or denied My name. (Rev. 3:8)

This body of believers has but a little strength. However, they have been faithful with what little they have. And because of this, God gave them a door of opportunity that no man can shut. Paul stated in I Corinthians 16:9, "That a great and effective door had been opened to him for service and with it many adversaries." (authors paraphrase) Sometimes an open door is an open door because along with it there is opposition. Just because God has opened the door does not mean the enemy is just going to let you walk through and take what is his. The purpose of this message is not to scare but to encourage. God opened the door, and no one can shut it. But often, resistance is the validation of your open door.

> Take note! I will make those of the synagogue of Satan who say they are Jews and are not, but lie—behold, I will make them come and bow down before your feet and learn and acknowledge that I have loved you. (Rev. 3:9)

God is going to vindicate this church. When a man's ways, or in this case a church's way, please the Lord, he makes even his enemies be at peace with him. (Prov. 16:7, author's paraphrase)

> Because you have guarded and kept My word of patient endurance [have held fast the lesson of My patience with the expectant endurance that I give you], I also will keep you [safe] from the hour of trial (testing) which is coming on the whole world to try those who dwell upon the earth. (Rev. 3:10)

This is another Scripture that the pre-Tribulation believers use as evidence for that viewpoint. However, once again, this is a picture or symbol of the Church, as we think of it today from that viewpoint. The plain reading is that God is specifically speaking to a church in Asia during the lifetime of John. It does not say how God is going to keep his people, and it does not state that he is rapturing his Church to heaven. Can this be a picture of the Rapture of the Church and keeping the Church from the time of the Tribulation? Absolutely! But there is only one who can say whether it is, and he left this open to interpretation.

Some are going to be kept safe while others, it seems, are going to be martyred for their Lord. Along with the hypothesis that each church represents a distinct Church age throughout history, there is the hypothesis that in every Church age, there are representatives of each type of church during that age.

> I am coming quickly; hold fast what you have, so that no one may rob you and deprive you of your crown. He who overcomes (is victorious), I will make him a pillar in the sanctuary of My God; he shall never be put out of it or go out of it, and I will write on him the name of My God and the name of the city of My God, the new Jerusalem, which descends from My God out of heaven, and My own new name. (Rev. 3:11–12)

God will reward the faithful. I am not sure if it depends on which type of church you are in or what you must overcome to get the different rewards. Maybe we will get all the different rewards, but God commends those who are faithful and gives them rewards.

> He who can hear, let him listen to and heed what the Spirit says to the assemblies (churches). (Rev. 3:13)

What have we gleaned from this church? God puts great value on those who have only a little strength yet remain faithful. It is not always the mighty by our standards who really impress him. God sees not as a human, according to the outward appearance, but God sees the heart

(1 Sam. 16:7). (authors paraphrase) So if you see yourself as small and not very mighty, but are holding on and remaining faithful, know that God sees you and your reward is with him.

> And to the angel (messenger) of the assembly (church) in Laodicea write: These are the words of the Amen, the trusty and faithful and true Witness, the Origin and Beginning and Author of God's creation: I know your [record of] works and what you are doing; you are neither cold nor hot. Would that you were cold or hot! (Rev. 3:14–15)

Have you ever had a nice lukewarm cup of coffee? Is there anything as good as a nice lukewarm can of soda? It's awful, and that is exactly the way God pictures this church.

> So, because you are lukewarm and neither cold nor hot, I will spew you out of My mouth! (Rev. 3:16)

You have set your coffee down and were busy for a while with other events of your day. Absentmindedly, you pick up that coffee and, without even thinking, spit it out because it has grown lukewarm. That is the picture here.

> For you say, I am rich; I have prospered and grown wealthy, and I am in need of nothing; and you do not realize and understand that you are wretched, pitiable, poor, blind, and naked. Therefore I counsel you to purchase from Me gold refined and tested by fire, that you may be [truly] wealthy, and white clothes to clothe you and to keep the shame of your nudity from being seen, and salve to put on your eyes, that you may see. (Rev. 3:17–18)

The following are Scriptures that deal with gold being refined in the fire. These verses dovetail Jesus's suggestion that we purchase gold refined in the fire to be truly wealthy.

But He knows the way that I take [He has concern for it, appreciates, and pays attention to it]. When He has tried me, I shall come forth as refined gold [pure and luminous]. (Job 23:10)

Anybody remember the trials of Job?

So that [the genuineness] of your faith may be tested, [your faith] which is infinitely more precious than the perishable gold which is tested and purified by fire. [This proving of your faith is intended] to redound to [your] praise and glory and honor when Jesus Christ (the Messiah, the Anointed One) is revealed. (1 Pet. 1:7)

The refining pot is for silver and the furnace for gold, but the Lord tries the hearts. (Prov. 17:3)

I the Lord search the mind, I try the heart, even to give to every man according to his ways, according to the fruit of his doings. (Jer. 17:10)

The Lord loves us just the way we are, but way too much to leave us that way.

Those whom I [dearly and tenderly] love, I tell their faults and convict and convince and reprove and chasten [I discipline and instruct them]. So be enthusiastic and in earnest and burning with zeal and repent [changing your mind and attitude]. (Rev. 3:19)

The following verse deals with the subject of God's discipline in our lives.

For the time being no discipline brings joy, but seems grievous and painful; but afterward it yields a peaceable fruit of righteousness to those who have been trained by it [a harvest of fruit which consists in righteousness—in conformity to God's will in purpose, thought, and action, resulting in right living and right standing with God]. (Heb. 12:11)

Behold, I stand at the door and knock; if anyone hears and listens to and heeds My voice and opens the door, I will come in to him and will eat with him, and he [will eat] with Me. (Rev. 3:20)

God is knocking, and if we are lukewarm, it is up to us to open that door and let him in. God is a gentleman and will patiently knock. He will not bust down the door and make us open the door. So if today you hear him knocking, do yourself a favor and open that door. It is interesting that for the Church of Philadelphia, he opened a door that no man could close. In the Church of Laodicea, he stands outside and knocks, waiting for us to open to him.

He who overcomes (is victorious), I will grant him to sit beside Me on My throne, as I Myself overcame (was victorious) and sat down beside My Father on His throne. He who is able to hear, let him listen to and heed what the [Holy] Spirit says to the assemblies (churches). (Rev. 3:21–22)

So what has the Spirit taught us about this church? They are in deception and need to ask God for gold refined in the fire to be truly wealthy. They are naked but think God has richly adorned them. God says they need white clothes—the righteousness of the saints, as Revelation 19:8 will later show us. That if we choose to remain lukewarm, God will spit us out of his mouth. Finally, that he stands at the door and knocks, and if we open, we will enjoy renewed fellowship.

There may be other things that God wants us to listen to concerning these churches. But it gives a very clear picture of some character qualities that God truly commends and some that he truly hates. If we look both corporally and individually, we have a Holy Spirit evaluation tool with which to measure ourselves and adjust as necessary. In all these churches, let us notice that God's love is for them—even the Church of Sardis, about whom God said, "You think you are alive but are dead. I have nothing good to say about anything you have accomplished." As already shown in Scripture, those whom God loves he disciplines and corrects. If he hated them, he would have said nothing, and they would have never known they needed to repent. Some say that the opposite of love is not hate but indifference. God is not indifferent with any of these churches but commends what he can and corrects what he must.

AFTER THIS I looked, and behold, a door standing open in heaven! And the first voice which I had heard addressing me like [the calling of] a war trumpet said, come up here, and I will show you what must take place in the future. (Rev. 4:1)

There has been much made of this one verse, which many theologians believe signifies the Rapture of the Church. The door that opened in heaven symbolizes God rapturing the Church. The Church's absence from the text after this chapter, and until Revelation 19:7–9, supports this interpretation, as noted earlier. That, according to the dispensational pre-Tribulation perspective, this verse is a prophetic picture of Christ calling his Church to come up, just as he told John to come up. While it is possible, it is not certain, and we need to consider what our response will be if this interpretation is not as accurate as we might wish.

Another thought to consider is that Revelation 4:1 is a cornerstone for the pre-Tribulation point of view, and as we have seen earlier, Jesus interprets many of the symbols that he gives . . . but not this one. The appeal that this is a picture of Christ calling his Church to heaven is understandable, but if that is the case, why does Jesus not interpret this symbol of an open door in heaven? If Christ rapturing the Church is as important as all that, why leave it open to interpretation? Jesus interprets the seven stars and the seven lampstands. There are many places in Revelation where the context of the passages gives you directly the effect of the thing being symbolized. Such is the case for the four horsemen of the Apocalypse:

1. First horseman: Someone who conquers . . . okay, a little vague.
2. Second horseman: Takes peace from the earth, people kill each other, and a great war.
3. Third horseman: Famine.
4. Fourth horseman: Death. And hell follows death! A quarter of the earth dies.

The angel of the abyss in chapter 9 is king over the locust army and is clearly called an angel in verse 11 when we get there. He cannot be a good angel in the context; therefore, it is a demon angel. There are many places in the book of Revelation where Jesus gives us the interpretation, either directly or through context. But neither Jesus nor context interprets the door standing open in heaven. We see no direct effect from the door being opened in heaven in the text except to show future events.

There is a door opened in heaven, and many consider this imagery of the Rapture of the Church, as we have explored in some detail earlier. Let's contrast this verse with a verse that includes the resurrection on the last day in the timing of the Rapture. Why do some people give more weight to one that is clearly imagery, and Jesus has not given us a definitive interpretation rather than ones that make good sense in the plain reading of the text?

> For this is My Father's will and His purpose, that everyone who sees the Son and believes in and cleaves to and trusts in and relies on Him should have eternal life, and I will raise him up [from the dead] at the last day. (John 6:40)

We are shifting gears here. Jesus has finished addressing personally the seven churches in Asia. But writing and sending this to them— doesn't this mean everything in the entirety of the letter affects these seven churches as representatives of all churches? Why bother sending this revelation to the churches if most of what is in it does not pertain to them? Isn't it more likely that the later omission of the Church is because Jesus has already made it clear this revelation is for the Church? If you are writing a long letter to your spouse, let's say, and it's sixteen pages long, do you keep referring to your spouse to make sure that they are the object of your concern? Or do you take it for granted that, even though you only mentioned them specifically in the beginning and the end, that they understand that the entire letter is for them?

Is it possible that God is doing what those theologians suggest, and that God divided this letter into two parts, one for the Church and one for the nation of Israel? Of course, it's possible; that's what makes this topic so challenging. There are a ton of possibilities. The prophecies of Christ's return are not as straightforward as, let's say, God's love for us. Most of us in the United States are familiar with the following verse, even if we have never gone to church:

> For God so loved the world that He gave His only begotten
> Son that whosoever believes in Him should not perish but have
> everlasting life. (John 3:16 KJV)

There is not an awful lot of ambiguity in that; God so loved that he gave. It's important to understand the main point. There are some elements that are bedrock: Jesus is coming again, to him who overcomes will I give, my reward is with me, be faithful until the end, I am the Alpha and the Omega, the Beginning and the End, etcetera. These are our foundation stones, and on these we are safe. Now what we choose to build upon this foundation, God has left room for interpretation. Again, what we choose to speculate on in our sincere attempts to interpret Scripture says a lot more about us than it does about the Lord—God already knows!

> At once I came under the [Holy] Spirit's power, and behold, a
> throne stood in heaven, with One seated on the throne! And
> He Who sat there appeared like [the crystalline brightness of]

jasper and [the fiery] sardius, and encircling the throne there was a halo that looked like [a rainbow of] emerald. (Rev. 4:2–3)

John is under the power of the Holy Spirit and sees a vision of someone on a throne. There can be little doubt that this is Father God. I leave it to others the significance of the jasper, sardius, and emerald.

Twenty-four other thrones surrounded the throne, and seated on these thrones were twenty-four elders (the members of the heavenly Sanhedrin), arrayed in white clothing, with crowns of gold upon their heads. (Rev. 4:4)

Numbers assuredly have significance, although I will not pretend to know what they are. Translators of the Amplified Bible may have gotten this one wrong. The Sanhedrin, comprising seventy people, originated in Moses's time, when God instructed Moses to choose seventy leaders and officials from among the people. This was to help him carry the load of deciding disputes among the people so that he did not wear himself out (Num. 11:16). However, they could be right, as this was a council of elders meant to govern, and it may not be all that important that in heaven there were twenty-four and on earth there were seventy-one: the seventy God said to appoint to help Moses, plus Moses, for seventy-one total. In Hebrews 9, the Holy Spirit speaks of the earthly tabernacle being a type or representative of the true tabernacle in heaven. Basically, what God told humans to build here on earth is a mirror of the true elements in heaven. So they may be right or not, but the concept of a governing body is similar. There are twenty-four elders surrounding the central throne, which would show God's council or government of some kind. It is okay to speculate; God knows we will. He gives us glimpses but does not break everything down, and it is in my heart that we don't need all the details. But he is painting a picture for us of some things that are transpiring in heaven, and while he mentions some things in passing, they are not what he is focusing on, so maybe we need not either.

Who are these elders? In all honesty, your guess is as good as mine. He does not feel the need to elaborate about them or their identities. There are clues—white raiment clothes the twenty-four elders, and later we see God clothes the saints in white, which represents the righteous deeds of the saints. We also see God gives the saints crowns. So these twenty-four elders could be saints God has given a place of authority to rule with him, which is also depicted in other places in Scripture. However, none of those clues are conclusive. While it is enjoyable to speculate, it is unnecessary to know their identities to see the picture God is painting and leave what he knows for a fact in his very capable hands and just enjoy the flow of the vision.

> Out from the throne came flashes of lightning and rumblings and peals of thunder, and in front of the throne seven blazing torches burned, which are the seven Spirits of God [the sevenfold Holy Spirit]. (Rev. 4:5)

This picture speaks of something profound that is about to transpire. If you were watching a movie, and you saw a throne and you saw flashes of lightning coming from the throne and heard loud rumblings and peals of thunder, wouldn't you expect something profound was about to happen—especially if the music in the movie got more intense?

Ancient of Days with Cherubim and the Glassy Sea

And before the throne there was a sea of glass like unto crystal: and in the midst of the throne, and round about the throne were four beasts full of eyes before and behind. (Rev. 4:6)

Cherub

The first living creature (being) was like a lion, the second living creature like an ox, the third living creature had the face of a man, and the fourth living creature [was] like a flying eagle. And the four living creatures, individually having six wings, were full of eyes all over and within [underneath their wings]; and day and night they never stop saying, Holy, holy, holy is the Lord God Almighty (Omnipotent), Who was and Who is and Who is to come. (Rev. 4:7–8)

We have seen these creatures or cherubim mentioned earlier in the Bible in Ezekiel chapter 1.

Just as the sun is what all the planets revolve around in our galaxy, in heaven everything revolves around him who sits on the throne.

> And whenever the living creatures offer glory and honor and thanksgiving to Him Who sits on the throne, Who lives forever and ever (through the eternities of the eternities), The twenty-four elders (the members of the heavenly Sanhedrin) fall prostrate before Him Who is sitting on the throne, and they worship Him Who lives forever and ever; and they throw down their crowns before the throne, crying out, Worthy are You, our Lord and God, to receive the glory and the honor and dominion, for You created all things; by Your will they were [brought into being] and were created. (Rev. 4:9–11)

There is much in the symbolism depicting this exceptional scene in heaven. There are people very gifted in understanding symbolism, and it's worth looking into, but we are here to just get a basic understanding. Taking in the majestic description of God, the twenty-four elders, the glassy sea, and the four living creatures should be enough.

Ancient of Days on the Throne with the Seven Sealed Scroll

CHAPTER 25

The Book of Revelation, Chapters 5-6

AND I saw lying on the open hand of Him Who was seated on the throne a scroll (book) written within and on the back, closed and sealed with seven seals. (Rev. 5:1)

The Ancient of Days has a scroll in his hand, and initially John sees this overview in heaven, but now we are focusing on that scene with much more specificity. We have arrived at the crux of what God wants to reveal. While we have enjoyed the great magisterial scene in heaven, God wants to draw our attention to a scroll that is in his hand and sealed with seven seals. The Bible often uses seven to denote completeness, a finished work, or perfection. God rested on the seventh day in the earth's creation, which gives us our complete week. During the time of Joseph, there were seven years of plenty, followed by seven years of famine. Jesus exhorted Peter to forgive his brother, who sinned against him seventy times seven. In Revelation, there are the seven churches, the sevenfold Spirit of God, seven seals, seven angels, seven trumpets, etcetera.

I am not sure how John can tell all this about the scroll unless it is by divine revelation or a word of knowledge. If God sealed the scroll with seven seals, how did John learn what was on the front and back of the scroll? This might have been "added" after the vision, resulting in the current account reflecting a later perspective on the scroll and seals. He appears to be recording this as he goes along, though, because in Revelation 10:4, he is about to write what the seven thunders just said and was told not to. There may be parts where he was and parts where he was not. This is important because how you see the scroll and the seals directly affect the interpretation. If God sealed the scroll on the outside with seven seals, then we do not actually see what is inside the scroll until after Jesus breaks the seventh seal. However, if you had seven separate pieces of parchment joined by seals, that would be different. Ancient people made seals by melting wax and then allowing the wax to harden. In your mind's eye, picture two pieces or more of parchment or paper side by side and then an amount of melted wax on both pieces. After the wax hardens, the two pieces join. If you did this seven times and then rolled it all together and sealed it to itself on the outside, you could not see what was inside until you broke the seal for each individual part. You would have to start at the end and work backward to the beginning to see each section.

Scrolls in ancient times were like our books. A scribe would take a long piece of parchment and, as they wrote, they would roll it, and that basically was a scroll. If a king were sending a letter in ancient times, it would be a scroll. Then the scribe, after writing the king's message, would melt wax where the scroll came together, and this would seal the letter. Normally, the king would use a ring with an insignia or some other device with an insignia, so whoever received the letter would know this was the mark or seal of the king. Only the addressee or someone with sufficient authority could break the seal and read the letter's contents. Some scrolls had more than one seal on the outside, which appears to be the case here, but the Scripture only states that God sealed it with seven seals and does not state where these seals are located. Some people say that after each seal broke, we glimpsed that part of the scroll until the next seal broke, allowing further reading. Others insist that someone must break the seven seals to reveal the scroll's contents. In either case, the breaking of each seal sequentially gives us insight and information. As an example, you would not see the fourth horseman of the Apocalypse, whoever he may be, until the first three horsemen of the Apocalypse had their appointed time on the world stage. That would be the natural reading of the text that one follows the other, as Jesus breaks open each seal.

We will follow this narrative as if someone breaks each seal and discloses another portion of the letter. We naturally read the text this way because each broken seal reveals previously undisclosed information. In the first four seals, we have one cherub telling John to come. As John obeys, he sees one of the four horsemen of the Apocalypse and what happens because of the rider and his horse on the earth.

> And I saw a strong angel announcing in a loud voice, who is worthy to open the scroll? And [who is entitled and deserves and is morally fit] to break its seals? And no one in heaven or on earth or under the earth [in the realm of the dead, Hades] was able to open the scroll or to take a [single] look at its contents. And I wept audibly and bitterly because no one was found fit to open the scroll or to inspect it. (Rev. 5:2–4)

The next scene has us looking around for someone who is worthy of breaking open the seven seals of the book and letting us look inside to its contents. We discover no one worthy—neither the twenty-four elders, nor the cherubim, nor the angels, nor any men on earth or among the dead, etcetera. We have come to a standoff.

> Then one of the elders [of the heavenly Sanhedrin] said to me, Stop weeping! See, the Lion of the tribe of Judah, the Root (Source) of David, has won (has overcome and conquered)! He can open the scroll and break its seven seals! (Rev. 5:5)

Ah, the Savior in more ways than one! Jesus is worthy of doing the honors, and absolutely no one else has the authority to do so.

> And there between the throne and the four living creatures (beings) and among the elders [of the heavenly Sanhedrin] I saw a Lamb standing, as though it had been slain, with seven horns and with seven eyes, which are the seven Spirits of God [the sevenfold Holy Spirit] Who have been sent [on duty far and wide] into all the earth. (Rev. 5:6)

This is a majestic picture of our Messiah as the Lamb of God, whom God slayed to redeem us back to himself. Now continuing with our cinematic picture as directed by God himself, we see Jesus right between the throne and the cherubim. Causing offense is not my intention, but much of this beauty and scope reminds me of a great cinematic movie where the camera repeatedly zooms in on certain elements, as if saying, "Pay special attention to this."

> He then went and took the scroll from the right hand of Him Who sat on the throne. (Rev. 5:7)

> The Father allows Jesus alone access to him and to the scroll that is sitting in his open hand.

And when He had taken the scroll, the four living creatures and the twenty-four elders [of the heavenly Sanhedrin] prostrated themselves before the Lamb. Each was holding a harp (lute or guitar), and they had golden bowls full of incense (fragrant spices and gums for burning), which are the prayers of God's people (the saints). And [now] they sing a new song, saying, you are worthy to take the scroll and to break the seals that are on it, for you were slain (sacrificed), and with your blood you purchased men unto God from every tribe and language and people and nation. (Rev. 5:8–9)

Can anyone say party or praise session? We have the best of the best assembled here in the throne room of God. As the Lamb takes the scroll, they all stop to worship and sing. We're celebrating because God's revelation is possible through the Lamb of God; without the Lamb, no one could have found a way.

And You have made them a kingdom (royal race) and priests to our God, and they shall reign [as kings] over the earth! (Rev. 5:10)

God honors his Son through the crowd in heaven, but then the Father includes redeemed humankind and his desire and design for humanity. Extraordinary!

Then I looked, and I heard the voices of many angels on every side of the throne and of the living creatures and the elders [of the heavenly Sanhedrin], and they numbered ten thousand times ten thousand and thousands of thousands. (Rev. 5:11)

This is an awe-inspiring image with ten thousand times ten thousand, which equals ten million, and then thousands of thousands on top of that.

Saying in a loud voice, deserving is the Lamb, who was sacrificed, to receive all the power and riches and wisdom and might and honor and majesty (glory, splendor) and blessing! (Rev. 5:12)

We have a group here over ten million strong, saying in a loud voice, "Deserving is the Lamb!" Have you ever been to a concert? The picture here is staggering! All of them with one voice crying out, "Deserving is the Lamb." What an image! If you stop to picture this, it can take your breath away!

And I heard every created thing in heaven and on earth and under the earth [in Hades, the place of departed spirits] and on the sea and all that is in it, crying out together, To Him Who is seated on the throne and to the Lamb be ascribed the blessing and the honor and the majesty (glory, splendor) and the power (might and dominion) forever and ever (through the eternities of the eternities)! (Rev. 5:13)

There is a Scripture in Philippians 2:5–11 that beautifully illustrates this concept. It says we are to have the same attitude in us that Jesus had. Even though he was equal to God, he did not feel that it was necessary to hold on and grasp that equality but emptied himself of his privileges and rights. He took on the form of a servant and then humbled himself even further and became obedient, even to the point of a humiliating death on a cross. But because he lowered himself, God has highly exalted him and given him a name that is above every other name. That at the name of Jesus, every knee shall bow, and every tongue confess that

Jesus Christ is Lord to the Father's glory. (authors paraphrase) We have the choice to do this willingly, or the time will come when we do so unwillingly. Every tongue would include Satan and his demons. One day, unwillingly, they will bow the knee and confess that Jesus Christ is Lord, glorifying the Father.

> Then the four living creatures (beings) said, amen (so be it)! And the elders [of the heavenly Sanhedrin] prostrated themselves and worshiped Him Who lives forever and ever. (Rev. 5:14)

> THEN I saw as the Lamb broke open one of the seven seals, and as if in a voice of thunder I heard one of the four living creatures call out, Come! (Rev. 6:1)

We have one of the four cherubim taking center stage at this point and telling John to come and see what is in the first of the seven seals. The first three chapters of Revelation show Jesus talking with John about the events and the churches of John's time, possibly a glimpse of all the churches throughout our history as falling roughly into one of these seven types of churches. Then, in chapter 4, we switch gears to a scene in heaven amid the throne room of God and the Lamb who is worthy to break the seals of the book to reveal what is inside. This book is the revelation of the future, as evidenced by the contents of what is in the book, and the characters that have yet to be revealed on the world stage. The Lamb has broken the first seal, and one cherub tells John to come.

Four Horsemen of the Apocalypse Rendition One

And I looked, and saw there a white horse whose rider carried a bow. And a crown was given him, and he rode forth conquering and to conquer. (Rev. 6:2)

Who is this white rider? Many say it is the Antichrist, but there are other theories. Jesus comes later in the book of Revelation on a white horse, so some have said this is Jesus going forth to conquer the hearts of men. In that section of Scripture, however, he has a sword coming out of his mouth with which to strike the nations and a scepter of iron. He also has many crowns in that passage, not just one. Could this still be Jesus? Possibly, but it does not seem likely, given the context, especially because the three horsemen that follow bring death and destruction, so if these were Jesus's fellow riders/companions, they do not share his Spirit.

Remember also though that the Antichrist will appear as an angel of light, so this could also be a picture of him trying to copy the accurate image of the King of kings and Lord of lords. The imagery here of the weapon is a bow, which is a long-range weapon, as compared to a sword, which is an up-close-and-personal weapon. It is also interesting to note that while he has a bow, there is no mention of an arrow. A bow alone cannot cause harm without an arrow. He conquers without using a weapon. A friend of mine stated he thought the bow was a rainbow and not a weapon at all. A friend of mine interprets this as a covenant that the Antichrist signs with Israel and is reminiscent of God making a covenant with the earth not to destroy it again with a flood:

> Then God spoke to Noah and to his sons with him, saying, Behold, I establish My covenant or pledge with you and with your descendants after you and with every living creature that is with you—whether the birds, the livestock, or the wild beasts of the earth along with you, as many as came out of the ark— every animal of the earth. I will establish My covenant or pledge with you: Never again shall all flesh be cut off by the waters of a flood; neither shall there ever again be a flood to destroy the earth and make it corrupt. And God said, this is the token of

the covenant (solemn pledge) which I am making between Me and you and every living creature that is with you, for all future generations: I set My bow [rainbow] in the cloud, and it shall be a token or sign of a covenant or solemn pledge between Me and the earth. And it shall be that when I bring clouds over the earth and the bow [rainbow] is seen in the clouds, I will [earnestly] remember My covenant or solemn pledge which is between Me and you and every living creature of all flesh; and the waters will no more become a flood to destroy and make all flesh corrupt. (Gen. 9:8–15)

Let's keep our options open for now and see what the flow is throughout the seals. It is hard to say what anything is at the beginning until you have looked at the entire picture and see it in context. At that point, context should narrow down the variables to give a more definitive probability.

And when He broke the second seal, I heard the second living creature call out, Come! (Rev. 6:3)

4 Horsemen of the Apocalypse Rendition Two

The next cherub calls John to come after Christ breaks open the second seal.

> And another horse came out, flaming red. And its rider was empowered to take the peace from the earth, so that men slaughtered one another; and he was given a huge sword. (Rev. 6:4)

Who is this rider? Some say it's the same rider but on a different horse. Many people have offered interpretations. What is important is not the identity of who this is, although, admittedly, that would be nice, but that this revelation is during the time of the Tribulation. Whoever this rider is, he is a man of war, and God has granted him the ability to take peace from the earth. If the first rider is masquerading as Jesus and is the Antichrist, this would kind of fit. We have talked before about the angel of light and how he enters a covenant with many people. Then, in the middle of the covenant, he breaks his promise and reveals his true colors. What if it is the same rider on a different horse? During the first three and one-half years, he uses peace and diplomacy to conquer, and in the next three and one-half years, his true colors emerge, and he comes out swinging?

On a side note, while both accomplish conquering through conquest, one appears to be using a long-range weapon and the other an up-close-and-personal weapon.

> When He broke open the third seal, I heard the third living creature call out, Come and look! And I saw, and behold, a black horse, and in his hand the rider had a pair of scales (a balance). (Rev. 6:5)

Now the third cherub calls John to come, and John sees a third rider and horse.

> And I heard what seemed to be a voice from the midst of the four living creatures, saying, A quart of wheat for a denarius [a whole day's wages], and three quarts of barley for a denarius; but do not harm the oil and the wine! (Rev. 6:6)

The third seal seems to involve the economy. More precisely, the economy is getting extremely bad. It basically appears to be saying a human's wages for one day would provide enough for a meal. However, while the necessities of life are scarce and costly, it would appear some luxuries in life are in abundance and relatively cheap. What are the natural consequences of war? Destroyed land and crops are natural consequences of war. The rider and horse of the second seal could take peace from the earth so that men slaughtered each other. This would appear to be on a worldwide scale, although that is not definite. That famine follows war is self-evident.

> When the Lamb broke open the fourth seal, I heard the fourth living creature call out, Come! (Rev. 6:7)

Now the fourth cherub calls John to come, and Jesus breaks open the fourth seal. John beholds a fourth horse and rider. It is interesting that there are four horsemen of the Apocalypse and four cherubim that call John to come and behold them. I am not exactly sure what this signifies, but it is interesting.

> So, I looked, and behold, an ashy pale horse [black and blue as if made so by bruising], and its rider's name was Death, and Hades (the realm of the dead) followed him closely. And they

were given authority and power over a fourth part of the earth to kill with the sword and with famine and with plague (pestilence, disease) and with wild beasts of the earth. (Rev. 6:8)

It is interesting to note that, of the four horsemen of the Apocalypse, we only know this rider's identity. Death naturally follows war and famine. Hades, or the realm of the dead, hell, naturally follows death. Is what we have here sequential? It appears to be that way. We have a scenario that if you take each element, the element that follows is not surprising. Jesus possesses one scroll, but seven seals require breaking. God gives us a vision or glimpse of something that happens at a particular time in humankind's future. This could be an actual person or a spiritual entity, a demon. The text will clearly interpret many symbols as demons. Demons sometimes inhabit humans, so a picture of a man can include himself and the spiritual being working in and through him.

The following are verses to illustrate this point.

But [then] Satan entered into Judas, called Iscariot, who was one of the Twelve [apostles]. (Luke 22:3)

Whoever or whatever this rider is, he has authority over a fourth of the earth to kill with some variety of means. Here are more verses on spiritual forces working behind the scenes.

For we are not wrestling with flesh and blood [contending only with physical opponents], but against the despotisms, against the powers, against [the master spirits who are] the world rulers of this present darkness, against the spirit forces of wickedness in the heavenly (supernatural) sphere. (Eph 6:12)

Since we consider and look not to the things that are seen but to the things that are unseen; for the things that are visible are temporal (brief and fleeting), but the things that are invisible are deathless and everlasting. (2 Cor. 4:18)

Let's go back to Revelation 6.

When the Lamb broke open the fifth seal, I saw at the foot of the altar the souls of those whose lives had been sacrificed for [adhering to] the Word of God and for the testimony they had borne. They cried in a loud voice, O [Sovereign] Lord, holy and true, how long now before You will sit in judgment and avenge our blood upon those who dwell on the earth? Then they were each given a long and flowing and festive white robe and told to rest and wait patiently a little while longer, until the number should be complete of their fellow servants and their brethren who were to be killed as they themselves had been. (Rev. 6:9–11)

So the fifth seal is martyrdom. Remember Jesus's words in Matthew 24?

Then they will hand you over to suffer affliction and tribulation and put you to death, and you will be hated by all nations for My name's sake. (Matt. 24:9)

And do not be afraid of those who kill the body but cannot kill the soul; but rather be afraid of Him who can destroy both soul and body in hell (Gehenna). (Matt. 10:28)

Sequentially, we have conquest, war, famine, death, and martyrdom. If we cross-reference these seals in Revelation with Matthew 24, they are close, wouldn't you say? Now let's go back to Revelation 6.

When He [the Lamb] broke open the sixth seal, I looked, and there was a great earthquake; and the sun grew black as sackcloth of hair, [the full disc of] the moon became like blood. (Rev. 6:12)

We have the heavens and the earth shaken here. The sun is black, the moon is like blood, and there is a great earthquake. Is this literal? The appearance of this imagery in Joel, Isaiah, and Matthew seems to confirm this. There are a lot of different places where God states the same thing, and the only real question becomes: Is it allegorical or literal? When God's judgment came to the people of Noah's day, was that literal or allegorical? Many sincere Christians would state it was literal. God sent a flood to destroy the earth. In Matthew 24, he states that as it was in the days of Noah, so will it be at the Son of Man's coming.

And the stars of the sky dropped to the earth like a fig tree shedding its unripe fruit out of season when shaken by a strong wind. (Rev. 6:13)

Everything is falling apart around you. How close to the end do you suppose we are now in this narrative? The Bible says we will not know the day or hour, but we will know the season. A season is relatively short: winter, spring, summer, and fall.

And the sky rolled up like a scroll and vanished, and every mountain and island was dislodged from its place. Then the kings of the earth and their noblemen and their magnates and their military chiefs and the wealthy and the strong and [everyone, whether] slave or free hid themselves in the caves and among the rocks of the mountains, and they called to the mountains and the rocks, fall on (before) us and hide us from the face of Him Who sits on the throne and from the deep-seated indignation and wrath of the Lamb. For the great day of His wrath (vengeance, retribution, indignation) has come, and who is able to stand before it? (Rev. 6:14–17)

This sounds like the day of the Lord, as previously shown in Isaiah and in Joel. Sequentially, then, after God glorifies a lot of martyrs for their testimony for Jesus, we have the day of God's judgment. Matthew 24:29 also speaks of these elements of the sun, moon, and stars not giving their light. The parallels between Revelation and Matthew 24 are so close that it is scary. There does not appear to be much more that can happen in humankind's history after this scenario. We are near the end.

CHAPTER 26

The Book of Revelation, Chapters 7-8

AFTER THIS I saw four angels stationed at the four corners of the earth, firmly holding back the four winds of the earth so that no wind should blow on the earth or sea or upon any tree. (Rev. 7:1)

Let's remember that we are still in the sixth seal, and after God shakes the heavens and earth, the angels have another job to do in the administration of God's kingdom. The Bible rarely reveals angels and their administration. We certainly have some references, especially in the life of Jesus. Most of the time, we see glimpses of them throughout the Scriptures as God's messengers, but they have other roles as well. In Revelation, we see angels doing many things not recorded for us previously. While they have been working primarily behind the scenes and will probably continue to do so, that does not mean that they are not active in the kingdom of God.

Then I saw a second angel coming up from the east (the rising of the sun) and carrying the seal of the living God. And with a loud voice he called out to the four angels who had been given authority and power to injure earth and sea, saying, Harm neither the earth nor the sea nor the trees, until we have sealed the bond servants of our God upon their foreheads. (Rev. 7:2–3)

Four angels have the power to harm the earth and the sea but are told to hold that thought until God applies his seal to his bond servants. We have already covered what it takes to become a bond servant, so anyone serious about a relationship with the Lord may want to carefully consider taking that next step in their walk with the Lord. We need to make a distinction here, as the ones who are being sealed are bond servants, and this seal is on their forehead and not their hearts or spirits. Is the seal on the forehead going to be visible? The Scriptures do not tell us, so it is unclear. It is probably not visible. However, that this seal differs from the seal of born-again believers is going to be evidenced in the paragraphs that follow.

The Holy Spirit of promise seals every believer, and various Scriptures testify to this:

[He has also appropriated and acknowledged us as His by] putting His seal upon us and giving us His [Holy] Spirit in our hearts as the security deposit and guarantee [of the fulfillment of His promise]. (2 Cor. 1:22)

In Him you also who have heard the Word of Truth, the glad tidings (Gospel) of your salvation, and have believed in and adhered to and relied on Him, were stamped with the seal of the long-promised Holy Spirit. (Eph. 1:13)

And do not grieve the Holy Spirit of God [do not offend or vex or sadden Him], by Whom you were sealed (marked, branded as God's own, secured) for the day of redemption (of final deliverance through Christ from evil and the consequences of sin). (Eph. 4:30)

However, not every believer is a bond servant. Earlier in the book of Revelation, the author explained what makes a bond servant. Jesus identifies John as a bond servant. All who come to know Jesus as Lord are children of God. Jesus considers those who submit to his will instead of their own as bond servants.

For it is by free grace (God's unmerited favor) that you are saved (delivered from judgment and made partakers of Christ's salvation) through [your] faith. And this [salvation] is not of yourselves [of your own doing, it came not through your own striving], but it is the gift of God; Not because of works [not the fulfillment of the Law's demands], lest any man should boast. [It is not the result of what anyone can possibly do, so no one can pride himself in it or take glory to himself.] (Eph. 2:8–9)

If you give me a gift of, let's say, a new car, can I do whatever I want with it? If it is a genuine gift and someone completely paid for it, and put it in my name, I can do what I want with it. The choice to be responsible with it, give it regular maintenance, keep it cleaned and waxed, and vacuumed and polished is mine. I can also smash it into a tree—not very advisable or productive, but I can choose to do that. I can loan it out or keep it in the garage and never use it. Once the car is in my name and fully paid for, with no liens, I can do what I want with it.

Many Christians have a nominal relationship with the Lord and Savior. This is not advisable or productive, but that is what they have chosen. There are also those who have said, "Here is my ear, Lord; drive through the nail and in this way let everyone know I am not for sale." The Bible, in many places, depicts our spiritual growth as like natural growth. Paul addresses some believers in Corinth and tells them, "I wanted to talk to you like spiritual men, but I was unable because you are unspiritual, still babes in Christ." (1 Cor. 3:1, author's paraphrase) In another place, he addresses the Galatians and says, "My children, I am going through birth pangs again until Christ is fully formed in you." (Gal. 4:19, author's paraphrase)

The book of I John is abounding in exhortations to the Church in three different levels of maturity. John addresses them as little children, young men, and fathers. We are free to choose whatever level of maturity we like, and God will not stop us. Do you remember that Scripture about how we have only one foundation upon which to build? That is Jesus? He says to be wise about how we build on this foundation. We can choose gold, silver, and precious stones or wood, hay, and stubble. We really have a choice. This group, whether you choose to take this number of 144,000 literally or symbolically, comprises bond servants: those who have sold out fully to the cause of Christ, those who have said, "I understand I am free, but I do not desire to be parted from you because I love you." This group of people that God chooses for a special task and administration before him, such as singing a new song that nobody else could learn—we will get to that in Revelation chapter 14—has first chosen to become bond servants. Paul, in many of his letters, at some point describes himself as a bond servant of Jesus Christ. In Romans, for instance, he starts out with "From Paul a bondservant of Jesus Christ."

As previously mentioned, God has had bond servants in every generation. In the last generation of humankind's history, God is going to raise up a small army of bond servants. It is in my heart—this is my opinion, and I am stating it as such—that these men and women may be alive and among us at the time of this writing. If it is not this generation, I believe it will be within a few generations of ours, if the signs of his appearing keep pace with where they are currently. We are going to have a small army of bond servants, like the apostles. It is possible that this army of bond servants will walk in miracles, signs, and wonders as a part of God's witness to all nations. It is possible that these bond servants will be like the two witnesses that God sends to vex the Antichrist and his kingdom later in the book.

This could be the point where the Lord's Spirit ceases striving with humanity, when everyone receives either the mark of the beast or the seal of the Holy Spirit. This is a sobering possibility.

And [then] I heard how many were sealed (marked) out of every tribe of the sons of Israel: there were 144,000. (Rev. 7:4)

Many argue, "See, it must refer to the nation of Israel, excluding the Church." We have already established that Jesus has said that "He has sheep not of this fold and he must gather them also and then there will be one flock and one Shepherd." (John 10:16, author's paraphrase) Also, Paul writes that "it is not only those who are born Jewish that are the true Israel." (Rom. 9:16, author's paraphrase) Then Paul states in Philippians 3:3; that "we (Christians) are the true circumcision who worship Christ from the spirit and have no confidence in the flesh." (author's paraphrase) Jesus states he is coming for his bride, the Church, and she is without spot or blemish. You and I are a part of the bride of Christ. Do you have any spots or blemishes in you? Apart from Christ, we are full of spots and blemishes, but in Christ, he makes us what we can never be apart from his gift of grace. The key part is at the beginning of this book of Revelation:

> [THIS IS] the revelation of Jesus Christ [His unveiling of the divine mysteries]. God gave it to Him to disclose and make known to His bond servants certain things which must shortly and speedily come to pass in their entirety. (Rev. 1:1) (emphasis mine)

God addresses the book of Revelation to his bond servants, and God seals them according to this passage.

Paul also states in Romans 2:28–29 that the person "is not a Jew because of circumcision of the skin but of the heart and spirit and receives his praise from God and not man." (author's paraphrase) Many say that this number is symbolic, and it is not to be taken literally, but it is a symbol of the twelve tribes squared and then multiplied by a thousand. And even that is not completely true, as God excludes the tribe of Dan. God lists Joseph twice in this list, first under his own name and then through his son, Manasseh. Many scholars believe Dan's exclusion is because of his consistent and unrepentant idol worship.

> Twelve thousand were sealed (marked) out of the tribe of Judah, 12,000 of the tribe of Reuben, 12,000 of the tribe of Gad, Twelve thousand of the tribe of Asher, 12,000 of the tribe of Naphtali, 12,000 of the tribe of Manasseh, Twelve thousand of the tribe of Simeon, 12,000 of the tribe of Levi, 12,000 of the tribe of Issachar, Twelve thousand of the tribe of Zebulun, 12,000 of the tribe of Joseph, 12,000 of the tribe of Benjamin. (Rev. 7:5–8)

Many say of the preceding verses that this is clearly about the nation of Israel, and others say that it is spiritual Israel. Either way, if you are here during this time, then you desire to be in this group somewhere. If you are not, you will want to be sealed with the Holy Spirit of God as a child of God. There are only two seals: the mark of the beast or the seal of the Holy Spirit. It is your call.

> After this I looked and a vast host appeared which no one could count, [gathered out] of every nation, from all tribes and peoples and languages. These stood before the throne and before the Lamb; they were attired in white robes, with palm branches in their hands. (Rev. 7:9)

Okay, so here is a second group within the sixth seal that is distinct from the first group, who God has identified as bond servants. This is a group that no one could count. The scene pictured here appears to suggest the people of God throughout all the ages, from Adam and Eve to the last person saved during the Tribulation. A Google search estimates our planet has a population of just over eight billion. It is impossible to quantify this group in Revelation 7:9. They are before the throne and the Lamb, so that should show that they are in heaven. However, they could be on the earth as pictured in the millennial reign or the eternal kingdom as well. But timelines are unclear: How long was it between the sealing of the bond servants and this second group in heaven? Could this be a snapshot of a picture after the tally is totally in?

This writer sees the book of Revelation as intermittently sequential. We do not see the events in the second seal come to pass on the world stage until after we have seen the events of the first seal come to pass on the world stage, and so on. However, after the seventh seal and its contents, the voices in heaven declared, "it is finished." After that, we have snapshots of different periods of time within one of the seven seals, and the landmarks contained within the prophecy identify these. For example, chapter 13 talks about the beast or the time of the Antichrist, which is probably contained in the first or second seal. Chapters 15 and 16 deal with the bowl judgments, which are the last of God's judgments, so this would be in the seventh seal or portion of the letter, etcetera.

Basically, it appears to be initially sequential: the first section of the letter or broken seal, which discloses the contents of that section. Then the second section of the letter, disclosed by the breaking of the second seal, and so on. However, in many places, we see elements that belong in other seals later in the book, as already mentioned. While it starts off sequentially, later it shifts in and out with distinct elements, almost like giving a closer view of a scene we have already seen before. My love for movies has shown me how films often revisit scenes, highlighting distinct elements previously unseen. If anyone has ever seen the movie Vantage Point, that is a perfect illustration of the concept, starting over from the beginning of the movie but from a different perspective, and then repeating that pattern multiple times.

What point in the book of Revelation does this start? We clearly see this after the seventh trumpet, which marks the end of humankind's history before the millennial reign; the text states that the kingdoms of this world have become the kingdoms of our Lord and of his Christ. This is a transfer of power and ownership. It could, however, start at this junction in the sixth seal because we have a picture of innumerable people before the throne of God, and the previous verse is about the sealing of the 144,000 bond servants during the period of the Tribulation.

In a loud voice they cried, saying, [Our] salvation is due to our God, Who is seated on the throne, and to the Lamb [to Them we owe our deliverance]! And all the angels were standing round the throne and round the elders [of the heavenly Sanhedrin] and the four living creatures, and they fell prostrate before the throne and worshiped God. Amen! (So be it!) they cried. Blessing and glory and majesty and splendor and wisdom and thanks and honor and power and might [be ascribed] to our God to the ages and ages (forever and ever, throughout the eternities of the eternities)! Amen! (So be it!). (Rev. 7:10–12)

A praise session in heaven now begins with this second group of believers; the angels, elders, and cherubim join in.

Then, addressing me, one of the elders [of the heavenly Sanhedrin] said, who are these [people] clothed in the long white robes? And from where have they come? (Rev. 7:13)

I replied, Sir, you know. And he said to me, these are they who have come out of the great tribulation (persecution), and have washed their robes and made them white in the blood of the Lamb. (Rev. 7:14)

They appear to be those who get saved during the Great Tribulation. It is more probable these are believers from every age because their number is innumerable. There will probably be a large number that are killed during the Great Tribulation, but that number is probably ascertainable.

There will come a point in time where the Spirit of God will stop striving with humans—this is a fact. It is not a fact that it will happen in the Great Tribulation, although that seems more probable than not. It would make very little sense to say it would happen in the eternal state when we have a new heaven and a new earth. At that point, everything, including Satan and his demons, God will seal for all eternity. That would only leave the millennial reign of Christ, when Satan leads a last-ditch revolt against God. Then God throws them into the lake of fire for all eternity.

> For this reason they are [now] before the [very] throne of God and serve Him day and night in His sanctuary (temple); and He Who is sitting upon the throne will protect and spread His tabernacle over and shelter them with His presence. (Rev. 7:15)

Have you ever been in the presence of God? There is absolutely nothing like it!

> They shall hunger no more, neither thirst any more; neither shall the sun smite them, nor any scorching heat. (Rev. 7:16)

No more hunger or thirst; our new bodies, which we have touched on before, are no longer frail and mortal. However, later in the book, God invites us to the marriage supper of the Lamb. We will enjoy eating but not need to. I am not in the least bit saying this to promote gluttony, but won't it be nice to eat whatever you desire without worrying about how it's going to make you look in that white robe?

> For the Lamb Who is in the midst of the throne will be their Shepherd, and He will guide them to the springs of the waters of life; and God will wipe away every tear from their eyes. (Rev. 7:17)

What a comfort our God is! Whether you believe this verse is speaking to those who come out of the Great Tribulation as spoken of in Matthew 24, or those who believe this speaks to all of God's covenant people of all ages.

> WHEN HE [the Lamb] broke open the seventh seal, there was silence for about half an hour in heaven. (Rev. 8:1)

Finally, we are up to the seventh seal, and the first thing that we encounter is silence, almost like the calm before the storm.

Seven Angels with the Seven Trumpets

Then I saw the seven angels who stand before God, and to them were given seven trumpets. (Rev. 8:2)

The seven trumpets are within the seventh seal, and they are a part of the ultimate act of God before the millennial reign of Christ. The Scriptures repeatedly claim that angels and demons exist. Just a casual read through the Gospels shows angels involved with Jesus's birth, his mother and father being visited by angels, and Jesus being ministered to by angels after Satan tempted him. Jesus cast out many demons in his ministry, and we should not assume he was playing for effect. If you believe in Jesus, you must believe what he says is true. He is the Savior of the world and the Lamb of God, slain before the foundations of the world for our salvation. Or he is the biggest liar in human history! You cannot have it both ways.

> And another angel came and stood over the altar. He had a golden censer, and he was given very much incense (fragrant spices and gums which exhale perfume when burned), that he might mingle it with the prayers of all the people of God (the saints) upon the golden altar before the throne. And the smoke of the incense (the perfume) arose in the presence of God, with the prayers of the people of God (the saints), from the hand of the angel. So, the angel took the censer and filled it with fire from the altar and cast it upon the earth. Then there followed peals of thunder and loud rumblings and blasts and noises, and flashes of lightning and an earthquake. (Rev. 8:3–5)

We have a cut scene here that has some interesting insights. It is an interaction among an administration of an angel, God's people, and God himself. In the book of Hebrews, among other places, we learn that what we have or had in the earthly tabernacle, altar, etcetera are only copies of the originals in heaven. They represent the genuine items before God. God gives the angel incense, and he mingles the incense with the prayers of God's people. Smoke arises in the presence of God with this mixture. After this mixture arises before God, the angel takes coals from the altar and casts it on the earth, and we have thunder, lightning, loud noises, and an earthquake. Every participant must play their part.

Here is what is interesting: In Matthew 16:19, Jesus teaches us that "what is bound in heaven is bound on the earth, and what we loose in heaven is loosed on the earth." (author's paraphrase) Our prayers have much greater significance in the world's state than we may have imagined.

> Then the seven angels who had the seven trumpets prepared to sound them. The first angel blew [his] trumpet, and there was a storm of hail and fire mingled with blood cast upon the earth. And a third part of the earth was burned up and a third of the trees was burned up and all the green grass was burned up. (Rev. 8:6–7)

What is this trumpet? What is the angel's name? Do we need to know? There is enough revealed here to occupy our minds and hearts without knowing every little detail. Unless you prefer a figurative interpretation, the hard, cold fact is that one-third of the world burned up. Could it be America? In God, we trust does not even sound sincere anymore. My purpose in saying this is not to promote sensationalism but to give a reality check. If this interpretation is literal, then we are going to be missing some continents. End-time events nowhere describe a land easily recognized as the United States. It talks of Russia, Iraq, Iran, Israel, China, and more. It is conceivable that this once-great nation, who is wallowing in sin and yet claims to be a Christian nation, is going to learn the lesson of ancient Israel. God allowed them to be taken into captivity repeatedly because of the Israelites' hard hearts and rebellious ways. A "stiff-necked people," I believe he called them. The Bible does not say America will not be around in end-time events. Omitting any mention of land recognizable as Canada or North or South America is curious.

However, to be fair, there are many Bible scholars who suggest that America will be a part of the revived Roman Empire of the Antichrist. There are even some who suggest that America is the beast. (There are a lot of interpretations of this book.) Fire incapacitates one-third of the earth.

> The second angel blew [his] trumpet, and something resembling a great mountain, blazing with fire, was hurled into the sea. (Rev. 8:8)

Do we need to know what this is before it happens? A great mountainlike object, perhaps a meteorite, hurls into the sea? Maybe what is important is what it does as it turns one-third of the sea to blood. Is this a literal depiction? That appears to be the case because whatever it is, it is not conducive to human or aquatic life. That is the important part.

> And a third of the sea was turned to blood, a third of the living creatures in the sea perished, and a third of the ships were destroyed. The third angel blew [his] trumpet, and a huge star fell from heaven, burning like a torch, and it dropped on a third of the rivers and on the springs of water—And the name of the star is Wormwood. A third part of the waters was changed into wormwood, and many people died from using the water, because it had become bitter. (Rev. 8:9–11)

I believe the star symbolizes an angel, and I will shortly provide evidence explaining why. However, the result is many people die from drinking the contaminated water.

> Then the fourth angel blew [his] trumpet, and a third of the sun was smitten, and a third of the moon, and a third of the stars, so that [the light of] a third of them was darkened, and a third of the daylight [itself] was withdrawn, and likewise a third [of the light] of the night was kept from shining. (Rev. 8:12)

> We have seen evidence of this before; we are getting very close now.

> Then I [looked and I] saw a solitary eagle flying in midheaven, and as it flew I heard it crying with a loud voice, Woe, woe, woe to those who dwell on the earth, because of the rest of the trumpet blasts which the three angels are about to sound! (Rev. 8:13)

CHAPTER 27

The Book of Revelation, Chapters 9-10

THEN THE fifth angel blew [his] trumpet, and I saw a star that had fallen from the sky to the earth; and to the angel was given the key of the shaft of the Abyss (the bottomless pit). (Rev. 9:1)

This Scripture is primarily why I have suggested that the former star was an angel. Stars do not use keys, and it says, "The star fell from heaven and to the angel was given." This is another symbol that Revelation unlocks for us. There are other symbols in the Scripture that represent angels, but this one is clear. Also, going back to Revelation chapter one, Jesus states that the seven stars in his right hand are the seven angels of the churches in Asia.

He opened the long shaft of the Abyss (the bottomless pit), and smoke like the smoke of a huge furnace puffed out of the long shaft, so that the sun and the atmosphere were darkened by the smoke from the long shaft. (Rev. 9:2)

What is being released here is a ton of demons, and as we go on, that will become more and more self-evident.

> Then out of the smoke locusts came forth on the earth, and such power was granted them as the power the earth's scorpions have. (Rev. 9:3)

The symbol of an angel is a star, but the symbol for these particular demons is locusts.

> They were told not to injure the herbage of the earth nor any green thing nor any tree, but only [to attack] such human beings as do not have the seal (mark) of God on their foreheads. (Rev. 9:4)

The bond slaves are not tormented, but it would suggest that the second group had better already be in heaven. Maybe the mid-Tribulation perspective has it right? Time will tell.

> They were not permitted to kill them, but to torment (distress, vex) them for five months; and the pain caused them was like the torture of a scorpion when it stings a person. And in those days people will seek death and will not find it; and they will yearn to die, but death evades and flees from them. (Rev. 9:5–6)

This pain will be excruciating enough that people will wish for death rather than endure this.

> The locusts resembled horses equipped for battle. On their heads was something like golden crowns. Their faces resembled the faces of people. They had hair like the hair of women, and their teeth were like lions' teeth. Their breastplates (scales)

resembled breastplates made of iron, and the [whirring] noise made by their wings was like the roar of a vast number of horse-drawn chariots going at full speed into battle. They have tails like scorpions, and they have stings, and in their tails lies their ability to hurt men for [the] five months. (Rev. 9:7–10)

Get a visual of these things; they sound ghastly! They have as king over them the king of the abyss, destruction, or destroyer, which is revealed in verse 11. If the king over them is a demon, what else can the locusts be? These appear to be demons, as what we see is temporary; what is unseen is eternal, as previously stated. For those who believe in the spiritual world, the concept that angels and demons exist goes hand-in-hand with the thought that God and Satan exist. Why does God allow Satan to exist? We would need another book to even broach that subject. God alone knows the depth and breadth of that elephant. What really grabs the attention is not their description as much as the angel opening the abyss and that they have a king over them known as the angel of the abyss, and his name is destruction or destroyer. It clearly states the king of the abyss is an angel in verse 11.

The King of the Abyss: Abaddon (Destruction) Apollyon (Destroyer)

Over them as king they have the angel of the Abyss (of the bottomless pit). In Hebrew his name is Abaddon [destruction], but in Greek he is called Apollyon [destroyer]. The first woe (calamity) has passed; behold, two others are yet to follow. (Rev. 9:11–12)

The first woe, then, is a release of demonic forces unlike anything the world has encountered before. Is there any evidence of this elsewhere in Scripture?

And angels who did not keep (care for, guard, and hold to) their own first place of power but abandoned their proper dwelling place—these He has reserved in custody in eternal chains (bonds) under the thick gloom of utter darkness until the judgment and doom of the great day. (Jude 1:6) (emphasis mine)

Then the sixth angel blew [his] trumpet, and from the four horns of the golden altar which stands before God I heard a solitary voice. (Rev. 9:13)

We have already mentioned what is in heaven is real and what the Jewish nation built were only earthly copies of the originals. We have these angels in various functions working around the actual altar and tabernacle with all that belong in it in heaven.

Saying to the sixth angel who had the trumpet, Liberate the four angels who are bound at the great river Euphrates. So the four angels who had been in readiness for that hour in the appointed day, month, and year were liberated to destroy a third of mankind. (Rev. 9:14–15)

One-third of humanity destroyed—that is a staggering number! No wonder Jesus said that unless God shortened those days, nobody would survive. The tragedy is that we bring this on ourselves. Just as the prayers of God's people mingled with incense have their repercussions on the earth, so does humankind's continued rebellion. The Bible states that "as it was in the days of Noah," and we have seen that they were thinking of only evil continuously, so it will be when the Son of Man returns. Obviously, this does not reflect the thoughts of God's elect, but the world at large. Let us consider that God's foreknowledge is not synonymous with predestination. God is not making us misbehave. He only knows ahead of time what we are going to choose. We are told not to accuse God of tempting us.

> Let no one say when he is tempted, I am tempted from God; for God is incapable of being tempted by [what is] evil and He Himself tempts no one. But every person is tempted when he is drawn away, enticed and baited by his own evil desire (lust, passions). Then the evil desire, when it has conceived, gives birth to sin, and sin, when it is fully matured, brings forth death. Do not be misled, my beloved brethren. (James 1:13–16)

> The number of their troops of cavalry was twice ten thousand times ten thousand (200,000,000); I heard what their number was. (Rev. 9:16)

It could be literal, or maybe these four angels appointed for this exact hour in humankind's history are influencing an army, or perhaps just its generals.

However, as we continue in the narrative, it appears more likely that the two hundred million mentioned in this verse are demons.

> And in [my] vision the horses and their riders appeared to me like this: the riders wore breastplates the color of fiery red and sapphire blue and sulphur (brimstone) yellow. The heads of the

horses looked like lions' heads, and from their mouths there poured fire and smoke and sulphur (brimstone). A third of mankind was killed by these three plagues—by the fire and the smoke and the sulphur (brimstone) that poured from the mouths of the horses. (Rev. 9:17–18)

These plagues kill one-third of humankind. Some might claim that three waves of plagues, each killing one-third of humanity, would cause annihilation. However, it seems each plague reduces the population, and the next plague takes one-third of the remaining population.

For the power of the horses to do harm is in their mouths and also in their tails. Their tails are like serpents, for they have heads, and it is by means of them that they wound people. (Rev. 9:19)

The description of these creatures appears again to be demonic. While we do not have something as focused as an angel of the abyss with a king over them, it would be likely as these creatures follow a similar pattern. If that is the case, as bad as the world is now, we have seen nothing yet!

For we are not wrestling with flesh and blood [contending only with physical opponents], but against the despotisms, against the powers, against [the master spirits who are] the world rulers of this present darkness, against the spirit forces of wickedness in the heavenly (supernatural) sphere. (Eph. 6:12)

And the rest of humanity who were not killed by these plagues even then did not repent of [the worship of] the works of their

[own] hands, so as to cease paying homage to the demons and idols of gold and silver and bronze and stone and wood, which can neither see nor hear nor move. And they did not repent of their murders or their practice of magic (sorceries) or their sexual vice or their thefts. (Rev. 9:20–21)

When we think of our American culture, one thing that is prominent is our pursuit of escape through illegal drugs. Pressures at this time are going to be enormous. The thought of many trying to escape this pressure through drugs is not a stretch at this point. The word "sorceries" in the preceding verse is Pharmakeia, which means medication, where we get the word "pharmacy" in English. By extension, it also means magic (literal or figurative), sorcery, and witchcraft, according to Strong's Exhaustive Concordance of the Bible.[11] The bath salts phenomenon has been an issue. Roadside witnesses saw a naked man eating another man's face in one extreme case. Who can say what is coming down the road next?

It is a powerful and sobering thought that God would give up on us. There comes a time, however, in the heart and mind of God, when enough is enough. He comes to the place of saying, "You want your way so much? Okay, it's yours!" This has always been a scary thought. The following Scriptures illustrate this truth poignantly.

For in the Gospel a righteousness which God ascribes is revealed, both springing from faith and leading to faith [disclosed through the way of faith that arouses to more faith]. As it is written, The man who through faith is just and upright shall live and shall live by faith. For God's [holy] wrath and indignation are revealed from heaven against all ungodliness and unrighteousness of men, who in their wickedness repress and hinder the truth and make it inoperative. For that which is known about God is evident to them and made plain in their inner consciousness, because God [Himself] has shown it to them. For ever since the creation of the world His invisible nature and attributes, that is, His eternal power and divinity, have been made intelligible and clearly discernible in and through the things that have been made (His handiworks). So [men] are without excuse [altogether without any defense or justification], because when they knew and recognized Him as God, they did not honor and glorify Him as God or give Him thanks. But instead they became futile and [godless in their thinking with vain imaginings, foolish reasoning, and stupid speculations] and their senseless minds were darkened. Claiming to be wise, they became fools [professing to be smart, they made simpletons of themselves]. And by them the glory and majesty and excellence of the immortal God were exchanged for and represented by images, resembling mortal man and birds and beasts and reptiles. Therefore God gave them up in the lusts of their [own] hearts to sexual impurity, to the dishonoring of their bodies among themselves [abandoning them to the degrading power of sin], because they exchanged the truth of God for a lie and worshiped and served the creature rather than the Creator, Who is blessed forever! Amen (so be it). For this reason God gave them over and abandoned them to vile affections and degrading passions. For their women exchanged their natural function for an unnatural and abnormal one, And the men also turned from natural relations with women and were set ablaze (burning out, consumed) with lust for one another— men committing shameful acts with men and suffering in their own bodies and personalities the inevitable consequences and penalty of their wrong-doing and going astray, which was [their] fitting retribution. And so, since they did not see fit to acknowledge God or approve of Him or consider Him worth the knowing, God gave them over to a base and condemned mind to do things not proper or decent but loathsome, until they were filled (permeated and saturated) with every kind of unrighteousness, iniquity, grasping and covetous greed, and malice. [They were] full of envy and jealousy, murder, strife, deceit and treachery, ill will and cruel ways. [They were] secret backbiters and gossipers, slanderers, hateful to and hating God, full of insolence, arrogance, [and] boasting; inventors of new forms of evil, disobedient and undutiful to parents. [They were] without understanding, conscienceless and faithless, heartless and loveless [and] merciless. Though they are fully aware of God's righteous decree that those who do such things deserve to die, they not only do them themselves but approve and applaud others who practice them. (Rom. 1:17–32) (emphasis mine)

Then the Lord said, My Spirit shall not forever dwell and strive with man. (Gen. 6:3)

God will give us what we want if we insist. He will not force us to choose him, although he does desire that we will.

Now let's continue with Revelation.

The Rainbow Angel

THEN I saw another mighty angel coming down from heaven, robed in a cloud, with a [halo like a] rainbow over his head; his face was like the sun, and his feet (legs) were like columns of fire. (Rev. 10:1)

Okay, so where were we? The sixth angel with the trumpet has loosed the four angels bound at the river Euphrates, and the event kills one-third of humankind. Now we have another cut scene before the blowing of the seventh trumpet.

> He had a little book (scroll) open in his hand. He set his right foot on the sea and his left foot on the land. (Rev. 10:2)

A mighty angel appears and has another scroll, but this one is open, and we will get to that shortly. There are those who believe that this mighty angel is Jesus himself, but that is doubtful, and we explore that in just a few verses.

> And he shouted with a loud voice like the roaring of a lion; and when he had shouted, the seven thunders gave voice and uttered their message in distinct words. And when the seven thunders had spoken (sounded), I was going to write [it down], but I heard a voice from heaven saying, Seal up what the seven thunders have said! Do not write it down! (Rev. 10:3–4)

God has excluded whatever these thunders uttered, so it is unwise of us to even speculate. It is interesting that the seven thunders seem to respond to the shout of the mighty angel.

> Then the [mighty] angel whom I had seen stationed on sea and land raised his right hand to heaven (the sky) And swore in the name of (by) Him Who lives forever and ever, Who created the heavens (sky) and all they contain, and the earth and all that it contains, and the sea and all that it contains. [He swore] that no more time should intervene and there should be no more waiting or delay. (Rev. 10:5–6)

Therefore, it is not probable that the mighty angel is Jesus because the angel swears by him who made heaven and earth and all that it contains. This is not conclusive because the Word of God has stated elsewhere that "since he could not swear by anything greater, he swore by himself." (Heb. 6:13, author's paraphrase) We have seen a lot of administrations performed by angels in this book. The natural reading would seem to support that it is an angel.

But that when the days come when the trumpet call of the seventh angel is about to be sounded, then God's mystery (His secret design, His hidden purpose), as He had announced the glad tidings to His servants the prophets, should be fulfilled (accomplished, completed). (Rev. 10:7)

This verse, and other verses like it, appear a few times throughout the book of Revelation. The book of Revelation appears to be a panorama rather than a story in chronological order, although the beginning appears to be sequential. We go in and out of different scenes that bring us ultimately back to this scene. Have you ever seen a movie that keeps flashing back, or sometimes forward, to a particular place in time? Then it will drop you off somewhere in the beginning or middle or toward the end and flash back to that place in time. There are movies that do this five or six times because that moment is of crucial importance. This same principle applies here; God drops us amid the seven seals and then builds until we return to the seventh trumpet sounding, and the kingdoms of this world become the kingdoms of our Christ and his God.

Then the voice that I heard from heaven spoke again to me, saying, Go and take the little book (scroll) which is open on the hand of the angel who is standing on the sea and on the land. (Rev. 10:8).

Okay, so now we are back to the mighty angel and the open scroll that is in his hand.

So I went up to the angel and asked him to give me the little book. And he said to me, Take it and eat it. It will embitter your stomach, though in your mouth it will be as sweet as honey. So I took the little book from the angel's hand and ate and swallowed it; it was as sweet as honey in my mouth, but once I had swallowed it, my stomach was embittered. Then they said to me, You are to make a fresh prophecy concerning many peoples and races and nations and languages and kings. (Rev. 10:9–11)

John is told to eat the book, and it will initially be sweet to the taste. However, once consumed, it becomes bitter. In eating this book, John is now enabled to make a fresh prophecy that includes many people, races, nations, languages, and kings.

We should keep this in mind as we approach the next chapter because this information, it seems, is beside the scroll that was sealed with seven seals. Or it's the same scroll, now fully opened because Jesus has broken the seals, and we are awaiting only the seventh trumpet of the seventh seal. In either case, we glean a much more up-close-and-personal look into events that are taking place on the earth at the time of the end.

CHAPTER 28

The Book of Revelation, Chapters 11-12

A REED [as a measuring rod] was then given to me, [shaped] like a staff, and I was told: Rise up and measure the sanctuary of God and the altar [of incense], and [number] those who worship there. (Rev. 11:1)

We will not be spending a lot of time here because there is considerable debate why God directs John to measure these various elements. Many believe God protects what John measured and does not protect what John did not measure. Given the following verse, that makes sense. The debate centers on exactly the elements symbolized by the sanctuary, the altar, and the worshippers.

But leave out of your measuring the court outside the sanctuary of God; omit that, for it is given over to the Gentiles (the nations), and they will trample the holy city underfoot for 42 months (three and one-half years). (Rev. 11:2)

Here we have a more detailed glimpse of the last three and a half years of humankind's history on earth. It does not appear to be the first three and a half years, when the Antichrist is relatively nice and appears to be a blessing for all humankind. Where he shows his true colors and makes war with the people of God and commits the abomination of desolation would be a more natural setting for this time, when the Gentiles or unbelievers tread the holy city and the sanctuary.

Remember the time of the Gentiles spoken of in Luke 21:24? The natural reading of Jerusalem being trod upon by Gentiles until the "time of the Gentiles is fulfilled" should include this setting, Jerusalem being trodden in 70 CE until the reign of the Antichrist. The natural reading of the prophecies in Daniel should be all the Gentile empires. That would be Babylon, the Medes and the Persians, Greece, and Rome, culminating in the revived Roman Empire with the last ten kings until the Messiah's kingdom.

The Two Witnesses

And I will grant the power of prophecy to My two witnesses for 1,260 days (42 months; three and one-half years), dressed in sackcloth, (Rev. 11:3)

Who are these two witnesses? The Bible does not identify them by name, although many say one of them will be Elijah. Malachi 4:5 states, "I will send you Elijah before the great day of the lord." (author's paraphrase) As we have seen, the day of the Lord is a Day of Judgment, some would say the Day of Judgment. There are also those who say he has already returned as John the Baptist, who came in the spirit and power of Elijah (Matt. 17:10–13) Elijah could come personally, as he was one of only two who did not taste of death. He was raptured into heaven, and God can do as he pleases. He could also develop a person like John the Baptist to come in the spirit and power of Elijah, out of the generation that will be a part of the end of the age. It is okay to speculate, but the truth is that we don't know for sure. We will only truly know when it is the appointed time.

These [witnesses] are the two olive trees and the two lampstands which stand before the Lord of the earth. (Rev. 11:4)

Olive trees produce oil, and oil is a symbol we have already established as an anointing of the Holy Spirit. We have also revealed lampstands to represent the Church, or light in the darkness. So these symbols depict the nature and essence of God's two witnesses.

And if anyone attempts to injure them, fire pours from their mouth and consumes their enemies; if anyone should attempt to harm them, thus he is doomed to be slain. (Rev. 11:5)

In 2 Kings 1:10, Elijah called down fire from heaven to consume the sacrifice on an altar in front of his enemies. This is another reason many have said that Elijah will be one of the two witnesses.

These [two witnesses] have power to shut up the sky, so that no rain may fall during the days of their prophesying (their prediction of events relating to Christ's kingdom and its speedy triumph); and they also have power to turn the waters into blood and to smite and scourge the earth with all manner of plagues as often as they choose. (Rev. 11:6).

ELIJAH THE Tishbite, of the temporary residents of Gilead, said to Ahab, As the Lord, the God of Israel, lives, before Whom I stand, there shall not be dew or rain these years but according to My word. (1 Kings 17:1)

We have mentioned before the miracles that accompanied Christ's First Coming. Is it hard to believe that miracles will usher in his Second Coming? Elijah had the grace of God on him to shut up heaven so that there was no rain in 1 Kings 17:1. This is another reason that people have said Elijah will be one of the two witnesses.

But when they have finished their testimony and their evidence is all in, the beast (monster) that comes up out of the Abyss (bottomless pit) will wage war on them, and conquer them and kill them. (Rev. 11:7)

Notice that the beast comes out of the bottomless pit. Regardless of what the man looks like, there is a demonic spirit that is operating through this man.

Now there is an encouraging word! After doing the Lord's work in the Lord's way, the beast from the bottomless pit conquers and kills them! Anybody want this job? Sometimes doing God's will does not exclude suffering or even dying. And it doesn't mean you're not doing it right! Jesus said in this passage:

> And going a little farther, He threw Himself upon the ground on His face and prayed saying, My Father, if it is possible, let this cup pass away from Me; nevertheless, not what I will [not what I desire], but as You will and desire. (Matt. 26:39)

Jesus then went to the cross to die for all the stupid, sinful things we all have done. Now back to Revelation 11.

> And their dead bodies [will lie exposed] in the open street (a public square) of the great city which is in a spiritual sense called [by the mystical and allegorical names of] Sodom and Egypt, where also their Lord was crucified. (Rev. 11:8)

We all know where the Romans crucified Christ, so this witnessing takes place in Jerusalem. This makes sense because the Antichrist sets up the abomination of desolation and proclaims that he is god in the temple.

> For three and a half days men from the races and tribes and languages and nations will gaze at their dead bodies and will not allow them to be put in a tomb. And those who dwell on the earth will gloat and exult over them and rejoice exceedingly, taking their ease and sending presents [in congratulation] to one another, because these two prophets had been such a vexation and trouble and torment to all the dwellers on the earth. (Rev. 11:9–10)

The world will have a party because those thorns in their sides have finally been silenced.

> But after three and a half days, by God's gift the breath of life again entered into them, and they rose up on their feet, and great dread and terror fell on those who watched them. Then [the two witnesses] heard a strong voice from heaven calling to them, Come up here! And before the very eyes of their enemies they ascended into heaven in a cloud. (Rev. 11:11–12)

Well, we are certainly having an early rapture here. It is not the last day yet, and God raptures the two witnesses up to heaven. There are exceptions to every rule. In the lives of Enoch and Elijah, for example, they were both transported to heaven without seeing death. (Gen. 5:24 and 1 Kings 2:11) This would appear to be in direct conflict with the Scripture found in Hebrews 9:27: "It is appointed that men are going to die once and then after that the judgment." (author's paraphrase) They did not die. Have they had God's judgment yet?

God is God, and no one can confine or limit him. Now God does not lie, but the Bible states, "His ways are above our ways and his thoughts are above our thoughts, even farther than the heavens are above us." (Isa. 55:8–9, author's paraphrase) Think of it this way: Insects have brains. Now, for the sake of argument, pretend that you can communicate with an ant. Imagine yourself trying to explain to the ant the concept of international banking procedures, or the vastness of the internet. That gives us just a tiny window into comparing God's ways and thoughts being above ours. There is always an angle we have not considered in our very limited understanding.

One way that God could reconcile these apparently opposing statements is to have Enoch and Elijah come back at the end of the age as his two witnesses. Then death would claim both of them, preserving both concepts. Is this what is going to happen? Probably not. It just illustrates one possibility among a multitude of others. The point is that God is so far beyond us, we are foolish to believe there are any apparent contradictions that he does not have an answer for. He reached out to us and revealed what he wanted us to know. The two dead witnesses rise, and the world watches in astonishment.

> And at that [very] hour there was a tremendous earthquake and one tenth of the city was destroyed (fell); seven thousand people perished in the earthquake, and those who remained were filled with dread and terror and were awe-struck, and they glorified the God of heaven. (Rev. 11:13)

Remember when Jesus died, and there was a huge earthquake? God ripped the veil in the temple from the top to the bottom. (Matt. 27:50–54) The very elements gave testimony that this was the Son of God they had just killed. That appears to be happening here: the Lord giving testimony concerning his two witnesses.

> The second woe (calamity) has passed; now the third woe is speedily to come. (Rev. 11:14)

The first woe was in the fifth trumpet with the release of the demonic horde. They had a king over them named Destroyer. Their power was to torment humankind for five months, but not to kill them.

> The seventh angel then blew [his] trumpet, and there were mighty voices in heaven, shouting, the dominion (kingdom, sovereignty, rule) of the world has now come into the possession and become the kingdom of our Lord and of His Christ (the

Messiah), and He shall reign forever and ever (for the eternities of the eternities)! (Rev. 11:15)

The seventh angel has sounded, and we are once again to the point of the kingdoms of the world, having become the kingdom of our Lord and of his Christ! This would appear to be the last trumpet spoken of in 1 Thessalonians. This is not conclusive, but the timing of both events appears to be similar, so it is possible.

> For this we declare to you by the Lord's [own] word, that we who are alive and remain until the coming of the Lord shall in no way precede [into His presence] or have any advantage at all over those who have previously fallen asleep [in Him in death]. For the Lord Himself will descend from heaven with a loud cry of summons, with the shout of an archangel, and with the blast of the trumpet of God. And those who have departed this life in Christ will rise first. (1 Thess. 4:15–16)

The strong and mighty angels found in Revelation, then, if this is correct, might be archangels. We only know of three archangels: Michael, the warrior-prince-protector over Israel; Gabriel, the herald or announcer of God; and Lucifer, the fallen. There is a strong probability that there are more than the three that are named.

> Then we, the living ones who remain [on the earth], shall simultaneously be caught up along with [the resurrected dead] in the clouds to meet the Lord in the air; and so always (through the eternity of the eternities) we shall be with the Lord! Therefore comfort and encourage one another with these words. (1 Thess. 4:17–18)

Now let's return to Revelation 11.

Then the twenty-four elders [of the heavenly Sanhedrin], who sit on their thrones before God, prostrated themselves before Him and worshiped, Exclaiming, To You we give thanks, Lord God Omnipotent, [the One] Who is and [ever] was, for assuming the high sovereignty and the great power that are Yours and for beginning to reign. (Rev. 11:16–17)

God has finally started reigning on earth! It is at this point that the millennial reign begins, though we have not gotten there yet in the text.

And the heathen (the nations) raged, but Your wrath (retribution, indignation) came, the time when the dead will be judged and Your servants the prophets and saints rewarded— and those who revere (fear) Your name, both low and high and small and great—and [the time] for destroying the corrupters of the earth. (Rev. 11:18)

There is a lot going on here: God's wrath has vanquished the ungodly. God will judge the dead. We will see later that at this point it is only believers whom God judges. God rewards his servants from every spectrum.

Then the sanctuary of God in heaven was thrown open, and the ark of His covenant was seen standing inside in His sanctuary; and there were flashes of lightning, loud rumblings (blasts, mutterings), peals of thunder, an earthquake, and a terrific hailstorm. (Rev. 11:19)

The true sanctuary in heaven is open, of which what has been on earth is only a representative. Have you ever seen professional wrestling? Someone comes down the ramp, the pyrotechnics are exploding, and the wrestler strikes a stunning pose. It speaks of excitement and anticipation: he has arrived! That is the picture here, and while professional wrestling is not real, it captures a similar ambience.

There is undoubtedly some deeper significance to the sanctuary being opened and all the thunder, lightning, etcetera. I will leave that to those who are much more gifted in this area and just enjoy the glory.

Okay, now we are shifting gears again, as the seventh trumpet has sounded. The kingdoms of this world have become the kingdom of our Christ and of his God. We are at the culmination of humankind's history on earth. God has finally taken his throne on earth. What follows are various glimpses into our past, but predominantly the time of the Great Tribulation. However, the first part of chapter 12 is more of an overview of humankind's entire history until verse 6, when we focus back in on the last three and a half years of the Tribulation.

Woman Clothed with the Sun

AND A great sign (wonder)—[warning of future events of ominous significance] appeared in heaven: a woman clothed with the sun, with the moon under her feet, and with a crownlike garland (tiara) of twelve stars on her head. (Rev. 12:1)

There is a dream that Joseph in the Old Testament had about the sun, moon, and eleven stars bowing down before him. If we included Joseph himself, that would make twelve stars. (Gen. 37:9) Jacob was his father and later, God changed his name to Israel. (Gen. 32:28) This, by itself, would not be conclusive. Later in verse 5, this woman brings forth a baby who shall rule all nations, and that can only be Jesus.

I love the Amplified Bible, but possibly they got this part wrong. As a lover of Scripture with a little knowledge of the original biblical Greek, Hebrew, and Aramaic, I believe the Amplified Bible's translators conscientiously strove to remain true to the original text while expanding upon it, giving a fuller flavor to those who struggle with other translations. We are all human, and in this text, it truly appears to be a picture of Israel giving birth to the Christ that Satan tries to destroy. So saying that it was a sign of future events may not be as accurate as the Amplified Bible would have liked. After many years of personal and some professional study, though, I believe the Amplified Bible truly attempts to be honest in its translation.

> She was pregnant and she cried out in her birth pangs, in the anguish of her delivery. Then another ominous sign (wonder) was seen in heaven: Behold, a huge, fiery-red dragon, with seven heads and ten horns, and seven kingly crowns (diadems) upon his heads. (Rev. 12:2–3)

Okay, we must include some of the prophecy of Daniel, for we are talking about both the Antichrist and Satan. We have already broached this prophecy earlier in the book. I will give a quick review: Daniel had a dream about a bunch of different beasts and the nations that would come to world power: Babylon, the Medes and Persia, Greece, Rome, and then the revived Roman Empire with ten rulers. Which is the last one before the messianic kingdom. We will look a little further at this prophecy as it parallels closely with Revelation and the Antichrist.

> After this I saw in the night visions, and behold, a fourth beast [the Roman Empire]—terrible, powerful and dreadful, and exceedingly strong. And it had great iron teeth; it devoured and crushed and trampled what was left with its feet. And it was different from all the beasts that came before it, and it had ten horns [symbolizing ten kings]. (Dan. 7:7)

The Bible symbolizes horns to denote power and aggressive strength. Think of two rams battling and locking horns. By extension, they also may signify kings or kingdoms.

> I considered the horns, and behold, there came up among them another horn, a little one, before which three of the first horns were plucked up by the roots; and behold, in this horn were eyes like the eyes of a man and a mouth speaking great things. (Dan. 7:8)

In this prophecy of the ten horns, we have one who destroys three of the horns, or kings. He talks a lot of smack. We had ten horns, and then from among the ten appears a little horn, so now we are at eleven. However, the little horn gets rid of three horns, so we have a new total of eight.

> I kept looking until thrones were placed [for the assessors with the Judge], and the Ancient of Days [God, the eternal Father] took His seat, whose garment was white as snow and the hair of His head like pure wool. His throne was like the fiery flame; its wheels were burning fire. (Dan. 7:9)

We have seen a similar image in this book of the Revelation.

A stream of fire came forth from before Him; a thousand thousands ministered to Him and ten thousand times ten thousand rose up and stood before Him; the Judge was seated [the court was in session] and the books were opened. (Dan. 7:10)

We have seen this image in Revelation as well.

I looked then because of the sound of the great words which the horn was speaking. I watched until the beast was slain and its body destroyed and given over to be burned with fire. And as for the rest of the beasts, their power of dominion was taken away; yet their lives were prolonged [for the duration of their lives was fixed] for a season and a time. I saw in the night visions, and behold, on the clouds of the heavens came One like a Son of man, and He came to the Ancient of Days and was presented before Him. And there was given Him [the Messiah] dominion and glory and kingdom, that all peoples, nations, and languages should serve Him. His dominion is an everlasting dominion which shall not pass away, and His kingdom is one which shall not be destroyed. As for me, Daniel, my spirit was grieved and anxious within me, and the visions of my head alarmed and agitated me. I came near to one of those who stood there and asked him the truth of all this. So he told me and made known to me the interpretation of the things. These four great beasts are four kings who shall arise out of the earth. But the saints of the Most High [God] shall receive the kingdom and possess the kingdom forever, even forever and ever. (Dan. 7:11–18)

In the end, this is true: the meek shall inherit the earth in the millennial kingdom. But during the time of this horn or king, the Antichrist will make war with God's people. The Antichrist will prevail against them until Christ's appearing brings his time to an end.

> Then I wished to know the truth about the fourth beast—which was different from all the others, exceedingly terrible and shocking, whose teeth were of iron and its nails of bronze, which devoured, broke and crushed, and trampled what was left with its feet—And about the ten horns, which represents kings, that were on its head, and the other horn which came up later and before which three of the horns fell, the horn which had eyes and a mouth that spoke great things and which looked greater than the others. As I looked, this horn made war with the saints and prevailed over them. Until the Ancient of Days came, and judgment was given to the saints of the Most High God, and the time came when the saints possessed the kingdom. (Dan. 7:19–22)

Here it is much clearer that the Antichrist has his moment until the Ancient of Days comes, and we possess the kingdom.

> Thus [the angel] said, The fourth beast shall be a fourth kingdom on earth, which shall be different from all other kingdoms and shall devour the whole earth, tread it down, and break it in pieces and crush it. And as for the ten horns, out of this kingdom ten kings shall arise; and another shall arise after them, and he shall be different from the former ones, and he shall subdue and put down three kings. And he shall speak words against the Most High [God] and shall wear out the saints of the Most High and think to change the time [of sacred feasts and holy

days] and the law; and the saints shall be given into his hand for a time, two times, and half a time [three and one-half years]. (Dan. 7:23–25)

The Antichrist will have his moment of power for three and a half years. This dovetails with Revelation.

But the judgment shall be set [by the court of the Most High], and they shall take away his dominion to consume it [gradually] and to destroy it [suddenly] in the end. And the kingdom and the dominion and the greatness of the kingdom under the whole heavens shall be given to the people of the saints of the Most High; His kingdom is an everlasting kingdom, and all the dominions shall serve and obey Him. (Dan. 7:26–27)

Okay, now that we have seen the Antichrist in this prophecy in Revelation dovetail with the prophecy in Daniel, let's look at how Satan figures into this as well:

His tail swept [across the sky] and dragged down a third of the stars and flung them to the earth. And the dragon stationed himself in front of the woman who was about to be delivered, so that he might devour her child as soon as she brought it forth. (Rev. 12:4)

This verse is talking about Satan himself. We have seen that stars are a symbol of angels, and he takes one-third with him. In keeping with this scene, we have Satan taking one-third of the angels with him. This leaves two-thirds on the side of God—not that God needs it, but I like those odds!

This cannot be the Antichrist, even though later we see Satan gives the Antichrist his own throne, power, might, and great dominion. Also, Satan sought the child's life when Jesus was born through Herod and probably others.

> And she brought forth a male Child, One Who is destined to shepherd (rule) all the nations with an iron staff (scepter), and her Child was caught up to God and to His throne. (Rev. 12:5)

This can be no one else but our Lord and Savior, Jesus.

> And the woman [herself] fled into the desert (wilderness), where she has a retreat prepared [for her] by God, in which she is to be fed and kept safe for 1,260 days (42 months; three and one-half years). (Rev. 12:6)

God himself prepares this sanctuary in the wilderness. Notice the jump here. We have been doing an overview of the nation of Israel giving birth to the Messiah. Spiritual warfare in heaven with Satan being cast out. However, now we are zeroing in on the last three and a half years of humankind's history with a retreat prepared by God for his people. It is places like this where we jump "time zones" that make Revelation difficult to follow.

Personally, I do not think we will know more until it is the proper season. Now while she was only Israel before bringing forth the child, as we have seen, the child changed some things before going back to his throne. We now have one flock and one shepherd. The woman, by Jesus's own admonition, has undergone a metamorphosis and comprises the Church and messianic Jewish people. She has a sanctuary prepared by God to keep her safe for three and a half years during the reign of the Antichrist. Not all the people of God take advantage of this sanctuary. We have seen that the Antichrist makes war with the saints and prevails. Later in Revelation, the Antichrist beheads many for their testimony to Jesus. Some are safe in this sanctuary, and some are safe through martyrdom. This may not sound very safe to some. Ultimately, we are safe, as the second death, which we shall get to, does not affect us, whether we are in the sanctuary or martyred for the Lord, and that truly is safe. The lessons throughout the Scriptures on this topic deal with preparedness. The difference between those martyred and those in the sanctuary may be the difference between those who prepare themselves and those who do not.

Michael the Archangel Battling the Dragon

Then war broke out in heaven; Michael and his angels went forth to battle with the dragon, and the dragon and his angels fought. (Rev. 12:7)

Again, this is Satan, not the Antichrist, and that part is plain.

But they were defeated, and there was no room found for them in heaven any longer. (Rev. 12:8)

The Dragon of Revelation 12

And the huge dragon was cast down and out—that age-old serpent, who is called the Devil and Satan, he who is the seducer (deceiver) of all humanity the world over; he was forced out and down to the earth, and his angels were flung out along with him. (Rev. 12:9)

The cross of Christ triumphed over the forces of darkness, and Satan is now limited to his influence on this world. We believers are wrestling not against what we can see but "against the spiritual forces of darkness of this present age," which are Satan and his demons. (Eph. 6:12, author's paraphrase) Notice, again, that we have jumped back into "overview" mode. This spiritual warfare between Micheal and Satan makes more sense at the cross where they were defeated. If it was at the end of the age, all the demonic forces would be cast into the lake of fire—which we will get to later in the book of Revelation—and Satan would be bound and cast into the bottomless pit.

> Then I heard a strong (loud) voice in heaven, saying, Now it has come—the salvation and the power and the kingdom (the dominion, the reign) of our God, and the power (the sovereignty, the authority) of His Christ (the Messiah); for the accuser of our brethren, he who keeps bringing before our God charges against them day and night, has been cast out! (Rev. 12:10)

This appears to be at the cross of Christ rather than the consummation of the age. We will see shortly that, after the kingdoms of this world become the kingdoms of our Christ and of his God, Satan is bound for a thousand years, then loosed briefly, and after the last attempt, God cast him into the lake of fire for all eternity. If Satan can see all this, why does he continue this path? Assuredly he can read. What else does he have but the opportunity to hurt God by hurting his children? Apparently, heaven no longer allows him entry, so he lacks direct access to God's throne room. All he has left is his rage and hate. While it must gall him to do what God has said he was going to do, that's all he has left. He'll strike any blow, even though it proves God right.

And they have overcome (conquered) him by means of the blood of the Lamb and by the utterance of their testimony, for they did not love and cling to life even when faced with death [holding their lives cheap till they had to die for their witnessing]. (Rev. 12:11)

One reason is that through him who loved us, we can grow and overcome Satan. That has significant eternal ramifications, from the cross to the sounding of the seventh trumpet. From the kingdoms of this world becoming the kingdoms of our Christ and of his God, this is our pattern of overcoming Satan.

1.   The blood of the Lamb. It has absolutely nothing to do with us except our acceptance of his sacrifice as payment for our sins.

2.   The word of our testimony. Here is where we come testifying to the goodness of the Lord in a lost world. Jesus said, "Whoever confesses him before men that he will also positively testify concerning that person before his Father and the angels in heaven." (Luke 12:8, author's paraphrase)

3.   They loved not their lives unto death. This is the ultimate level, of course, in any Christian's quest for maturity. It, of course, applies to being a martyr during the time of the Great Tribulation. It probably applies also throughout all the ages of God's people. This verse doesn't mention dying to self, but that principle might also apply here.

Therefore be glad (exult), O heavens and you that dwell in them! But woe to you, O earth and sea, for the devil has come down to you in fierce anger (fury), because he knows that he has [only] a short time [left]! (Rev. 12:12)

Heaven rejoices that Christ's cross banished Satan from heaven at last, but the earth is in trouble because Satan understands the implications.

> And when the dragon saw that he was cast down to the earth, he went in pursuit of the woman who had given birth to the male Child. (Rev. 12:13)

Being kicked out of heaven and full of spite, Satan goes after what is available to him: the object of God's love that Jesus has just redeemed. God could throw Satan into the lake of fire now. However, the priority for God appears to be in raising a kingdom of kings and priests for his purposes through redeemed humankind. And there is something in the testing and trying of our faith that other means cannot duplicate. Peter tells us, "The trying of our faith is infinitely more precious than fine gold, which is going to rebound to our honor and glory when Jesus is revealed." (1 Pet. 1:7, author's paraphrase) As already discussed, Satan is on a leash. He cannot do whatever comes into his twisted mind. But for some, those limits are less than others. God knows what we can handle if we will rely on him. Many of us would ask God to not trust us so much. However, we need to see this, considering eternity and trust, that even though God does not spell out all the whys of what he allows the enemy and evil men and women to do, there are reasons.

Woman with Eagles Wings in the Desert

But the woman was supplied with the two wings of a giant eagle, so that she might fly from the presence of the serpent into the desert (wilderness), to the retreat where she is to be kept safe and fed for a time, and times, and half a time (three and one-half years, or 1,260 days). (Rev. 12:14)

The serpent in the garden and in many other places is Satan, of course. God gives people wings to evade the serpent for three and a half years. What are the wings? I don't have a clue. It is enough for me that at least some of God's people have protection during this period. As we draw closer to these events, time itself might make it apparent. Maybe those gifted with symbolism can shed light. The point is, we do not need to understand it all to be prepared and obedient.

> Then out of his mouth the serpent spouted forth water like a flood after the woman that she might be carried off with the torrent. (Rev. 12:15)

Again, I will not attempt the symbolism here. It is sufficiently clear that Satan tries to destroy the people of God.

> But the earth came to the rescue of the woman, and the ground opened its mouth and swallowed up the stream of water which the dragon had spouted from his mouth. (Rev. 12:16)

Sorry again. God rescues the people of God. See, that much is clear, regardless of whether you see all this as allegorical or literal. We don't need to have an answer for everything. It is very possible that those who do not know the Lord or are seekers will have more respect for people who can admit that we don't have all the answers. Statistically speaking, in school while you were taking tests, did you always score one hundred? Seekers are not stupid; they know we can't possibly know it all. Let's just admit that.

So then the dragon was furious (enraged) at the woman, and he went away to wage war on the remainder of her descendants—[on those] who obey God's commandments and who have the testimony of Jesus Christ [and adhere to it and bear witness to Him]. (Rev. 12:17)

Satan attacks God's people—no surprise there. What other choice does he have? We should also note that, while Israel was the woman who gave birth to the child, this verse clearly states that her descendants possess the testimony of Jesus Christ. As Christians, we now have the testimony of Jesus Christ.

Seven Headed Beast coming out of the Sea

[AS] I stood on the sandy beach, I saw a beast coming up out of the sea with ten horns and seven heads. On his horns he had ten royal crowns (diadems) and blasphemous titles (names) on his heads. (Rev. 13:1)

CHAPTER 29

The Book of Revelation, Chapters 13-14

O kay, now we're back to dealing with the Antichrist and the last ten rulers of the new world order. According to the prophecy in Daniel and now here in Revelation, we have left the overview of the battle in heaven with Satan and his demons being cast to the earth. We have dropped back into the narrative of the Tribulation period.

> And the beast that I saw resembled a leopard, but his feet were like those of a bear and his mouth was like that of a lion. And to him the dragon gave his [own] might and power and his [own] throne and great dominion. (Rev. 13:2)

If you read Daniel and the descriptions of these beasts, it stays true to the principle of interpreting symbols we have described before. That the symbols of the beasts capture the essence and nature of the kingdom being symbolized. The book of Daniel depicts the fourth beast as iron; this fourth beast will act like iron, breaking and smashing all things.

Rome had those characteristics. Then the last kingdom that is partly strong and partly weak: the ten toes. (like the ten horns, though, the analogy differs) (Dan. 2:40–44)

This beast differs from the others because to this one, Satan gives his own might, power, throne, and great dominion. Now are we talking about the whole beast or just the horn? As we continue in this discourse, it becomes more focused on one horn.

> And one of his heads seemed to have a deadly wound. But his death stroke was healed; and the whole earth went after the beast in amazement and admiration. (Rev. 13:3)

Remember, in Matthew 24, where Jesus talked about miracles, signs, and wonders that were so convincing, they would fool even the elect if that were possible? We have touched briefly on stem cell research and cloning. Not that this is what will happen here, but we have more modern-day advances so that things of this nature are plausible. Whether it is this or something else, we will see the miraculous. Can anyone believe we will not advance beyond what we have seen to date? We cannot predict what advancements the future holds. Will we Christians seem outdated and out of touch with reality if science, not miracles, achieves this? If the world pursued this or something similar, would the world see Christians as obstacles to human advancement? People would see us as barriers to be swept aside by our antiquated ideas of God and morality. Christians have stepped up in some sensitive areas, such as abortion, stem cell research, cloning, and other moral issues. How will Christians respond when we are told we are going to have a one-world currency? We will resist, and they will claim that we are holding on to fairy tales and that these steps are necessary and rational for humankind.

We will go close to the brink of disaster before the Antichrist is to be revealed. If he comes along and takes us away from the brink of disaster, what are we going to look like to those who support him, as he just saved our butts? We will look fanatical and sorely outdated and out of touch with the needs of the world. Ultimately, removing us serves everyone. We need to remember that he will have a lot of solutions for humankind's troubles. Many people are simply practical: if it works, don't fix it.

> They fell down and paid homage to the dragon, because he had bestowed on the beast all his dominion and authority; they also praised and worshiped the beast, exclaiming, who is a match for the beast, and, who can make war against him? (Rev. 13:4)

There will be some, no doubt, who will worship Satan, for his time has come. However, the humanistic man will not knowingly worship Satan, as this is right along with the same antiquated thinking of God and morality.

> And the beast was given the power of speech, uttering boastful and blasphemous words, and he was given freedom to exert his authority and to exercise his will during forty-two months (three and a half years). (Rev. 13:5)

He, according to Daniel and other prophecies, will have seven years total. He remains reserved during the first half. In the second half, he has complete liberty to do whatever he wishes.

> And he opened his mouth to speak slanders against God, blaspheming His name and His abode, [even vilifying] those who live in heaven. (Rev. 13:6)

This would appear to be about the time he commits the abomination of desolation that Scripture foretells is coming.

> He was further permitted to wage war on God's holy people (the saints) and to overcome them. And power was given him to extend his authority over every tribe and people and tongue and nation. (Rev. 13:7)

Notice, first, that the Bible states he is permitted to overcome God's people. God gives this power to him; it is not inherently his. Why God allows this is vexing, especially as there are many verses that speak of God's protection for his children and our authority over the enemy. However, for this period, God allows this exception, for whatever his reasons are. He does not start out dominating the world; what world leader in their right mind would abdicate power and authority? However, with lawlessness increasing and society out of control, if someone in power finds a path of apparent peace and prosperity, would you not yield to him? If you were a world leader—let's just say the leader of Timbuktu had created order out of chaos—wouldn't that make you stand up and take notice? If the only way you could save yourself and your people from disaster was to cede your power to this light of humanity, would you not do so? The Antichrist extends his authority over the entire world, but that is not how he begins. It is scary what he is permitted to do. There is a similar verse found in Daniel.

> And he [the angel] said, Go your way, Daniel, for the words are shut up and sealed till the time of the end. Many shall purify themselves and make themselves white and be tried, smelted, and refined, but the wicked shall do wickedly. And none of the

wicked shall understand, but the teachers and those who are wise shall understand. (Dan. 12:9–10)

Do you remember the gold that is refined in the fire that Jesus said we might purchase from him to escape the deception of the Laodicean Church? This verse just mentioned in Daniel has very similar qualities. The pressures of this time are going to refine and make white those who choose to stand for the Lord.

And from the time that the continual burnt offering is taken away and the abomination that makes desolate is set up, there shall be 1,290 days. Blessed, happy, fortunate, spiritually prosperous, and to be envied is he who waits expectantly and earnestly [who endures without wavering beyond the period of tribulation] and comes to the 1,335 days! (Dan. 12:11–12)

There is a month and a half difference between these two dates, but both are approximately three and a half years. Could the difference between the two be the season of our Lord's return?

But you [Daniel, who was now over ninety years of age], go your way until the end; for you shall rest and shall stand [fast] in your allotted place at the end of the days. (Dan. 12:13) (emphasis mine)

The text also informs Daniel that he will stand at the end of days after his death. God will raise him up with the others on the last day. It is amazing how all over the Scriptures this theme keeps coming up. Job says:

For I know that my redeemer liveth, and that he shall stand at the latter day upon the earth: And though after my skin worms destroy this body, yet in my flesh shall I see God: Whom I shall see for myself, and mine eyes shall behold, and not another; though my reins be consumed within me. (Job 19:25–27 KJV)

Jesus has obviously talked to others, including Mary and Martha, about raising people up on the last day.

Now we will go back to Revelation 13:

And all the inhabitants of the earth will fall down in adoration and pay him homage, everyone whose name has not been recorded in the Book of Life of the Lamb that was slain [in sacrifice] from the foundation of the world. (Rev. 13:8)

Many say that this is a clear description of the Antichrist, whom Satan gives his own might and power. God gives the Antichrist freedom to do as he wills for three and a half years. The following verse is the response God wants his people to have during this time.

Here [comes in a call for] the steadfastness of the saints [the patience, the endurance of the people of God], those who [habitually] keep God's commandments and [their] faith in Jesus. (Rev. 14:12)

But the people who know their God shall prove themselves strong and shall stand firm and do exploits [for God]. (Dan. 11:32)

Now we go back to Revelation 13:

If anyone is able to hear, let him listen: Whoever leads into captivity will himself go into captivity; if anyone slays with the sword, with the sword must he be slain. Herein is [the call for] the patience and the faith and fidelity of the saints. (God's people) (Rev. 13:9–10)

"Be careful, for God is not made a fool of, that which a man sows he shall also reap." (Gal. 6:7, author's paraphrase) If you turn in your brother in the Lord to the powers that be, your turn is coming when someone will do the same to you. If you commit murder, someone will murder you. Currently, a delay exists between sowing and reaping, but it seems this germination period has sped up.

The False Prophet

Then I saw another beast rising up out of the land [itself]; he had two horns like a lamb, and he spoke (roared) like a dragon. He exerts all the power and right of control of the former beast in his presence, and causes the earth and those who dwell upon it to exalt and deify the first beast, whose deadly wound was healed, and to worship him. (Rev. 13:11–12)

As the false prophet is in the presence of the Antichrist, he has the same amount of power as the Antichrist. The false prophet is the one who incites the world to worship the Antichrist.

He performs great signs (startling miracles), even making fire fall from the sky to the earth in men's sight. (Rev. 13:13)

He can duplicate the miracles of God's two witnesses, which makes choosing sides a little more challenging for the average person. After all, they can both do miracles, so whom do you believe? If, on one hand, you have restrictions, such as trying to live a holy life before God, the opposite position is freedom to do as you please because we have tapped into our latent human potential or some other plausible possibility. What would the average person choose? The Bible predicts that most of the world will choose the latter.

And because of the signs (miracles) which he is allowed to perform in the presence of the [first] beast, he deceives those who inhabit the earth, commanding them to erect a statue (an image) in the likeness of the beast who was wounded by the [small] sword and still lived. (Rev. 13:14)

The false prophet deceives most people on earth through his miracles, and the world erects an image of the Antichrist. And as we have seen previously, the world worships this man, our savior. Just because we see a miracle or prophecies come to pass, that does not make it of God. Satan also can perform miracles, and here are Scriptures that tell us to be careful.

IF A prophet arises among you, or a dreamer of dreams, and gives you a sign or a wonder, And the sign or the wonder he foretells to you comes to pass, and if he says, let us go after other gods—gods you have not known—and let us serve them, you shall not listen to the words of that prophet or to that dreamer of dreams. For the Lord your God is testing you to know whether you love the Lord your God with all your [mind and] heart and with your entire being. You shall walk after the Lord your God and [reverently] fear Him, and keep His commandments and obey His voice, and you shall serve Him and cling to Him. But that prophet or that dreamer of dreams shall be put to death, because he has talked rebellion and turning away from the Lord your God, who brought you out of the land of Egypt and redeemed you out of the house of bondage; that man has tried to draw you aside from the way in which the Lord your God commanded you to walk. So shall you put the evil away from your midst. (Deut. 13:1–5)

When Pharaoh says to you, prove [your authority] by a miracle, then tell Aaron, throw your rod down before Pharaoh, that it may become a serpent. So Moses and Aaron went to Pharaoh and did as the Lord had commanded; Aaron threw down his rod before Pharaoh and his servants, and it became a serpent. Then Pharaoh called for the wise men [skilled in magic and divination] and the sorcerers (wizards and jugglers). And they also, these magicians of Egypt, did similar things with their enchantments and secret arts. For they cast down every man his rod and they became serpents; but Aaron's rod swallowed up their rods. (Exod. 7:9–12)

BELOVED, DO not put faith in every spirit, but prove (test) the spirits to discover whether they proceed from God; for many false prophets have gone forth into the world. (1 John 4:1)

Now let's go back to Revelation 13.

And he is permitted [also] to impart the breath of life into the beast's image, so that the statue of the beast could actually talk and cause to be put to death those who would not bow down and worship the image of the beast. (Rev. 13:15)

The false prophet is the one who establishes the death penalty for those who will not worship the Antichrist. As a Christian, you now have a choice: Worship the Antichrist or die. That is not a straightforward decision, but the stakes are higher than just your life; this decision affects all of eternity.

Also he compels all [alike], both small and great, both the rich and the poor, both free and slave, to be marked with an inscription [stamped] on their right hands or on their foreheads. (Rev. 13:16)

Once again, it is the false prophet and not the Antichrist that institutes the mark of the beast. The false prophet is the Antichrist's public relations person. He is the one who lifts the Antichrist up as the savior of the world.

So that no one will have power to buy or sell unless he bears the stamp (mark, inscription), [that is] the name of the beast or the number of his name. (Rev. 13:17)

This part seems straightforward. The mark of the beast or the seal of the Holy Spirit—it's your call! It could be a microchip or anything else we can imagine. There is a microchip already available to be implanted in human beings to help us. It appears reasonable to implement this device. People could see this as increasingly necessary, as lawlessness increases in frequency and intensity. As identity theft and the need to feel secure in an increasingly unstable world increase, what price is too high for safety and security once again? While it may not be the microchip, it will be something that enables us to feel stability and order coming back into the world. The world will know for sure soon enough. Whatever comes down the road that says, "Without this, you cannot buy or sell," be cautious. We need to keep in mind that any mark, or microchip, that has your personal information to help identify you is not at issue here. The name and number that we need to be concerned about is his (the beast's) name and number. A microchip with your personal information may very well be an intermediate state before taking his name or number, but if you want any chance of salvation, you do not take his.

> Here is [room for] discernment [a call for the wisdom of interpretation]. Let anyone who has intelligence (penetration and insight enough) calculate the number of the beast, for it is a human number [the number of a certain man]; his number is 666. (Rev. 13:18)

Concerning the Antichrist, whoever he is, there are enough identifying remarks in the Bible to know he is not good. He will initially appear good, though. In our modern age, there has never been one person in an official position for the entire world. When this happens—and it must happen—he is the man.

THEN I looked, and behold, the Lamb stood on Mount Zion, and with Him 144,000 [men] who had His name and His Father's name inscribed on their foreheads. (Rev. 14:1)

Okay, another cut scene, and this time we are back with the 144,000 bond servants who God seals with the mark of the living God on their foreheads. Will the average person be able to see this mark? Probably not, but you can bet that the spiritual forces on both sides will be able to. Remember, we are told, "that the things that are seen are temporary, but the things which are not seen are eternal." (2 Cor. 4:18, author's paraphrase)

And I heard a voice from heaven like the sound of great waters and like the rumbling of mighty thunder; the voice I heard [seemed like the music] of harpists accompanying themselves on their harps. And they sang a new song before the throne [of God] and before the four living creatures and before the elders [of the heavenly Sanhedrin]. No one could learn [to sing] that song except the 144,000 who had been ransomed (purchased, redeemed) from the earth. (Rev. 14:2–3)

On a side note, since music must have its origin and inspiration from God himself (the new song that the 144,00 are singing is what inspired this thought), and we have eternity to spend with him, what do you think the chances are that at some point we will see a billboard or heaven's equivalent announcing, God in concert? We think we know music and singing now, but, since God is the source, how mind-blowing do you think that concert will be?

This time they are in heaven before the throne and not on earth like they were the last time. After their work on earth is complete, we see them singing a new song, a song no one else can learn.

> These are they who have not defiled themselves by relations with women, for they are [pure as] virgins. These are they who follow the Lamb wherever He goes. These are they who have been ransomed (purchased, redeemed) from among men as the firstfruits for God and the Lamb. (Rev. 14:4)

The firstfruits are a biblical concept that God instituted for Israel. Therefore, by extension, to the Church to give God the first of your harvest. Pretend that you owned a farm in biblical times. When it was time to harvest, you would take the first of your harvest—grain, corn, etcetera—and offer it as a sacrifice in the sanctuary to God. This was to symbolize that all the good stuff you were about to harvest ultimately came from the goodness of God. (Deut. 26:1–10)

> No lie was found to be upon their lips, for they are blameless (spotless, untainted, without blemish) before the throne of God. (Rev. 14:5)

It bears stating that whoever these bond servants are; they are not blameless through their own righteousness. None of God's former bond servants (Peter, Paul, Luke, Mary, John, Priscilla, and all the others) were perfect within themselves. We have read about some of their human weaknesses; however, the Bible still considers them bond servants. I believe these bond servants will have similar weaknesses. Like the others mentioned, God will make them pure "in Christ," not trusting in their own righteousness. Many look at these particular individuals and see them as something mystical, and yes, they are a special group. The Bible is clear on that, but if the symbol of the 144,000 is representing actual people, then they have similarities with the rest of the people of God. Obviously, they also have differences.

> Then I saw another angel flying in midair, with an eternal Gospel (good news) to tell to the inhabitants of the earth, to every race and tribe and language and people. (Rev. 14:6)

Okay, another cut scene. God has good news: Judgment is coming. Why is this good news? It all seems like bad news, doesn't it? Well, it is an extremely hard time for God's people. The ungodly are going to be brought to their knees. So the immediate sensation is unpleasant, but the result is exquisite! The kingdoms of this world become the kingdoms of our Christ and of his God, so it is ultimately good news.

> And he cried with a mighty voice, Revere God and give Him glory (honor and praise in worship), for the hour of His judgment has arrived. Fall down before Him; pay Him homage and adoration and worship Him Who created heaven and earth, the sea and the springs (fountains) of water. Then another angel, a second, followed, declaring, Fallen, fallen is Babylon the great! She who made all nations drink of the [maddening] wine of her passionate unchastity [idolatry]. (Rev. 14:7–8)

We will get to Babylon in much more detail soon, but for now, we will just take note she makes the world drink of her passionate unfaithfulness. We are not figuratively talking about a woman who occasionally messes up, who has a few moments of questionable judgment and consequently affairs. This woman goes full bore into adultery and revels in it.

Then another angel, a third, followed them, saying with a mighty voice, Whoever pays homage to the beast and his statue and permits the [beast's] stamp (mark, inscription) to be put on his forehead or on his hand, He too shall [have to] drink of the wine of God's indignation and wrath, poured undiluted into the cup of His anger; and he shall be tormented with fire and brimstone in the presence of the holy angels and in the presence of the Lamb. And the smoke of their torment ascends forever and ever; and they have no respite (no pause, no intermission, no rest, no peace) day or night—these who pay homage to the beast and to his image and whoever receives the stamp of his name upon him. (Rev. 14:9–11)

If you choose to be faithful to the Antichrist and the false prophet, God will also be faithful to you. You do not want his faithfulness in this case because he will be faithful in pouring out his anger on you with no reprieve. I thought he was a loving God. Where did that go? God is both love and justice. You can choose either, but after your decision, you live with that decision for all eternity. Choose wisely. He has done everything in his love to spare you from his justice, but the scary part is he has left the choice up to you.

Here [comes in a call for] the steadfastness of the saints [the patience, the endurance of the people of God], those who [habitually] keep God's commandments and [their] faith in Jesus. (Rev. 14:12)

This is self-explanatory: Hold on tight. Don't give in to the pressures to betray your brothers and sisters in the Lord or take the mark of the beast.

Then I heard further [perceiving the distinct words of] a voice from heaven, saying, write this: Blessed (happy, to be envied) are the dead from now on who die in the Lord! Yes, blessed (happy, to be envied indeed), says the Spirit, [in] that they may rest from their labors, for their works (deeds) do follow (attend, accompany) them! (Rev. 14:13)

If you must die, and the truth is we all must—except, of course, those who get raptured. Since only God knows whom he will rapture and who will die as martyrs, prepare for either possibility. You might just as well die standing up for the one who stood up for you.

Again I looked, and behold, [I saw] a white cloud, and sitting on the cloud One resembling a Son of Man, with a crown of gold on His head and a sharp scythe (sickle) in His hand. (Rev. 14:14)

This is probably not Jesus, although it does state the one resembles the son of man. But Jesus, in the passage that follows, states that the angels are reapers. This is not a dogmatic statement; it also could be the Lord. He is obviously free to do whatsoever he chooses.

And another angel came out of the temple sanctuary, calling with a mighty voice to Him Who was sitting upon the cloud, Put in Your scythe and reap, for the hour has arrived to gather the harvest, for the earth's crop is fully ripened. So He Who was sitting upon the cloud swung His scythe (sickle) on the earth, and the earth's crop was harvested. (Rev. 14:15–16)

This dovetails beautifully with what Jesus spoke of in Matthew 13.

Then He left the throngs and went into the house. And His disciples came to Him saying, Explain to us the parable of the darnel in the field. He answered, He Who sows the good seed is the Son of Man. The field is the world, and the good seed means the children of the kingdom; the darnel is the children of the evil one, And the enemy who sowed it is the devil. The harvest is the close and consummation of the age, and the reapers are angels. Just as the darnel (weeds resembling wheat) is gathered and burned with fire, so it will be at the close of the age. The Son of Man will send forth His angels, and they will gather out of His kingdom all causes of offense [persons by whom others are drawn into error or sin] and all who do iniquity and act wickedly, And will cast them into the furnace of fire; there will be weeping and wailing and grinding of teeth. Then will the righteous (those who are upright and in right standing with God) shine forth like the sun in the kingdom of their Father. Let him who has ears [to hear] be listening, and let him consider and perceive and understand by hearing. (Matt. 13:36–43)

Now let's go back to Revelation 14.

Then another angel came out of the temple [sanctuary] in heaven, and he also carried a sharp scythe (sickle). And another angel came forth from the altar, [the angel] who has authority and power over fire, and he called with a loud cry to him who had the sharp scythe (sickle), Put forth your scythe and reap the fruitage of the vine of the earth, for its grapes are entirely ripe. (Rev. 14:17–18)

Okay, we have two harvests here. In the first one, with the one resembling the son of man, God harvests the earth's crop. For the second one, it is the fruit of the vine. In the following verse, the one resembling the Son of man throws them into the winepress of God's wrath. Going back to an earlier question which gets harvested first, it would appear that the godly get harvested first and the ungodly follow. This, of course, is not conclusive, as this book shows time and time again that we move in and out of time periods so swiftly, you can't really say too much dogmatically regarding timing, only about some things concerning the result.

Angel Like the Son of Man Harvesting the World

So the angel swung his scythe on the earth and stripped the grapes and gathered the vintage from the vines of the earth and cast it into the huge winepress of God's indignation and wrath. And [the grapes in] the winepress were trodden outside the city, and blood poured from the winepress, [reaching] as high as horses' bridles, for a distance of 1,600 stadia (about two hundred miles). (Rev. 14:19–20)

CHAPTER 30

The Book of Revelation, Chapters 15-16

THEN I saw another wonder (sign, token, symbol) in heaven, great and marvelous [warning of events of ominous significance]: There were seven angels bringing seven plagues (afflictions, calamities), which are the last, for with them God's wrath (indignation) is completely expressed [reaches its climax and is ended]. (Rev. 15:1)

As this finishes the judgment of God, we must be in the seventh seal. It would seem the seventh trumpet introduces the seven bowls of judgment because they are the last. Once again, we have taken a time warp.

Then I saw what seemed to be a glassy sea blended with fire, and those who had come off victorious from the beast and from his statue and from the number corresponding to his name were standing beside the glassy sea, with harps of God in their hands. And they sang the song of Moses the servant of God and the song of the Lamb, saying, Mighty and marvelous are Your works, O Lord God the Omnipotent! Righteous (just) and true are Your ways, O Sovereign of the ages (King of the nations)! Who shall not reverence and glorify Your name, O Lord [giving You honor and praise in worship]? For You only are holy. All the nations shall come and pay homage and adoration to You, for Your just judgments (Your righteous sentences and deeds) have been made known and displayed. (Rev. 15:2–4)

Okay, we have a cut scene: a glassy sea, blended with fire, that surrounds those who overcame the beast—whether through martyrdom or patient endurance until the Rapture. These overcomers sing before God, praising him for who he is and the victory he has enabled them to get.

After this I looked and the sanctuary of the tent of the testimony in heaven was thrown open. (Rev. 15:5)

Now we have another cut scene, and the tabernacle in heaven is open. The "tent of testimony" is another term for the tabernacle.

And there came out of the temple sanctuary the seven angels bringing the seven plagues (afflictions, calamities). They were arrayed in pure gleaming linen, and around their breasts they wore golden girdles. (Rev. 15:6)

Okay, now we cut back to the seven angels we were looking at in verse one with the last of the plagues.

Seven Angels with the Seven Bowls of Wrath

And one of the four living creatures [then] gave the seven angels seven golden bowls full of the wrath and indignation of God, who lives forever and ever (in the eternities of the eternities) And the sanctuary was filled with smoke from the glory (the radiance, the splendor) of God and from His might and power, and no one was able to go into the sanctuary until the seven plagues (afflictions, calamities) of the seven angels were ended. (Rev. 15:7–8)

Seven angels, seven bowls: Let's see what is in those bowls.

THEN I heard a mighty voice from the temple sanctuary saying to the seven angels, Go and empty out on the earth the seven bowls of God's wrath and indignation. So the first [angel] went and emptied his bowl on the earth, and foul and painful ulcers (sores) came on the people who were marked with the stamp of the beast and who did homage to his image. (Rev. 16:1–2)

Bowl one is painful ulcers directed at those who have aligned themselves with the Antichrist.

The second [angel] emptied his bowl into the sea, and it turned into blood like that of a corpse [thick, corrupt, ill-smelling, and disgusting], and every living thing that was in the sea perished. (Rev. 16:3)

The second bowl targets the sea. It's unclear whether this affects all salt water, but the results are devastating. Everything within this sea dies, so there is no food from this body of water.

Then the third [angel] emptied out his bowl into the rivers and the springs of water, and they turned into (became) blood. (Rev. 16:4)

The third bowl appears to hurt our freshwater supply and food sources within it.

And I also heard the angel of the waters say, Righteous (just) are You in these Your decisions and judgments, You Who are and were, O Holy One! Because they have poured out the blood of Your people (the saints) and the prophets, and You have given them blood to drink. Such is their due [they deserve it]! (Rev. 16:5–6)

These plagues that affect our food and water supply seem to be a direct judgment of the people whose allegiance is with the Antichrist. Because they have poured out the blood of God's people. This is another example of God's principle of sowing and reaping.

And [from] the altar I heard [the] cry, Yes, Lord God the Omnipotent, your judgments (sentences, decisions) are true and just and righteous! Then the fourth [angel] emptied out his bowl upon the sun, and it was permitted to burn (scorch) humanity with [fierce, glowing] heat (fire). (Rev. 16:7–8)

Something directs the fourth bowl toward the sun directly and against the earth's inhabitants indirectly as the sun's virulence increases.

People were severely burned (scorched) by the fiery heat, and they reviled and blasphemed the name of God, who has control of these plagues, and they did not repent of their sins [felt no regret, contrition, and compunction for their waywardness, refusing to amend their ways] to give Him glory. Then the fifth [angel] emptied his bowl on the throne of the beast, and his kingdom was [plunged] in darkness; and people gnawed their tongues for the torment [of their excruciating distress and severe pain]. (Rev. 16:9–10)

The fifth bowl strikes the Antichrist and his kingdom, plunging them into darkness. Whether this is a huge power outage or part of the heavenly bodies not giving their light, they are in darkness.

And blasphemed the God of heaven because of their anguish and their ulcers (sores), and they did not deplore their wicked deeds or repent [for what they had done]. (Rev. 16:11)

Humans harden their hearts—no surprise there. We do this more often than not.

Then the sixth [angel] emptied his bowl on the mighty river Euphrates, and its water was dried up to make ready a road for [the coming of] the kings of the east (from the rising sun). (Rev. 16:12)

The sixth bowl is preparation for Armageddon, which even those unfamiliar with the Scriptures have heard of.

And I saw three loathsome spirits like frogs, [leaping] from the mouth of the dragon and from the mouth of the beast and from the mouth of the false prophet. (Rev. 16:13)

Here, we see the unholy trinity: the dragon or Satan, the beast or the Antichrist, and the false prophet. For everything that God has, Satan has a counterfeit. Satan enjoys the perversion of the genuine article.

For really they are the spirits of demons that perform signs (wonders, miracles). And they go forth to the rulers and leaders all over the world, to gather them together for war on the great day of God the Almighty. (Rev. 16:14)

Miracles, signs, and wonders convince the world leaders to gather for battle at Armageddon, but demonic design inspires these.

Behold, I am going to come like a thief! Blessed (happy, to be
envied) is he who stays awake (alert) and who guards his clothes,
so that he may not be naked and [have the shame of being] seen
exposed! (Rev. 16:15)

He is coming like a thief to those who are asleep, as previously noted.
The wise person will be awake. To the person who is awake, he will not
be coming as a thief.

And they gathered them together at the place which in Hebrew
is called Armageddon. (Rev. 16:16)

The Battle of Armageddon is infamous; it is the last battle of
humankind before the millennial reign.

Then the seventh [angel] emptied out his bowl into the air,
and a mighty voice came out of the sanctuary of heaven from
the throne [of God], saying, It is done! [It is all over, it is all
accomplished, it has come! (Rev. 16:17)

The seventh angel with the bowls of God's judgment would appear
to be the seventh trumpet mentioned earlier. If we look back, it does
not say exactly what the seventh trumpet accomplishes in Revelation
10:7 and 11:15. It suggests that it signifies the end of God's judgment.
After the pouring out of the seventh bowl, the seventh angel says, "It
is done!" While it is not definitive, it appears reasonable that the seven
bowls are part of the seventh trumpet, for we are back to "It is done!"
Or the kingdoms of this world have become the kingdoms of our Christ
and of his God.

And there followed lightning flashes, loud rumblings, peals of thunder, and a tremendous earthquake; nothing like it has ever occurred since men dwelt on the earth, so severe and far-reaching was that earthquake. The mighty city was broken into three parts, and the cities of the nations fell. And God kept in mind mighty Babylon, to make her drain the cup of His furious wrath and indignation. (Rev. 16:18–19)

Who is "mystery Babylon"? Many scholars say this city is Rome. Mystery Babylon is on seven hills, and Rome also sits on seven hills. Others argue this city is Jerusalem, also built on seven hills—the great city where our Lord sacrificed his life and which has now become the Antichrist's seat of power, where he committed the abomination of desolation. Almost everyone agrees it is a symbol of an anti-God, humanistic religious system that controls most of the earth during the time of the end. This city, whether one of the two or one that has yet to rise to power, will break into three sections through an earthquake—the likes of which this world has never seen before. Technically, while many writers refer to this city as "mystery Babylon," it says the name "Babylon, the great mother of prostitutes," which is itself a mystery.

The Whore of Babylon

And on her forehead there was inscribed a name of mystery [with a secret symbolic meaning]: Babylon the great, the mother of prostitutes (idolatresses) and of the filth and atrocities and abominations of the earth. (Rev. 17:5)

And every island fled and no mountains could be found. And great (excessively oppressive) hailstones, as heavy as a talent [between fifty and sixty pounds], of immense size, fell from the sky on the people; and men blasphemed God for the plague of the hail, so very great was [the torture] of that plague. (Rev. 16:20–21)

The seventh bowl unleashes lightning, peals of thunder, and a devastating earthquake that wipes out the cities of the nations.

If this is literal, then Hawaii, the Philippines, the Fiji Islands, etcetera are gone at this point. While extreme, this is the last bowl in the seventh trumpet in the seventh seal and things are about to be wrapped up for all eternity, so it kind of makes sense. Jesus's return is imminent.

Seven bowls of God's wrath and indignation: "Oh, to have been born in a different place and time," the wicked will say.

CHAPTER 31

The Book of Revelation, Chapters 17-18

O NE OF the seven angels who had the seven bowls then came and spoke to me, saying, Come with me! I will show you the doom (sentence, judgment) of the great harlot (idolatress) who is seated on many waters. (Rev. 17:1)

Okay, another cut scene, as we have just come from "It is finished" with the conclusion of the seventh bowl judgment. We are going from the pronouncement that "it is finished" to a different scene with the great harlot. The activities of the great harlot must occur before "it is finished." We are stepping back in time. Let's back this narrative up a bit. Focus a little closer on an element that occurs before the kingdoms of this world become the kingdoms of Christ and his God.

[She] with whom the rulers of the earth have joined in prostitution (idolatry) and with the wine of whose immorality (idolatry) the inhabitants of the earth have become intoxicated. (Rev. 17:2)

The rulers of the earth have joined with this harlot. This shows she has universal influence or, as many have heard, a one-world religion. This symbol of the harlot is clearly a world system. The Scriptures here tell us the rulers and inhabitants of the world have gotten drunk with her immorality. The Bible repeatedly throughout the Old Testament relates idolatry to spiritual adultery, that God is jealous over his people. Much like a married couple, his people have been unfaithful to him. Committing idolatry is equivalent to spiritual adultery. There is a passage in Jeremiah 3:1–14 that gives a clear accounting of this. This includes God calling himself a husband to his people who have played the harlot with other gods. The harlot, it would appear, has a hand in uniting the world together under this false religion as the rulers of the world join her. However, these rulers will destroy her.

Now let us inspect this world system.

Seven Headed Beast and the Whore of Babylon in the Desert

And [the angel] bore me away [rapt] in the Spirit into a desert (wilderness), and I saw a woman seated on a scarlet beast that was all covered with blasphemous titles (names), and he had seven heads and ten horns. (Rev. 17:3)

We know this beast because we introduced him earlier in this narrative; he is the Antichrist. Now we will investigate the relationship between the Antichrist and the harlot.

> The woman was robed in purple and scarlet and bedecked with gold, precious stones, and pearls, [and she was] holding in her hand a golden cup full of the accursed offenses and the filth of her lewdness and vice. (Rev. 17:4)

On the outside she looks hot: beautiful and totally decked out. What she has in her hands, however, is lewd, crude, and rude. Where have we seen a picture similar to this? When Jesus was talking to the religious leaders of his day, he said, "You are like whitewashed tombs that look good on the outside but inside are full of dead people's bones and everything rotten." (Matt. 23:27) (author's paraphrase)

> And on her forehead there was inscribed a name of mystery [with a secret symbolic meaning]: Babylon the great, the mother of prostitutes (idolatresses) and of the filth and atrocities and abominations of the earth. (Rev. 17:5)

This is a false world religion that the rulers of the earth have joined because it promotes unity. The exception to this unity is the believers. As it tells us in the next verse, they get drunk off the blood of God's people. Notice as well that the woman rides the beast. These are two separate entities. One is a religious system. The other is a political system. As we will see later in the prophecy, the political system will turn on the religious system. At the beginning of their relationship, they use one another. Most of the material I have seen believes that this great false religious system is the Roman Catholic Church. Especially when you look at medieval Europe and the Inquisition, this appears to be a fair assessment. No other religious institution even comes close to killing more of God's people than the Roman Catholic Church. I have known some very good and honorable Catholics; let's not assume everyone in that institution is part of the falseness. However, unless a new rival picks up some steam and surpasses what this religious institution has done, it looks like we have our mystery, Babylon the Great. This institution also functions as a political powerhouse besides being a religious powerhouse.

> I also saw that the woman was drunk, [drunk] with the blood of the saints (God's people) and the blood of the martyrs [who witnessed] for Jesus. And when I saw her, I was utterly amazed and wondered greatly. (Rev. 17:6)

This world system enables the death of many of God's people, as she is drunk on the blood of the saints and martyrs.

> But the angel said to me, why do you wonder? I will explain to you the [secret symbolic meaning of the] mystery of the woman, as well as of the beast having the seven heads and ten horns that carries her. (Rev. 17:7)

The angel gives us an interpretation of the Antichrist and the harlot.

> The beast that you saw [once] was, but [now] is no more, and he is going to come up out of the Abyss (the bottomless pit) and proceed to go to perdition. And the inhabitants of the earth whose names have not been recorded in the Book of Life from the foundation of the world will be astonished when they look at the beast, because he [once] was, but [now] is no more, and he is [yet] to come. (Rev. 17:8)

I find this interpretation spoken by the angel to be more confusing than the symbol of the whore and the beast themselves. In just a little bit, we will explore a plausible explanation when we go through the scenario of the ten kings. However, in this specific Scripture, let us notice that the beast comes out of the bottomless pit. The spirit operating through the Antichrist is clearly demonic in nature. Regardless of what the *shell* looks like, this is a spirit being who has ruled through a different man in our history.

A time of judgment is coming, and what we really need to know is which side we are on. There are many interpretations of who the harlot and the beast are. Only God knows for sure. What clearly is being revealed here is not what all the symbols are. This passage reveals two opposing sides, requiring a choice.

> And if it seems evil to you to serve the Lord, choose for yourselves this day whom you will serve, whether the gods which your fathers served on the other side of the River, or the gods of the Amorites, in whose land you dwell; but as for me and my house, we will serve the Lord. (Josh. 24:15)

> Now we'll go back to Revelation 17.

> This calls for a mind [to consider that is packed] with wisdom and intelligence [it is something for a particular mode of thinking and judging of thoughts, feelings, and purposes]. The seven heads are seven hills upon which the woman is sitting. (Rev. 17:9)

> The Scriptures often use hills to denote a place of refuge, an elevated position offering an advantage, and a refuge. You might interpret these literally. You could also view them symbolically, looking at the

relationship between the governmental aspect of the last world empire and the false religious system allied with it.

Tradition holds that they built Rome on seven hills, so many say this symbolizes Rome. Therefore, some say this points us to a revived Roman Empire. Remember the prophecy of Daniel in which he talks about the fourth kingdom? Daniel depicted the fourth kingdom as legs of iron, symbolizing Rome, as iron breaks and crushes all things, but the feet and toes were of both iron and clay. The theory is that the last kingdom comes out of the legs. (Rome) This last kingdom is partly strong and partly weak. The ten toes would correlate to the ten rulers or horns of the Antichrist kingdom. The last kingdom on earth until Jesus sets up his throne here on earth. One of the other things that we must keep in mind is that only God knows the end from the beginning. These kings or rulers are seven positions of powers that the religious system allied itself with. Whether these seven rulers are in a city like Rome which has seven actual hills, or the hills are simply symbolic of being an elevated position of power, remains to be seen. If it is symbolic, then these kings or rulers could operate out of virtually any city in the world. Then the religious system is operating in unison with this ruler. Where they would end up is anybody's guess. This is like picturing a game of chess, except only God knows in advance where all the various pieces on the chessboard will move for their final destination.

Seven hills also form the base of Jerusalem. Many say this symbolizes Jerusalem since the Antichrist commits the abomination of desolation in Jerusalem. The two witnesses are in Jerusalem, vexing the powers that be (Rev. 11:8); Jesus shall stand on the Mount of Olives on the day when he gathers all nations to battle against Jerusalem. (Zech. 14:3–4) The Battle of Armageddon is just outside Jerusalem. (Rev. 16:6) Scripturally, this is our center. I know it is said that "all roads lead to Rome." However, in this case, it looks like all roads lead to Jerusalem. This is not a definitive statement, but the scriptural support for the theory is there.

> And they are also seven kings, five of whom have fallen, one still exists [and is reigning]; the other [the seventh] has not yet appeared, and when he does arrive, he must stay [but] a brief time. (Rev. 17:10)

There are Bible teachers who see this as kingdoms. They use the kings to represent these kingdoms. However, we have very distinctive words in the Greek for kings and kingdoms. While plausible, it may or may not be correct.

> And as for the beast that [once] was, but now is no more, he [himself] is an eighth ruler (king, head), but he is of the seven and belongs to them, and he goes to perdition. (Rev. 17:11)

This passage is admittedly hard. The Scripture is saying the beast is a former ruler, and he is going to reign again. He is an eighth ruler, but one of the first seven. It could look like this if we were talking about ten kings who are going to be the last ten of the Antichrist's kingdom. The ten kings who are represented by the ten horns of the Beast. I selected these names purely at random; they bear absolutely no relation to anyone alive now.

The hypothetical Antichrist's kingdom:

1.   King Ken
2.   King Ben
3.   King Mark
4.   King Nicholas

5. King Jerry

6. King Peter

7. King Alex

8. King Simon

9. King Frank

10. King George

Now for the sake of argument, let's say that these kings represent all the world's nations. They represent even distribution among the kings. Now let's say that King Ben assassinates King Nicholas. However, miraculously, King Nicholas rises back to life. This happens fairly frequently, with a person flatlining and then someone shocking the heart back to beating again. However, this appears to be different because the Bible says his fatal wound healed, and the entire world marveled at him. (Rev. 13:3) After rising from the dead, King Nicholas has King Ben, King Simon, and King George assassinated, as the latter three were involved in the conspiracy to have him assassinated. This is purely hypothetical but serves as an example of what this could look like. There are now seven kings left out of the original ten. In this context, Nicholas was once a ruler, but then died and later resurrected. It is very apparent how far-fetched this sounds. However, there are advances today that make this type of apparent science fiction an actual possibility. Besides, it is not this author, or any other making the claim. It is the Scriptures themselves that make this claim.

Also the ten horns that you observed are ten rulers (kings) who have as yet received no royal dominion, but together they are to receive power and authority as rulers for a single hour, along with the beast. These have one common policy (opinion, purpose), and they deliver their power and authority to the beast. (Rev. 17:12–13)

These last six rulers yield everything that they have to the Antichrist.

They will wage war against the Lamb, and the Lamb will triumph over them; for He is Lord of lords and King of kings—and those with Him and on His side are chosen and called [elected] and loyal and faithful followers. (Rev. 17:14)

If you read to the end of the book, we win, even though this end-time scenario is scary, and everybody will have to endure some stuff that nobody really wants to go through. He is the King of kings and Lord of lords, and he triumphs over the Antichrist and his kingdom.

And [the angel further] said to me, the waters that you observed, where the harlot is seated, are races and multitudes and nations and dialects (languages). (Rev. 17:15)

This again emphasizes that this harlot, the false religion, has almost universal influence. This is also one of the few places where the symbol is interpreted for us. As noted earlier, if the interpretation had not been given to us, how many of us would have the correct interpretation for that one?

And the ten horns that you saw, they and the beast will [be the very ones to] hate the harlot (the idolatrous woman); they will make her cheerless (bereaved, desolate), and they will strip her and eat up her flesh and utterly consume her with fire. For God has put it into their hearts to carry out His own purpose by acting in harmony in surrendering their royal power and authority to the beast, until the prophetic words (intentions and promises) of God shall be fulfilled. (Rev. 17:16–17)

So even though the false religious harlot helps set up the Antichrist's kingdom, once she is no longer needed, they turn on her and destroy her.

And the woman that you saw is herself the great city which dominates and controls the rulers and the leaders of the earth. (Rev. 17:18)

We have touched briefly on a couple of scenarios about which city this is. It is very possible that, once again, Jerusalem will be the center of the world's activities. As shown before, there is a lot in this book that points to Jerusalem once again becoming a world center of activity. While it is not conclusive, this is a strong possibility. If it turns out to be accurate, the scenario that Jerusalem is once again the center of political and religious power could be what the Jewish nation has been waiting for. The Jewish nation is still waiting for the coming of their Messiah and reestablished preeminence among the cities of the world. However, if it turns out to be the Muslim equivalent of the Messiah in this scenario, that makes Jerusalem front and center on the world stage. That would make sense as well. If a strong Muslim leader could make a peace treaty that restored the nation of Israel's ability to fully practice their faith, including temple sacrifices, this could give Israel something that its people dearly wanted. This could be grounds for a successful peace treaty. I am not speculating what he would give his Muslim colleagues, but it would have to be substantial. Then, three and a half years into the treaty, he commits the abomination of desolation and takes Jerusalem over. The world will know soon enough. It could be one of those scenarios previously mentioned or something entirely different. Both the harlot and the beast are evil, yet one turns on the other. We, as Christians, will do no better, as Jesus foretold.

> And then many will be offended and repelled and will begin to distrust and desert [Him Whom they ought to trust and obey] and will stumble and fall away and betray one another and pursue one another with hatred. (Matt. 24:10)

Now back to Revelation 18.

> THEN I saw another angel descending from heaven, possessing great authority, and the earth was illuminated with his radiance and splendor. And he shouted with a mighty voice, she is fallen! Mighty Babylon is fallen! She has become a resort and dwelling place for demons, a dungeon haunted by every loathsome spirit, an abode for every filthy and detestable bird. (Rev. 18:1–2)

What was once beautiful is no longer!

> For all nations have drunk the wine of her passionate unchastity, and the rulers and leaders of the earth have joined with her in committing fornication (idolatry), and the businessmen of the earth have become rich with the wealth of her excessive luxury and wantonness. (Rev. 18:3)

We have seen before how all the nations of the world are intimately involved with her, emphasizing once more the key role she plays in end-time events.

I then heard another voice from heaven saying, come out from her, my people, so that you may not share in her sins, neither participate in her plagues. (Rev. 18:4)

God exhorts us to come out from this false religious harlot, that we do not share in the judgment of God upon her. Better than going in and then getting back out would be to never go in.

For her iniquities (her crimes and transgressions) are piled up as high as heaven, and God has remembered her wickedness and [her] crimes [and calls them up for settlement]. Repay to her what she herself has paid [to others] and double [her doom] in accordance with what she has done. Mix a double portion for her in the cup she mixed [for others]. (Rev. 18:5–6)

Remember that principle of reaping and sowing? God's judgment on the harlot is to reap twice the amount she has sown.

To the degree that she glorified herself and reveled in her wantonness [living deliciously and luxuriously], to that measure impose on her torment and anguish and tears and mourning. Since in her heart she boasts, I am not a widow; as a queen [on a throne] I sit, and I shall never see suffering or experience sorrow. (Rev. 18:7)

She sees herself as invincible. God, it would appear, has a different point of view.

So shall her plagues (afflictions, calamities) come thick upon her in a single day, pestilence and anguish and sorrow and famine; and she shall be utterly consumed (burned up with fire), for mighty is the Lord God Who judges her. And the rulers and leaders of the earth who joined her in her immorality (idolatry) and luxuriated with her will weep and beat their breasts and lament over her when they see the smoke of her conflagration. They will stand a long way off, in terror of her torment, and they will cry, Woe and alas, the great city, the mighty city, Babylon! In one single hour how your doom (judgment) has overtaken you! And earth's businessmen will weep and grieve over her because no one buys their freight (cargo) any more. Their merchandise is of gold, silver, precious stones, and pearls; of fine linen, purple, silk, and scarlet [stuffs]; all kinds of scented wood, all sorts of articles of ivory, all varieties of objects of costly woods, bronze, iron, and marble. (Rev. 18:8–12)

This city that is symbolized by Babylon is the center of the political, religious, and economic world at the end of the age. It is most probably Jerusalem. As we look, the evidence appears to be building to that conclusion, although there is room for other interpretations.

Of cinnamon, spices, incense, ointment and perfume, and frankincense, of wine and olive oil, fine flour and wheat; of cattle and sheep, horses and conveyances; and of slaves (the bodies) and souls of men! The ripe fruits and delicacies for which your soul longed have gone from you, and all your luxuries and dainties, your elegance and splendor are lost to you, never again to be recovered or experienced! The dealers who handled these articles, who grew wealthy through their business with her, will stand a long way off, in terror of her doom and torment, weeping and grieving aloud, and saying, Alas, alas for the great city that was robed in fine linen, in purple and scarlet, bedecked and glittering with gold, with precious stones, and with pearls! Because in one [single] hour all the vast wealth has been destroyed (wiped out). And all ship captains and pilots, navigators and all who live by seafaring, the crews and all who ply their trade on the sea, stood a long way off. (Rev. 18:13–17)

If it is Jerusalem, then the fact they stood a far way off makes sense. Jerusalem is inland, about an hour away from a seaport.

And exclaimed as they watched the smoke of her burning, What city could be compared to the great city! And they threw dust on their heads as they wept and grieved, exclaiming, Woe and alas, for the great city, where all who had ships on the sea grew rich [through her extravagance] from her great wealth! In one single hour she has been destroyed and has become a desert! Rejoice (celebrate) over her, O heaven! O saints (people of God) and apostles and prophets, because God has executed vengeance for you upon her! (Rev. 18:18–20)

What is bad news for the world is good news for God's people because God judges her, who drank the blood of God's people.

Then a single powerful angel took up a boulder like a great millstone and flung it into the sea, crying, with such violence shall Babylon the great city be hurled down to destruction and shall never again be found. And the sound of harpists and minstrels and flute players and trumpeters shall never again be heard in you, and no skilled artisan of any craft shall ever again be found in you, and the sound of the millstone shall never again be heard in you. And never again shall the light of a lamp shine in you, and the voice of bridegroom and bride shall never be heard in you again; for your businessmen were the great and prominent men of the earth, and by your magic spells and poisonous charm all nations were led astray (seduced and deluded). And in her was found the blood of prophets and of saints, and of all those who have been slain (slaughtered) on earth. (Rev. 18:21–24)

Whatever this city is (and there are many interpretations) God brings severe judgment. Many say it is not the physical city of Babylon, but that it is a symbol in our modern day of prominence, like Babylon was in ancient times. This city may not even have come into its full power yet. However, the fact that musicians will not be heard in her anymore, the voice of the bridegroom and bride will not be heard in her anymore kind of rules out that Babylon is Jerusalem. The New Jerusalem becomes the central focus point in the millennial reign.

CHAPTER 32

The Book of Revelation, Chapters 19-20

AFTER THIS I heard what sounded like a mighty shout of a great crowd in heaven, exclaiming, Hallelujah (praise the Lord)! Salvation and glory (splendor and majesty) and power (dominion and authority) [belong] to our God! Because His judgments (His condemnation and punishment, His sentences of doom) are true and sound and just and upright. He has judged (convicted, pronounced sentence, and doomed) the great and notorious harlot (idolatress) who corrupted and demoralized and poisoned the earth with her lewdness and adultery (idolatry). And He has avenged (visited on her the penalty for) the blood of His servants at her hand. (Rev. 19:1–2)

There is rejoicing in heaven because of God's judgment of this city, which is also symbolized as the harlot.

And again, they shouted, Hallelujah (praise the Lord)! The smoke of her [burning] shall continue to ascend forever and ever (through the eternities of the eternities). Then the twenty-four elders [of the heavenly Sanhedrin] and the four living creatures fell prostrate and worshiped [paying divine honors to] God, Who sits on the throne, saying, Amen! Hallelujah (praise the Lord)! Then from the throne there came a voice, saying, praise our God, all you servants of His, you who reverence Him, both small and great! After that I heard what sounded like the shout of a vast throng, like the boom of many pounding waves, and like the roar of terrific and mighty peals of thunder, exclaiming, Hallelujah (praise the Lord)! For now the Lord our God the Omnipotent (the All-Ruler) reigns! (Rev. 19:3–6).

We are back once again to the kingdoms of this world having become the kingdoms of our Christ and of his God.

The Marriage Supper of the Lamb

Let us rejoice and shout for joy [exulting and triumphant]! Let us celebrate and ascribe to Him glory and honor, for the marriage of the Lamb [at last] has come, and His bride has prepared herself. (Rev. 19:7)

We, as the Church, the body of believers throughout all ages, are the bride of Christ.

As the church is subject to Christ, so let wives also be subject in everything to their husbands. Husbands, love your wives, as Christ loved the church and gave Himself up for her, So that He might sanctify her, having cleansed her by the washing of water with the Word, That He might present the church to Himself in glorious splendor, without spot or wrinkle or any such things [that she might be holy and faultless]. Even so husbands should love their wives as [being in a sense] their own bodies. He who loves his own wife loves himself. For no man ever hated his own flesh, but nourishes and carefully protects and cherishes it, as Christ does the church, because we are members (parts) of His body. For this reason a man shall leave his father and his mother and shall be joined to his wife, and the two shall become one flesh. This mystery is very great, but I speak concerning [the relation of] Christ and the church. (Eph. 5:24–32)

Now we will go back to Revelation 19.

She has been permitted to dress in fine (radiant) linen, dazzling and white—for the fine linen is (signifies, represents) the righteousness (the upright, just, and godly living, deeds, and conduct, and right standing with God) of the saints (God's holy people). Then [the angel] said to me, write this down: Blessed (happy, to be envied) are those who are summoned (invited, called) to the marriage supper of the Lamb. And he said to me [further], These are the true words (the genuine and exact declarations) of God. (Rev. 19:8–9)

God calls blessed the people he invites to be a part of the marriage supper of the Lamb. There will at last be a man—ladies, you can rejoice now—who is faithful, attentive, and totally honest, who always has your best interest at heart.

> Then I fell prostrate at his feet to worship (to pay divine honors) to him, but he [restrained me] and said, Refrain! [You must not do that!] I am [only] another servant with you and your brethren who have [accepted and hold] the testimony borne by Jesus. Worship God! For the substance (essence) of the truth revealed by Jesus is the spirit of all prophecy [the vital breath, the inspiration of all inspired preaching and interpretation of the divine will and purpose, including both mine and yours]. After that I saw heaven opened, and behold, a white horse [appeared]! The One Who was riding it is called Faithful (Trustworthy, Loyal, Incorruptible, Steady) and True, and He passes judgment and wages war in righteousness (holiness, justice, and uprightness) (Rev. 19:10–11).

I love this picture of Jesus! He is now more in the persona of the Lion of Judah than the Lamb of God—though both are vitally important—and it is time for war.

> His eyes [blaze] like a flame of fire, and on His head are many kingly crowns (diadems); and He has a title (name) inscribed which He alone knows or can understand. He is dressed in a robe dyed by dipping in blood, and the title by which He is called is The Word of God. And the troops of heaven, clothed in fine linen, dazzling and clean, followed Him on white horses (Rev. 19:12–14).

The troops of heaven follow him to war, but who are they? One can safely assume this army includes the angelic administration we've seen in heaven. This may be the only time in human history that there is an army that is a joint venture that includes both angels and saints.

Many have said, "What is the point of being raptured at Jesus's return as he is heading for the earth? Is there any significance to doing a complete U-turn? Wouldn't it be an honor to join God as he fights the war?" Sometimes it seems like all we want is the good stuff: the marriage feast of the Lamb, eternal rewards, and positions of influence in the millennial or eternal kingdom, etcetera. What about some things that are not so appealing? Jesus is coming to face and destroy the Antichrist and his kingdom. After the butt kicking, the Antichrist was just allowed to do, why would you not want a piece of that action? We will not be what we are now. We will have our glorified bodies, as previously discussed. There is a verse that says, "Brothers (sisters also) we are, even as we stand right now, God's children, but it has not yet been manifested what the fullness of that is. But when we see him, we shall be like him for we are going to see him as he truly is." (1 John 3:2, author's paraphrase) Whoever this army is, they are standing alongside the King of kings and Lord of lords, which sounds like a high privilege to me.

> From His mouth goes forth a sharp sword with which He can smite (afflict, strike) the nations; and He will shepherd and control them with a staff (scepter, rod) of iron. He will tread the winepress of the fierceness of the wrath and indignation of God the All-Ruler (the Almighty, the Omnipotent). (Rev. 19:15)

God at war: Whose side do you want to be on?

Jesus Coming with his Army

And on His garment (robe) and on His thigh He has a name (title) inscribed, KING OF KINGS AND LORD OF LORDS. Then I saw a single angel stationed in the sun's light, and with a mighty voice he shouted to all the birds that fly across the sky, Come, gather yourselves together for the great supper of God. (Rev. 19:16–17)

The great supper of God is in stark contrast to the marriage feast of the Lamb.

That you may feast on the flesh of rulers, the flesh of generals and captains, the flesh of powerful and mighty men, the flesh of horses and their riders, and the flesh of all humanity, both free and slave, both small and great! Then I saw the beast and the rulers and leaders of the earth with their troops mustered to go into battle and make war against Him Who is mounted on the horse and against His troops. And the beast was seized and overpowered, and with him the false prophet who in his presence had worked wonders and performed miracles by which he led astray those who had accepted or permitted to be placed upon them the stamp (mark) of the beast and those who paid homage and gave divine honors to his statue. Both of them were hurled alive into the fiery lake that burns and blazes with brimstone. And the rest were killed with the sword that issues from the mouth of Him Who is mounted on the horse, and all the birds fed ravenously and glutted themselves with their flesh. (Rev. 19:18–21)

Satan Being Bound in the Bottomless Pit

THEN I saw an angel descending from heaven; he was holding the key of the Abyss (the bottomless pit) and a great chain was in his hand. And he gripped and overpowered the dragon, that old serpent [of primeval times], who is the devil and Satan, and [securely] bound him for a thousand years. Then he hurled him into the Abyss (the bottomless pit) and closed it and sealed it above him, so that he should no longer lead astray and deceive and seduce the nations until the thousand years were at an end. After that he must be liberated for a short time. (Rev. 20:1–3)

Why does God allow Satan to be loosed again after the millennial reign? One reason may be—and this is pure speculation—that all of God's people throughout all the ages will have settled for all eternity, that we would not have done any better than Adam and Eve in their place. We are going to live in a utopian society with God right in our midst, with immediate access. Even as Adam and Eve walked in the garden with God and had unbroken fellowship with him, so shall we. But even with all that, after a thousand years of paradise, Satan is still going to raise a rebellion among the people.

Who will populate the earth and turn from God? The Bible is not clear on that subject, so it is only speculation how this all works out. Because God does not connect all the dots in a scenario, that does not mean we can dismiss it. Just because God does not tell us all the reasons he allows evil to exist, that does not mean there are none. There is not one subject God has completely revealed. His writing mentioned the Messiah's arrival, but the details about the Messiah were incomplete. When the people looked for the Messiah, they were expecting him to behave one way; he behaved another. Somehow, he expects us to adjust to him.

> Then I saw thrones, and sitting on them were those to whom authority to act as judges and to pass sentence was entrusted. Also, I saw the souls of those who had been slain with axes [beheaded] for their witnessing to Jesus and [for preaching and testifying] for the Word of God, and who had refused to pay homage to the beast or his statue and had not accepted his mark or permitted it to be stamped on their foreheads or on their hands. And they lived again and ruled with Christ (the Messiah) a thousand years. (Rev. 20:4)

This is where we see that beheading is the primary means of martyrdom during the reign of the Antichrist.

Now back to Revelation 20.

The remainder of the dead were not restored to life again until the thousand years were completed. This is the first resurrection. (Rev. 20:5)

The coming of the Lord resurrects the godly. Here we see the wicked remain unraised until the end of the millennial reign. The following verses confirm the resurrection of the godly first.

For this we declare to you by the Lord's [own] word, that we who are alive and remain until the coming of the Lord shall in no way precede [into His presence] or have any advantage at all over those who have previously fallen asleep [in Him in death]. For the Lord Himself will descend from heaven with a loud cry of summons, with the shout of an archangel, and with the blast of the trumpet of God. And those who have departed this life in Christ will rise first. Then we, the living ones who remain [on the earth], shall simultaneously be caught up along with [the resurrected dead] in the clouds to meet the Lord in the air; and so always (through the eternity of the eternities) we shall be with the Lord! Therefore, comfort and encourage one another with these words. (1 Thess. 4:15–18)

Now we go back to Revelation 20.

Blessed (happy, to be envied) and holy (spiritually whole, of unimpaired innocence and proved virtue) is the person who takes part (shares) in the first resurrection! Over them the second death exerts no power or authority, but they shall be ministers of God and of Christ (the Messiah), and they shall rule along with Him a thousand years. (Rev. 20:6)

We all physically die in our lives—except Enoch, Elijah, and those whom God takes in the Rapture—that is the first death. However, the ungodly die twice: their physical, earthly death and then the spiritual death of complete separation from God for all eternity. God judges them and throws them into the lake of fire.

Who populates the millennial kingdom? The Scriptures do not plainly speak on this subject. It would be hard to believe that any of us who have gone through this life and seen the atrocities of Satan, and the goodness of God, would follow Satan into a rebellion against God. Since the Bible speaks little on the subject, we will leave this in God's very capable hands. We, obviously, are a part of that millennial kingdom as we rule and reign with him. But exactly who we are ruling and reigning over is not so clear.

And when the thousand years are completed, Satan will be released from his place of confinement, and he will go forth to deceive and seduce and lead astray the nations which are in the four quarters of the earth—Gog and Magog—to muster them for war; their number is like the sand of the sea. (Rev. 20:7–8)

It is amazing that, just as Adam and Eve were in paradise, we have people who have never seen death. They live in a utopian society with God himself. In just a thousand years, humankind is ready to rebel again.

And they swarmed up over the broad plain of the earth and encircled the fortress (camp) of God's people (the saints) and the beloved city; but fire descended from heaven and consumed them. (Rev. 20:9)

Why would Satan do this, knowing that God will cast him into the lake of fire? As we have previously looked at this before, what actual choice does he have? He knows he is going into the Lake of Fire and probably thinks, "Spite dictates I take as many with me as I can." Do you think he could resist this one last chance to hurt his enemy? Hate, spite, and malice are not reasonable, and they are Satan's very nature!

Lake of Fire with God's Enemies

Then the devil who had led them astray [deceiving and seducing them] was hurled into the fiery lake of burning brimstone, where the beast and false prophet were; and they will be tormented day and night forever and ever (through the ages of the ages). (Rev. 20:10)

Finally, Satan is out of the picture for all eternity and will trouble God's people no more.

Then I saw a great white throne and the One Who was seated upon it, from Whose presence and from the sight of Whose face earth and sky fled away, and no place was found for them. I [also] saw the dead, great and small; they stood before the throne, and books were opened. Then another book was opened, which is [the Book] of Life. And the dead were judged (sentenced) by what they had done [their whole way of feeling and acting, their aims and endeavors] in accordance with what was recorded in the books. (Rev. 20:11–12)

God opens the books. Were you aware that you would have to recount your life for every idle word you say?

But I tell you, on the Day of Judgment men will have to give account for every idle (inoperative, nonworking) word they speak. (Matt. 12:36)

For we must all appear and be revealed as we are before the judgment seat of Christ, so that each one may receive [his pay] according to what he has done in the body, whether good or evil [considering what his purpose and motive have been, and what he has achieved, been busy with, and given himself and his attention to accomplishing]. (2 Corinthians 5:10)

Now back to Revelation 20.

And the sea delivered up the dead who were in it, death and Hades (the state of death or disembodied existence) surrendered the dead in them, and all were tried and their cases determined by what they had done [according to their motives, aims, and works]. Then death and Hades (the state of death or disembodied existence) were thrown into the lake of fire. This is the second death, the lake of fire. And if anyone's [name] was not found recorded in the Book of Life, he was hurled into the lake of fire. (Rev. 20:13–15)

The wicked are part of the second resurrection and then the second death. Let's be part of the first group.

CHAPTER 33

The Book of Revelation, Chapters 21-22

The New Jerusalem

THEN I saw a new sky (heaven) and a new earth, for the former sky and the former earth had passed away (vanished), and there no longer existed any sea. And I saw the holy city, the new Jerusalem, descending out of heaven from God, all arrayed like a bride beautified and adorned for her husband; Then I heard a mighty voice from the throne and I perceived its distinct words, saying, See! The abode of God is with men, and He will live (encamp, tent) among them; and they shall be His people, and God shall personally be with them and be their God. God will wipe away every tear from their eyes; and death shall be no more, neither shall there be anguish (sorrow and mourning) nor grief nor pain any more, for the old conditions and the former order of things have passed away. And He Who is seated on the throne said, See! I make all things new.

Also He said, Record this, for these sayings are faithful (accurate, incorruptible, and trustworthy) and true (genuine). (Rev. 21:1-5)

We have a glimpse of the eternal state. All things are new. We are finally in paradise, our original destination. There is no more hurting, sickness, or death! What we went through does not compare to the glory that God has for us. More importantly, that longing to be truly one with God that feels like a long-distance relationship is a thing of the past. There are no more doubts or fears. We will spend the rest of eternity with the Prince of Peace with nothing to disturb our tranquility.

And He [further] said to me, it is done! I am the Alpha and the Omega, the Beginning and the End. To the thirsty I [Myself] will give water without price from the fountain (springs) of the water of Life. He who is victorious shall inherit all these things, and I will be God to him and he shall be My son. (Rev. 21:6–7)

We have everything back, and what was once denied us is now ours permanently.

Lake of Fire with God's Enemies including Fallen Humanity

But as for the cowards and the ignoble and the contemptible and the cravenly lacking in courage and the cowardly submissive, and as for the unbelieving and faithless, and as for the depraved and defiled with abominations, and as for murderers and the lewd and adulterous and the practicers of magic arts and the idolaters (those who give supreme devotion to anyone or anything other than God) and all liars (those who knowingly convey untruth by word or deed)—[all of these shall have] their part in the lake that blazes with fire and brimstone. This is the second death. (Rev. 21:8)

All the things that we hated about our life before eternity will never trouble us again. All the irritations of anger, lust, murder, and the like that we found so annoying in others—and ourselves—have no place in our new home!

Then one of the seven angels who had the seven bowls filled with the seven final plagues (afflictions, calamities) came and spoke to me. He said, Come with me! I will show you the bride, the Lamb's wife. Then in the Spirit He conveyed me away to a vast and lofty mountain and exhibited to me the holy (hallowed, consecrated) city of Jerusalem descending out of heaven from God, Clothed in God's glory [in all its splendor and radiance]. The luster of it resembled a rare and most precious jewel, like jasper, shining clear as crystal. It had a massive and high wall with twelve [large] gates, and at the gates [there were stationed] twelve angels, and [on the gates] the names of the twelve tribes of the sons of Israel were written: On the east side three gates, on the north side three gates, on the south side three gates, and on the west side three gates. And the wall of the city had twelve foundation [stones], and on them the twelve names of the twelve apostles of the Lamb. And he who spoke to me had a golden measuring reed (rod) to measure the city and its gates and its wall. The city lies in a square, its length being the same as its width. And he measured the city with his reed—12,000 stadia (about fifteen hundred miles); its length and width and height are the same. He measured its wall also—144 cubits (about 72 yards) by a man's measure [of a cubit from his elbow to his third fingertip], which is [the measure] of the angel. The wall was built of jasper, while the city [itself was of] pure gold, clear and transparent like glass. The foundation [stones] of the wall of the city were ornamented with all of the precious stones.

The first foundation [stone] was jasper, the second sapphire, the third chalcedony (or white agate), the fourth emerald, The fifth onyx, the sixth sardius, the seventh chrysolite, the eighth beryl, the ninth topaz, the tenth chrysoprase, the eleventh jacinth, the twelfth amethyst. And the twelve gates were twelve pearls, each separate gate being built of one solid pearl. And the main street (the Broadway) of the city was of gold as pure and translucent as glass. I saw no temple in the city, for the Lord God Omnipotent [Himself] and the Lamb [Himself] are its temple. And the city has no need of the sun nor of the moon to give light to it, for the splendor and radiance (glory) of God illuminate it, and the Lamb is its lamp. The nations shall walk by its light and the rulers and leaders of the earth shall bring into it their glory. And its gates shall never be closed by day, and there shall be no night there. They shall bring the glory (the splendor and majesty) and the honor of the nations into it. But nothing that defiles or profanes or is unwashed shall ever enter it, nor anyone who commits abominations (unclean, detestable, morally repugnant things) or practices falsehood, but only those whose names are recorded in the Lamb's Book of Life. (Rev. 21:9–27)

It would appear as though the bride of Christ is the New Jerusalem. God does not have a love relationship with a city—the buildings and such—but with his covenant people who populate the New Jerusalem. We have no need for external lights anymore because he whose very nature is light now dwells with us. We have twelve angels, one stationed at each of the gates. What would it be like to have a one-on-one conversation with Michael or Gabriel and their perspective on our struggles?

THEN HE showed me the river whose waters give life, sparkling like crystal, flowing out from the throne of God and of the Lamb. Through the middle of the Broadway of the city; also, on either side of the river was the tree of life with its twelve varieties of fruit, yielding each month its fresh crop; and the leaves of the tree were for the healing and the restoration of the nations. There shall no longer exist there anything that is accursed (detestable, foul, offensive, impure, hateful, or horrible). But the throne of God and of the Lamb shall be in it, and His servants shall worship Him [pay divine honors to Him and do Him holy service]. They shall see His face, and His name shall be on their foreheads. And there shall be no more night; they have no need for lamplight or sunlight, for the Lord God will illuminate them and be their light, and they shall reign [as kings] forever and ever (through the eternities of the eternities). And he [of the seven angels further] said to me, These statements are reliable (worthy of confidence) and genuine (true). And the Lord, the God of the spirits of the prophets, has sent His messenger (angel) to make known and exhibit to His servants what must soon come to pass. And behold, I am coming speedily. Blessed (happy and to be envied) is he who observes and lays to heart and keeps the truths of the prophecy (the predictions, consolations, and warnings) contained in this [little] book. (Rev. 22:1–7)

Again, it is noteworthy that the Bible does not say blessed are those who understand fully the prophecy (symbols and everything). It is the person who observes the truths of the prophecy, who holds on to the end, returns to our first love, repents, remains faithful, etcetera. These truths are of much greater importance than understanding everything in the prophecy. There are twelve varieties of fruit, one for each season; I am looking forward to finding out what those varieties will be. Think of the most succulent, sweetest fruit you have ever had. The restoration of paradise will probably make that memory taste like dust in comparison.

> And I, John, am he who heard and witnessed these things. And when I heard and saw them, I fell prostrate before the feet of the messenger (angel) who showed them to me, to worship him. But he said to me, Refrain! [You must not do that!] I am [only] a fellow servant along with yourself and with your brethren the prophets and with those who are mindful of and practice [the truths contained in] the messages of this book. Worship God! And he [further] told me, Do not seal up the words of the prophecy of this book and make no secret of them, for the time when things are brought to a crisis and the period of their fulfillment is near. (Rev. 22:8–10).

Many people will say it has been two thousand years and more. Does God not understand the concept of time? He does; however, he reckons time differently than we do.

> Nevertheless, do not let this one fact escape you, beloved, that with the Lord one day is as a thousand years and a thousand years as one day. (2 Pet. 3:8)

So from God's point of view, it has been a little over two days since we murdered his son.

> He who is unrighteous (unjust, wicked), let him be unrighteous still; and he who is filthy (vile, impure), let him be filthy still; and he who is righteous (just, upright, in right standing with

God), let him do right still; and he who is holy, let him be holy still. (Rev. 22:11)

God placed this here as a warning for us to choose sides. Be careful what you choose. For the time being, the choice is ours. Once we are on the God side of the equation, we will have to live with those choices for all eternity.

Behold, I am coming soon, and I shall bring My wages and rewards with Me, to repay and render to each one just what his own actions and his own work merit. I am the Alpha and the Omega, the First and the Last (the Before all and the End of all). Blessed (happy and to be envied) are those who cleanse their garments, that they may have the authority and right to [approach] the tree of life and to enter through the gates into the city. (Rev. 22:12–14)

The Lord has rewards for us. While it is our love that should be the motivation for our service to him, is it not extremely satisfying that he is so generous? We work with him to cleanse our garments in cooperation with the Holy Spirit. That is part of the sanctification process while we live, but ultimately it is his blood and finished work that makes us clean.

[But] without are the dogs and those who practice sorceries (magic arts) and impurity [the lewd, adulterers] and the murderers and idolaters and everyone who loves and deals in falsehood (untruth, error, deception, cheating). (Rev. 22:15)

There is a new heaven and a new earth. We have the New Jerusalem inhabited by God himself. We will rule with him. How far away is the lake of fire that houses all the evil spirits and humans? The Scriptures do not clearly say, but it would appear it is close enough to be a reminder... just outside.

> I, Jesus, have sent My messenger (angel) to you to witness and to give you assurance of these things for the churches (assemblies). I am the Root (the Source) and the Offspring of David, the radiant and brilliant Morning Star. (Rev. 22:16)

Jesus signs this, stating: "I, Jesus, have sent my messenger as a witness to the churches." It would seem odd to address this to the Church if we have nothing to do with the revelation he has just revealed, because we are in heaven for these events recorded in the book of Revelation, according to the pre-Tribulation perspective. If you are going to send a witness to testify, does it not make sense to send your witness to the group of people that is your intended audience?

> The [Holy] Spirit and the bride (the church, the true Christians) say, Come! And let him who is listening say, Come! And let everyone come who is thirsty [who is painfully conscious of his need of those things by which the soul is refreshed, supported, and strengthened]; and whoever [earnestly] desires to do it, let him come, take, appropriate, and drink the water of Life without cost. (Rev. 22: 17)

We have a call to come and drink freely of the water of life. Remember the legend of the fountain of youth? In heaven we have paradise restored and can drink and eat freely of its life-giving water and delicious fruit.

> I [personally solemnly] warn everyone who listens to the statements of the prophecy [the predictions and the consolations

and admonitions pertaining to them] in this book: If anyone shall add anything to them, God will add and lay upon him the plagues (the afflictions and the calamities) that are recorded and described in this book. And if anyone cancels or takes away from the statements of the book of this prophecy [these predictions relating to Christ's kingdom and its speedy triumph, together with the consolations and admonitions or warnings pertaining to them], God will cancel and take away from him his share in the tree of life and in the city of holiness (purity and hallowedness), which are described and promised in this book. (Rev. 22: 18–19)

It is a tricky thing to touch God's Word and this book in particular. We have this statement that those who add to the book will have God's plagues that are in the book added to them. Conversely, if we take away from this book, God will take away the blessings that are contained. This book, in particular, needs to be approached with reverence and awe. We are told specifically what happens, should we attempt to alter the contents.

He Who gives this warning and affirms and testifies to these things says, Yes (it is true). [Surely] I am coming quickly (swiftly, speedily). Amen (so let it be)! Yes, come, Lord Jesus! The grace (blessing and favor) of the Lord Jesus Christ (the Messiah) be with all the saints (God's holy people, those set apart for God, to be, as it were, exclusively His). Amen (so let it be)! (Rev. 22:20–21)

"Even so, Lord, come quickly" is the cry of every heart that groans over the hurt and pain in our world that knows deep down in their spirit that this world is not our true home. We love this world too much, even with its faults and obvious inequities. Brothers and sisters, what we have here is the palest reflection of what God intends for us. Let us do what we can to touch others in Jesus's name and make a difference while we have breath. Let our hearts echo our brother John's words and say, "Come, Lord Jesus!"

CHAPTER 34

The Conclusion: Signposts of the End Times

(Not Necessarily in This Order)

1. The beginning of birth pangs

There will be an increase in frequency and intensity of natural disasters.

2. The increase of lawlessness

Society will spiral out of control, and lawlessness will be the law of the land.

3. The falling away of the Church

There will be a great falling away from the Church because of the increased lawlessness among other factors. Many people will leave the Church en masse.

4. The Gospel being preached to the entire world

Preachers will preach the Gospel to all nations, including those who are antagonistic to the message of Christ's salvation before the end comes.

5. **The signing of the peace agreement between Israel and other nations—this starts the prophetic clock of God in the seventieth week of Daniel.**

As previously noted in the chapter of the seventy weeks of Daniel, God has one week (of years, or seven years) left in bringing fulfillment to God's covenant people, Israel, and by extension, the rest of the world. At the end of the seven-year reign, Jesus returns and destroys the Antichrist. The seven-year Tribulation period is a common name for this time. It begins with the signing of the agreement, and then approximately three and a half years into the treaty, the Antichrist breaks his word. All hell breaks loose.

6. **The resuming of the temple sacrifice in Jerusalem**

The temple sacrifice will resume in Jerusalem. There are currently still many obstacles that would have to be overcome before this could happen. This sets up the Antichrist declaring himself to be god in the temple.

7. **The abomination of desolation**

The Antichrist will declare himself to be god in the temple at Jerusalem. This is the abomination of desolation that Jesus foretold in Matthew 24, approximately three and a half years into the Antichrist's reign.

8. **The days of Noah**

Violence and lawlessness characterized Noah's days. The people of Noah's day were blind to their impending judgment until there was no escape.

9. The persecution of the Church

Persecution will come to the Church from without and from within. Brother and sister will rise against brother and sister (Christian brother and sister against Christian brother and sister) and against anyone sympathetic to the Christian faith. The powers that be will martyr and behead many for standing with Jesus.

10. A human's wages for a loaf of bread

A human's wage will be enough to feed him, leaving nothing for his wife or children, if he has any. The mortgage, vehicles, gas, and electricity, etcetera, will take a back seat to eating. We are talking about poverty and famine of historic proportions.

11. A one-world government

We have not seen a one-world government in what is considered modern times. What nation would want to give up its sovereignty? A global crisis and someone stepping forward to solve this crisis could convince nations to give up their sovereignty. Averting World War III would be a potential candidate. When the Antichrist appears on the global scene, he will appear as an angel of light, as previously mentioned. A savior, if you will, this angel of light will appear to be the answer to humankind's troubles.

12. A one-world religion

Revelation 17:1–6 depicts a harlot. The passage in verse two is where the concept of a one-world religion stems from. She will rise, and her immorality (idolatry) will intoxicate the earth's inhabitants. Although symbolic, it suggests a nearly universal influence, and the world government controls it until the beast and ten rulers destroy it. The beast and the ten rulers are saying something like, "We don't need you anymore!"

13. A one-world currency

We have never had one currency for the entire world—at least not in modern times. This is vastly significant! What nation wants to give up its individuality? It is a lot easier to tell people they cannot buy or sell without the mark of the beast when everyone is using the same monetary system. Imagine trying to implement that with everybody using different methods of payment. So when this unity takes place, religiously, nationally, monetarily . . . call out to God because he warned us ahead of time.

14. The two witnesses

There will be two witnesses to vex the rulers and the Antichrist. These two will have the gift of miracles and signs and wonders. The Antichrist and his minions will overcome them after their testimony and kill them. Three and a half days later, God will raise them from the dead. They will rise to heaven in the plain sight of all.

15. True and false demonstrations of signs and wonders

There will be false signs and wonders or miracles from the Antichrist and his minions. Signs and wonders are not necessarily of God and godliness. The question we need to be asking is this: Do they point us to Jesus?

16. The Battle of Armageddon

The Battle of Armageddon is the last great battle of humankind.

17. The return of the Lord

The Lord will return on the last day of human history as we know it. It will be an unpleasant surprise for some and a joyous occasion for others.

18. The millennial reign

The kingdoms of this world become the kingdom of our Christ and of his God! He will set up his rule on earth and live among humankind. The faithful—scholars and theologians differ on who exactly these people are—will be kings and priests to our God for a thousand years. God allows Satan one more time to seduce humankind into rebellion against him after they have lived with him for a thousand years. How stupid the human heart is! God casts Satan into the lake of fire as his ultimate punishment, never to disturb God's people again.

19. A new heaven and a new earth: God establishes everything for all eternity

God ushers us into our ultimate state, into the eternity of eternities with a new heaven and a new earth. He shall wipe away every tear. There will be no more sickness or disease. The former things are gone and will never be again!

CHAPTER 35

Final Thoughts

I f it's going to happen as plainly and as straightforwardly as that, won't most people even vaguely familiar with the Bible recognize what is going on?

Let no one deceive or beguile you in any way, for that day will not come except the apostasy comes first [unless the predicted great falling away of those who have professed to be Christians has come], and the man of lawlessness (sin) is revealed, who is the son of doom (of perdition), Who opposes and exalts himself so proudly and insolently against and over all that is called God or that is worshiped, [even to his actually] taking his seat in the temple of God, proclaiming that he himself is God. Do you not recollect that when I was still with you, I told you these things? And now you know what is restraining him [from being revealed at this time]; it is so that he may be manifested (revealed) in his own [appointed] time. For the mystery of lawlessness (that hidden principle of rebellion against constituted authority) is already at work in the world, [but it is] restrained only until he who restrains is taken out of the way. And then the lawless one (the antichrist) will be revealed and the Lord Jesus will slay him with the breath of His mouth and bring him to an end by His appearing at His coming. The coming [of the lawless one, the antichrist] is through the activity and working of Satan and will be attended by great power and with all sorts of [pretended] miracles and signs and delusive marvels—[all of them] lying wonders—And by unlimited seduction to evil and with all wicked deception for those who are perishing (going to perdition) *because they did not welcome the Truth but refused to love it that they might be saved. Therefore, God sends upon them a misleading influence, a working of error and a strong delusion to make them believe what is false.* (2 Thess. 2:3–11) (emphasis mine)

In 2 Thessalonians Paul is talking about the Antichrist and Jesus destroying him when he returns. Then the Bible says that because the unbelievers did not receive the love of the truth so they could be saved, God sends them a strong delusion that they will believe lies. (2 Thess. 2:8–11)

It is sometimes a fearful thing when God says, "Okay, you can have what you want," especially if it's for all eternity. Here's a word on God not appointing us to wrath, as previously discussed. Eternally, God has appointed us for blessing beyond our wildest dreams, not wrath, no matter what we go through here.

[But what of that?] For I consider that the sufferings of this present time (this present life) are not worth being compared with the glory that is about to be revealed to us and in us and [for us] and conferred on us! (Rom. 8:18)

But, on the contrary, as the Scripture says, What eye has not seen and ear has not heard and has not entered into the heart of man, [all that] God has prepared (made and keeps ready) for those who love Him [who hold Him in affectionate reverence, promptly obeying Him and gratefully recognizing the benefits He has bestowed]. (1 Cor. 2:9)

In light of eternity, we are not objects of God's wrath—the unbelievers are. If you have ever read the Bible, you notice that there are times God saves his people out of trouble. Other times, God saves his people through trouble. God saved Noah out of the flood. He saved Shadrach, Meshach, and Abednego out of the fiery furnace. God saved Daniel out of the lions' den. God rescued Peter from prison before the authorities could do what they wanted. Many more examples exist. When the Lord visited Egypt with plagues, he distinguished between them and his people. The plagues did not touch the people of Israel.

However, God saved Job through his trials. God saved Jonah through the belly of the great fish. He saved Jesus and all of us who believe in his name through the cross. God saved the early Church fathers, despite their persecution; most died as martyrs for him. Were they appointed for wrath? There is a thief who comes to "steal, kill, and destroy!" He is not called the "accuser of the brothers" for no reason. But God, for whatever his reasons, sometimes takes his people through hard situations and sometimes out of hard situations.

These new believers who get saved in the Great Tribulation and have their heads chopped off for their steadfastness to their Lord and Savior—are they now appointed to wrath? The new believers, who some say will get saved after the Rapture of the Church—are they appointed to wrath? If they are correct, and the Rapture occurs because the Church escapes God's wrath, what have these new Christians done to incur his wrath? No, sorry, God reserves his wrath for his enemies. However, we are the objects of Satan's wrath; he has no love for us! In the book of Job, if you read the first few chapters, God allows Satan to put Job through great testing and tribulation. God was very proud of his servant Job. God knew that even though he allowed Satan to test Job, he was going to come out much better than he went in. At the end of the book, God restored to Job twice what Satan had stolen. The example of Job continues to inspire us Christians throughout the centuries, resulting in exponential eternal rewards for Job, as he touches lives thousands and thousands of years later.

But even within that testing, God allowed Satan only so much leeway. Satan may not do just anything he wants. God says, "This far and no farther!" Truth be told, we would tell God to have Satan stop much sooner. However, God is the master weaver, and our job is not to evaluate God's job performance but to trust that he knows what he is doing. Why God allows Satan the room to test us may vex you. Only God knows all those answers, so we can choose to trust him or not.

> Beloved, never avenge yourselves, but leave the way open for [God's] wrath; for it is written, Vengeance is Mine, I will repay (requite), says the Lord. (Rom. 12:19)

> Therefore, those who are ill-treated and suffer in accordance with God's will must do right and commit their souls [in charge as a deposit] to the One Who created [them] and will never fail [them]. (1 Pet. 4:19)

Peter chose crucifixion upside down on a cross. Martyrdom was how all the apostles died (except John) for living for Jesus. It is not God's wrath that does these things, but Satan.

> The thief comes only in order to steal and kill and destroy. I came that they may have and enjoy life, and have it in abundance (to the full, till it overflows). I am the Good Shepherd. The Good Shepherd risks and lays down His [own] life for the sheep. (John 10:10–11)

Why does God allow the enemy to do these things? He alone knows all the answers to that question. We would need another book to even address this topic.

However, there is a story that may or may not help. A child was watching a mother weave a tapestry when he was very young and could not see what his mother was looking at. Quietly, day after day, he was underneath the loom, just looking at this tapestry until one day he spoke up. "Mother," he said, "what are you making? I have to tell you, it does not look very good from under here." There were a lot of dangling threads. Nothing looked like it went with the next thing. "Why do you spend so much time each day working on this?" His mother smiled and picked her son up and set him on her lap. She showed him the top of the tapestry. It was beautiful, with majestic mountains and streams and wildlife. It took his breath away because it was so beautiful. The child gained a new perspective and did not ask his mother again what she was creating. It is possible that the questions we mean to ask God are going to be very similar when he shows us his perspective.

Hard times are coming, people. Regardless of which position you hold, somebody is going through the Tribulation and the reign of the

Antichrist. Either we as the Church or the people who get saved after the body of believers gets raptured are going through this period. It would appear there are going to be prominent signs and wonders on both sides. The test is to know the origin of the power that is providing the miracles, signs, and wonders—by God or Satan. All that glitters is not gold.

Matthew 25 encourages us to be prepared and have enough oil for the wait. Many times, oil is symbolic of the Holy Spirit. In this study, we have not delved into symbolism too much, but we may need to here. If we are just hunkered down in our foxholes, waiting to be delivered from this time, and it does not happen the way we thought, how will we fare? Would it not be wiser to be prepared to go through the Great Tribulation holding onto our Lord and then unexpectedly get raptured before the Tribulation—instead of not being prepared for that possibility and then finding ourselves in the Great Tribulation?

Is this topic scary? Without a doubt! We have but a little time on this earth. We do the best we know how. But this life is only the beginning; eternity lies before us. How we have lived this life directly affects how we will spend our eternity.

Here is a thought for those who do not believe in heaven and hell. What the Bible says about salvation in Jesus. If you are right and there is no heaven or hell or salvation in Jesus, what has the Christian lost? Christians have lost a lot of sinful pleasures, and let's be real: sin can be fun. But the beginning of that sinful season is more pleasurable than the end. Ask any alcoholic or substance abuse user. What started out as them having power over the intoxicant eventually becomes the intoxicant having power over them.

Choosing rather to suffer affliction with the people of God, than to enjoy the pleasures of sin for a season. (Heb. 11:25 KJV)

So Christians lost out on some fun they could have had. We don't want to pretend that Christians are perfect. We all know they are not. But even the ones who never grew into all that God wanted for them—and that is most of us, myself included—abstained from many things when we were trying to please God. So the end of the story is we missed out on some fun we could have had. Now if Christians are wrong—there is nothing after this life. We lie in a hole somewhere and there is nothing—no pleasure, but no pain either.

Now let's turn this around to the opposite possibility. What if Christians are right?

> For God so greatly loved and dearly prized the world that He [even] gave up His only begotten (unique) Son, so that whoever believes in (trusts in, clings to, relies on) Him shall not perish (come to destruction, be lost) but have eternal (everlasting) life. (John 3:16)

> And there is salvation in and through no one else, for there is no other name under heaven given among men by and in which we must be saved. (Acts 4:12)

> But now the righteousness of God has been revealed independently and altogether apart from the Law, although actually it is attested by the Law and the Prophets, Namely, the righteousness of God which comes by believing with personal trust and confident reliance on Jesus Christ (the Messiah). [And it is meant] for all who believe. For there is no distinction, Since all have sinned and are falling short of the honor and glory which God bestows and receives. [All] are justified and made

upright and in right standing with God, freely and gratuitously by His grace (His unmerited favor and mercy), through the redemption which is [provided] in Christ Jesus. (Rom. 3:21–24)

Because if you acknowledge and confess with your lips that Jesus is Lord and in your heart believe (adhere to, trust in, and rely on the truth) that God raised Him from the dead, you will be saved. For with the heart a person believes (adheres to, trusts in, and relies on Christ) and so is justified (declared righteous, acceptable to God), and with the mouth he confesses (declares openly and speaks out freely his faith) and confirms [his] salvation. The Scripture says, No man who believes in Him [who adheres to, relies on, and trusts in Him] will [ever] be put to shame or be disappointed. (Rom. 10:9–11)

And do not be afraid of those who kill the body but cannot kill the soul; but rather be afraid of Him who can destroy both soul and body in hell (Gehenna). (Matt. 10:28)

If Christians are right, and you—if you are not a Christian—unfortunately are wrong, what have you lost? Forgiveness of your sins, your place in heaven, and the honor of having your name recorded in the Lamb's Book of Life, to mention a few. Are you a gambling man or woman? The stakes are enormously high and for all of eternity. I'm saying this not for sensationalism but out of sincerity. God loved you so much that he gave. He kept nothing back. He gave that which was dearest to him to purchase you back from sin and Satan. You will never outgive God, no matter what you must go through. If we must go through the Great Tribulation, we have good company. Here are Scriptures that assure us of that.

> For He [God] Himself has said, I will not in any way fail you nor [give you up nor] leave you without support. [I will] not, [I will] not, [I will] not in any degree leave you helpless nor forsake nor [let [you] down (relax My hold on you)! [Assuredly not!]. (Heb. 13:5)

> Go ye therefore, and teach all nations, baptizing them in the name of the Father, and of the Son, and of the Holy Ghost: Teaching them to observe all things whatsoever I have commanded you: *and, lo, I am with you always, even unto the end of the world.* Amen. (Matt. 28:19–20 KJV) (emphasis mine)

Jesus is with us right up to the end.

Giving your life and heart is one of the easiest and hardest things to do, all at the same time. We must admit to ourselves that we are basically wrong. Others have taught us we are basically good by nature. Take another look at current events or, scarier still, inside your own heart, and then ask yourself if you believe that. We must admit to ourselves that we need him. We are proud by nature and dislike admitting that we need anything outside ourselves.

> But He gives us more and more grace (power of the Holy Spirit, to meet this evil tendency and all others fully). That is why He says, God sets Himself against the proud and haughty, but gives grace [continually] to the lowly (those who are humble enough to receive it). (James 4:6)

Do not be proud; take the help that is freely offered to you. If you fell off a large ship into the ocean, would you take the life preserver or say, "No, thank you"? This is of even greater importance because, in that scenario, you lose your life. In this scenario, you lose your eternal soul.

For what will it profit a man if he gains the whole world and forfeits his life [his blessed life in the kingdom of God]? Or what would a man give as an exchange for his [blessed] life [in the kingdom of God]? (Matt. 16:26)

If today there is a stirring in your heart, a desire to set things right with your Creator, rejoice, for God's spirit is still striving with humankind! Take the opportunity and get right with God. The day is coming when he will no longer strive with humankind, and then it is too late.

> Therefore, as the Holy Spirit says: Today, if you will hear His voice, Do not harden your hearts, as [happened] in the rebellion [of Israel] and their provocation and [embitterment [of Me] in the day of testing in the wilderness. (Heb. 3:7–8)

The heart's ability to stir is cause for celebration! God is calling you to himself, to respond simply say in your own words, with a sincere heart, "God, you have given everything to me in Jesus. I do not begin to understand why you would love me. You have seen every wrong thing I have done, and every wrong thing I have thought and somehow you love me anyway. I acknowledge that you have placed the punishment I deserved on your Son, Jesus. That he was dead, buried, and resurrected by your power for my benefit. He did not need it; I did. Thank you. Forgive me of my sins and make me your child. In Jesus's name, amen."

I have learned this principle of hearing what we want to hear personally and intimately. There have been times while I have read the

Word that the Holy Spirit has made a particular section stand out and come to life. Too often, I have thought I understood what God meant by what he said. I later discovered that God meant what he said, but what I initially understood was coming from my perspective or filter and not his. What are even more delicate are those things that God drops into your spirit. All who have a vital relationship with God will attest that there are times God speaks to us, although not in an audible voice. Every person I have talked to admits that occasionally, those things they thought were God's voice were their own human inclination. Nobody bats 100 percent in this area. The other hard part is timing. God meant what he said. However, I presumed I knew when God was going to accomplish this or that, and later learned I was wrong!

In writing this book, I do not intend to portray myself as more than I actually am. I have had seasons when I was very close to the Lord. It was during these times that I gleaned the insights I have shared in this book. I have made many mistakes in my life. God gets the glory when repentance and restoration occur. If I am honest, God has taught me more through some of my mistakes than places where I got it right. One amazing thought that has captured my heart lately has been that God knows the beginning from the end. Back when I was a teenager, God looked down the path of my life and saw all my difficulties. He saw the places that, like Peter, I was going to fail him and fall flat on my face, and he chose me anyway. The grace of God is unfathomable. The Lord knows my heart and sees the inside. I relate well with the Samaritan woman who gathered her town. She said, "Come see a man who has told me everything about myself! Could this be the Messiah?" As previously mentioned, she had had five husbands, and the man she was living with was not her husband. She was a very unlikely candidate to be chosen by Jesus to spearhead an evangelistic crusade. Jesus chose her anyway.

If My people, who are called by My name, shall humble themselves, pray, seek, crave, and require of necessity My face and turn from their wicked ways, then will I hear from heaven, forgive their sin, and heal their land. (2 Chron. 7:14)

That Scripture is my stance for writing this book. I have run and walked zealously with God. I have fallen flat on my face more times than I care to admit. Fortunately for all of us, God does not need perfect vessels.

What are we to do, and how are we to respond as the times get tougher? The purpose of sharing the following story is to encourage us as the time continues to draw near. There once was a man who lived on the beach and was a genuine lover of marine life. One day, there was a tropical storm. Tens of thousands of starfish got washed up on the beach. He tossed them back into the ocean. A tourist came to him after a while and asked him what he was doing. He said he was saving the starfish. The tourist looked at the magnitude of what was before this man and said, "You cannot really make a difference to all those starfish!" The man thought about that for a moment and then reached down and picked up another starfish. He gently put the starfish in front of the tourist's face. Then he gently tossed the starfish into the ocean. He turned back to the tourist and stated, "Maybe not, but to that starfish, I made a difference!" He then went back to doing as much as he could. (This is an adaptation of the starfish story.)

No, we cannot do it all. Be faithful to what you can do. Jesus did not save the entire nation of Israel. He got ahold of twelve of them, and look what a difference that has made!

Brothers and sisters, while we have looked at many things that are scary and unpleasant, keep in mind that this is the dark before the eternal dawn. We lost our place in paradise through the choice made by Adam and Eve, even though we were not personally there. God is the hero and has redeemed us back to himself at substantial cost to himself. Our path is hard . . . Jesus's path was hard as well. Keep in mind our example "for the joy that was before him he endured the cross" for our sakes. (Heb. 12:2) (author's paraphrase) There will be no more war, starving people, abused and exploited children. No more grave misfortune, stubbing our toes, financial troubles, losing a loved one. No more heartache in our true home. We will have perfect weather every day and enough food and fellowship, as we fellowship with believers of all ages for eternity in our new home. Most importantly, he whom we have longed for, but seen through a glass dimly (1 Cor. 13:12), we will see fully and know, as he knows us. (authors paraphrase) No matter how close your walk with God has been, it is only a pale comparison to the intimacy we truly long for. He will be in our midst and make all things new. We have touched on only a few things briefly that will be our joy for all eternity. Is that not worth the darkness of the night to get to the eternal dawn?

Here are some final Scriptures concerning the time that is ahead.

And he [the angel] said, Go your way, Daniel, for the words are shut up and sealed till the time of the end. Many shall purify themselves and make themselves white and be tried, smelted, and refined, but the wicked shall do wickedly. And none of the wicked shall understand, but the teachers and those who are wise shall understand. (Dan. 12:9–10)

And will not [our just] God defend and protect and avenge His elect (His chosen ones), who cry to Him day and night? Will He defer them and delay help on their behalf? I tell you, He will defend and protect and avenge them speedily. However, when the Son of Man comes, will He find [persistence in] faith on the earth? (Luke 18:7–8)

Now when these things begin to occur, look up and lift up your heads, because your redemption (deliverance) is drawing near. (Luke 21:28)

Many things are going to come to pass, and we will not know the day or the hour, but we will know the season.

We must work the works of Him Who sent Me and be busy with His business while it is daylight; night is coming on, when no man can work. (John 9:4)

ACKNOWLEDGMENTS

I am grateful most of all to God for working in the hearts of women and men to reconcile us back to our Creator. He inspires all of us who love him to do what we can to help both those in the church and those outside the church. Thank you, Lord God, for the gifts you have given me, and it is my sincere desire that this book will bless your people and those who are not yet your people.

I am very grateful to Carly Catt from Catt Editing for the editing in this book. I found her and her team to be gracious, professional, and easy to work with. I loved that your process was user-friendly and that you were willing to talk through things I did not understand. In every instance where you were not quite sure the idea I was trying to convey, your suggestions to clarify were spot on. Thank you!

My point person at selfpublishing.com, Karen Pina, I want to thank for all your assistance in bringing this book to life. You and I have been in lockstep since day one. Even in the one area where we had an artistic difference of opinion, we are of a similar spirit to defer and be gracious. Thank you for all your support throughout this process.

Endnotes

1   Notes Cheish Merryweather, "Top 10 Horrific True Crime Cases You Should Never Web Search," List Verse, listverse.com, December 10, 2019, https://listverse.com/2019/12/10/10-horrific-true-crime-cases-you-should-never-web-search/.

2   Emma Henderson Vaughan, "40 Years of Hope," National Center for Missing & Exploited Children (blog), MissingKids.org, December 23, 2024, https://www.missingkids.org/blog/2024/40-years-of-hope.

3   Nellah Bailey McGough, "36 Most Memorable Forrest Gump Quotes," *Southern Living* magazine, updated April 30, 2024, https://www.southernliving.com/travel/forrest-gump-quotes.

4   "Riots: David Cameron's Commons statement in full," BBC News, bbc.com, August 11, 2011, https://www.bbc.com/news/uk-politics-14492789.

5   James Strong, *Exhaustive Concordance of the Bible* (Hendrickson Publishers, 2007).

6   Editors of The American Heritage Dictionaries, *The American Heritage Dictionary: Second College Edition* (Houghton Mifflin Company, 1982).

7   Strong, *Exhaustive Concordance of the Bible.*

8   Matthew Kelly, "Star Wars: Palpatine's Journey to the Dark Side, Explained," Game Rant, gamerant.com, December 5, 2023, https://gamerant.com/star-wars-palpatine-becoming-darth-sidious-explained/.

9   Strong, *Exhaustive Concordance of the Bible.*

10   David Noel Freedman, *Eerdmans Dictionary of the Bible* (William B. Eerdmans Publishing Company, 2000).

11   Strong, *Exhaustive Concordance of the Bible.*

www.ingramcontent.com/pod-product-compliance
Lightning Source LLC
Chambersburg PA
CBHW071659120626
46550CB00001B/43